Church-going, going, gone!

**Also by Michael Horan
and published by Imprint Academic:**

*Jesus and the Trojan War:
Myth and meaning for today*

CHURCH-GOING, GOING, GONE!

A Movement of the Human Spirit Begins

MICHAEL HORAN

imprint-academic.com

Copyright © Michael Horan, 2015

The moral rights of the author have been asserted.
No part of this publication may be reproduced in any form
without permission, except for the quotation of brief passages
in criticism and discussion.

Published in the UK by
Imprint Academic, PO Box 200, Exeter EX5 5YX, UK

Distributed in the USA by
Ingram Book Company,
One Ingram Blvd., La Vergne, TN 37086, USA

ISBN 9781845407711

A CIP catalogue record for this book is available from the
British Library and US Library of Congress

Biblical quotations are from the Holy Bible,
New International Version ®
copyright © 1973, 1978, 1984
by International Bible Society.
Used by permission of Hodder & Stoughton.
All rights reserved.

If someone comes to you and asks your help, you shall not turn him away with pious words, saying, 'Have faith and take your troubles to God!' You shall act as though there were no God, as though there were only one person in all the world who could help this man—only yourself.
—Moshe Leib of Sasov, Hasidic rabbi, d.1807

The kingdom of God does not come with your careful observation, nor will people say, 'Here it is,' or 'There it is,' because the kingdom of God is within you.
—Luke 17:21

Contents

Preface: Church-going is going	ix

Part One

Chapter 1: An invitation to the fulfilment society	1
Chapter 2: Closing down: Everything must go!	13
Chapter 3: Opening shortly: A new enterprise	26
Chapter 4: Learners wanted: Now recruiting	41
Chapter 5: In place of teaching: Learning to learn	57

Part Two

Chapter 6: But *that* I can't believe	67

Sketches:

1. The gods and God	73
2. Jesus, the man from Galilee	80
3. A young woman shall give birth	87
4. The death of Jesus	94
5. Resurrection	100
6. Ascending to heaven	106
7. Judgment day	110
8. The spirit of the divine	114
9. The church	119
10. Forgiveness	125
11. An afterlife	132

Part Three

Chapter 7: Social construction	139
Jottings:	
1. Children and young people	148
2. Crime	152
3. Disablement	156
4. Ecology and the environment	160
5. Education	164
6. Employment	168
7. Equality of opportunity	172
8. Ethnicity, 'race' and immigration	176
9. Family and marriage	180
10. Gender and sexuality	184
11. Health	188
12. Housing and homelessness	192
13. Media	196
14. Old age	200
15. Poverty	204
16. Other concerns	208
Epilogue: Where to now?	209
Appendix 1: A Supreme Court opinion on 'religion'	211
Appendix 2: Developing the effective working group	213
Appendix 3: A learning review	216
Appendix 4: A personal check-up	218
Bibliography	220
Acknowledgments	224
Index	225

Preface

Church-going is going

Whether or when the theological, political organisations known collectively as the Christian church in Britain[1] will finally wither and die cannot yet be known. It may well be that the question will be answered within a generation or two from now.[2]

Meanwhile, one possible future—in Britain at least, but other countries with an historically 'Christian' culture might give thought to this—could develop along these lines: the disestablished Church of England has lost its political status (bishops no longer sit in the Lords at Westminster) and has ceased to be the 'national church'. Those who retain their Roman Catholic identity take for granted that they can now in conscience and with impunity ignore the impotent strictures of a paternalistic Vatican, although Rome maintains a nominal presence in this outpost of its empire. Nonconformist church-goers, whose forebears prided themselves on their centuries-old separatist, dissenting tradition, have dropped their divisive denominational labels, put their differences behind them,[3] and now join with newly-formed local groups of secular and Christian humanists, together with one-time members of the Church of England and of the Roman Catholic church, with a few liberal Jews perhaps, a Buddhist possibly, and maybe others. They meet, not in dedicated buildings, which have become too expensive to maintain, but in hired halls or in private homes, and not always on Sundays. There they share their insights, based on their beliefs in and experiences of what they variously call God or some other name for the 'Other-than-oneself', joining in informal celebration of joy and gratitude, and expression of their hopes and concerns. More and more of these groups are forming, and more and more people are attending them.

It is taken as read here that 'spiritual' communities such as these, or something like them, historically but no longer the church's unique role, will continue to be important to many people. For them, worship and prayer — or whatever new words they coin to give meaning to joyous celebration and to meditation and quiet — will remain central to spiritual thought and practice, as a source of peace and personal renewal, and as an expression of spiritual and social values. However, over time and irreversibly, the traditional, outdated teachings of the Christian church will have been replaced by new concepts and language, none of it requiring individual or corporate acceptance as fixed or 'official' doctrine or dogma, or forming a prerequisite to membership.

This will be among the beginnings of an emergent movement of the human spirit, committed to personal growth, creating and maintaining loving relationships (both personally and socially), working toward equality, peace and reconciliation, and dedicated to unselfish and imaginative social action.

We are witnessing the terminal decline of the Christian church in Britain. However, the argument which follows is that 'religion' itself is far from dead. The church structure may be crumbling, the form of its teaching now seen to be irrelevant, but the essence of belief and spirituality remains.

We are in transition, moving towards a radically different future, in a time of unprecedented change. So this is not an end. It is a beginning.

---

[1] By 'the Christian church in Britain' I mean British churches as a whole. Only when there is a need to refer to a specific church is its denominational name used. 'The church' is *not* to be read as a synonym for the Church of England, for example, as the press does, both regularly and misleadingly. While the focus of this book is on the British scene, other western countries whose culture, historically at least, has been based on a Christian tradition will do well to think about the implications of the argument within their own context.

[2] A view taken by the former Archbishop of Canterbury, George Carey, is that the Church of England could be one generation away from extinction if it cannot attract young people into its membership. It is a statement of the obvious, of course. His speech at the Shropshire churches conference was widely reported in British national newspapers and on their websites on 19 November 2013.

[3] In this possible future, a few conservative evangelical congregations continue with their services, but their numbers are small, and are getting smaller. Within

a generation or so these groups will also have gone. Meanwhile, they have an unfortunate and unfounded sense of being under threat from what they think of as a godless society. Their literalist and dogmatic biblical fundamentalism emphasises apocalyptic expectation; and a defensive belief in their being 'the elect' regrettably precludes dialogue with any whose beliefs are at variance with theirs.

Part One

Chapter 1

An invitation to the fulfilment society

This book is about belief and the practical relevance of belief. Its aim is to contribute to the growth of a new movement of the human spirit, based on the acceptance that the practices of traditional Christian faith are dying.

First, something that I believe. I believe that the issues explored in these pages are both urgent and important. Urgent, because our world, locally, nationally and internationally, is increasingly in need of solutions to increasingly complex problems, but time is not on our side if those problems are to be resolved. Important, because what I shall be calling spiritual values and beliefs (and which some will continue to think of as religious values and beliefs) have far more direct and practical relevance to these problems, including individuals' personal problems, than the great majority of us have so far applied our hearts and minds and hands to.

An early task, therefore, will be to clarify if not define what is meant by spiritual values and spirituality, so that we can stop tripping over our language, and so resolve once and for all the historical believer/unbeliever dichotomy.

Moreover, I believe that these values are to be found far more widely in the population than is commonly supposed. Indeed it may even be said that to one extent or another, little or much, spiritual values are to be found somewhere in all people, aware or unaware, whether high or low in our consciousness.

It will be objected immediately that every day national newspapers and radio and television news programmes provide more than enough evidence to the contrary, with the darkest reports of evil actions. It may be that there is a potential for that in all of us.

Some will wish to pick up again the well-rehearsed discussion about the part that 'religion' has played across the centuries in confrontation and persecution and conflict and worse, citing Northern Ireland or Israel as evidence in our day. It may be questioned, of course, what is meant by 'religion' in this context, when it is possible to speak of an atheist Ulsterman who was a fanatical Protestant, for example;[1] or secular, non-observant Jews in Israel who quote the Hebrew scriptures to authenticate the borders of a land promised by God to the patriarch Abraham and to Moses the lawmaker and to their descendants.[2]

Meanwhile, in another part of the forest, claims are made for an increase in belief in the occult, astrology, witchcraft and the so-called New Age cults. There may be some truth in that, and perhaps it needs to form a part of the exploration to find new meanings for belief and religion.

In spite of all of that, the evidence that will be presented here argues that a majority of Britons believe in some form of Ultimate Reality, whether they call it (him/her) 'God' or use some other name for the 'Other-than-oneself'. The position is taken here that there is a spark of the 'divine' in every one of us—and here is the first opportunity for you to substitute your own word for divine, if you will—a spark which has to be nurtured and fanned into a flame.

That positive and optimistic view of humanity is held by Quakers, for example, who like to quote the words of their founder, George Fox: 'walk cheerfully over the world, answering *that of God in every one*' [my emphasis].[3] In more recent times a rabbi has asserted that 'the most sublime idea I know is to see the trace of God in the face of the human other'.[4] A mirror image of that notion finds popular expression in a familiar song, 'To love another person is to see the face of God'.[5] (At every point from now on, I have to ask those readers who need to, to substitute their own word or phrase whenever I write 'God'.)

These 'promptings of love and truth in [our] hearts'[6] may be what we call conscience, that still, small voice within me, telling me what is required by the highest that I know. And that is the essential theme of the book, a dual challenge to each of us: one, to commit to the 'highest

An invitation to the fulfilment society

that we know' — what some will think of as God and others will conceive as the 'Other-than-oneself' or Ultimate Reality — and two, to love our neighbour as ourselves.

Given that it is true, then, that all men and women have some degree of spiritual awareness, however badly we may behave in practice, it follows that these values (still to be defined) are by no means limited to religious organisations, since only a small minority of people have church affiliations and their numbers continue to fall. Richard Holloway, former bishop of Edinburgh, has observed that an 'enormous group of people has not left the church for the simple reason they were never in it', but 'they do not cease to be interested in spirituality or the inner life of the human community just because they are not members of any of the religions on offer'.[7]

While it may be dismissed as slender, anecdotal evidence, it is none the less interesting to quote a report of the atheist 'Sunday Assembly' first held in London early in 2013, described by its organisers as 'a godless congregation that meets... to hear great talks, sing songs and generally celebrate life'. One of its co-founders was quoted as saying that there was 'clearly a thirst for community' and that he felt 'words such as awe and transcendence shouldn't be the preserve only of religious people'. A little more than a year later, the assembly's founders were predicting that, by the end of 2014, one hundred of these 'godless' congregations would have been established.[8]

If the proposition holds good, that it is a universal experience and not only 'the preserve of religious people' to have a degree of belief in or awareness of something 'Other-than-oneself', then almost limitless world-changing resources are available, if only they can be tapped, and if the social relevance of those beliefs can be turned into action. That will be a task for the fulfilment society.

The 'fulfilment society' is a concept introduced by Julian Huxley in an essay titled 'The Coming New Religion of Humanism', first published in *The Humanist* magazine in January/February 1962. In this essay, Huxley made clear his conviction that 'this world and the life in it can be improved, and that it is our duty to try to improve it, socially, culturally, and politically'. A humanist religion, he proposed, 'will uphold the ideal of equality... of richness and variety... and of active, open and continuous development, personal, social, and evolutionary'. More concisely, Huxley described the fulfilment society as being

> organized in such a way as to give the greatest number of people the fullest opportunities of realizing their potentialities — of achievement and enjoyment, morality and community. It will do so by providing opportunities for education, for adventure and achievement, for co-operating in worthwhile projects, for meditation and withdrawal, for self-development and unselfish action.[9]

There is ample evidence for the truth of the opening statement of this chapter, that the *practices* of the traditional Christian religion are dying,[10] although questions remain about *belief*. Equally, there is a sense of the early stirrings of an emergent movement of the human spirit, developing what Bonhoeffer may have meant by his notion of 'religionless Christianity'[11] and giving evidence for Huxley's 'coming new religion of humanism'.

Just what is to be understood by religion, and by religious or spiritual beliefs and values, may defy an agreed definition, of course. Certainly it can be expected that there will be widely differing views or theories.[12] The word supernatural will crop up from time to time in what follows, but there will be no place for it as new, relevant meaning is sought for 'religion' and 'spiritual values'. The old language has to be deconstructed, and replaced by a new vocabulary. A word more appropriate to this discussion is metaphysical, both as *transcendence*, meaning that ultimate reality lies beyond ordinary experience, and *immanence*, meaning that reality consists only as an object of experience.[13]

However, for the fulfilment society project to get off the ground, let alone make progress, it is vital that the age-old, limiting definitions of words such as religion and (more significantly) 'God'[14] are no longer permitted to draw go/no-go demarcation lines between 'believers', agnostics and atheists. Without doubt, common ground exists between these groups, but unnecessary and long-standing misunderstandings and arguments and disagreements over language have hindered collaboration and prevented so much that might otherwise have been achieved in the vital task of mending a broken world.

An invitation to the fulfilment society

It is relevant to note the ease with which the eminent humanist Huxley accepted humanism as a religion. By contrast, high-profile present-day atheists are actively critical of religion, but I suggest that they expend unwarranted amounts of intellectual energy on protesting too much about beliefs which they mistakenly consider to be key religious concepts. Do people really still believe in the literal truth of a six day creation? Do people really still believe that a first couple was created, named Adam and Eve? Do people really still believe that many of the biblical stories are literally or historically true? (Some of them may be, of course.) For his part, A.C. Grayling is prepared to go firm: he is quite clear that there is no God, and exhorts us to stop worrying about it.[15] By contrast, Richard Dawkins is more cautious in his approach; while he is clearly aware that negatives cannot be proved, his position is that he thinks God's existence to be extremely improbable.[16]

One atheist at least has declared that it is time to 'Call off the faith wars', suggesting to his fellow non-believers that 'it's time we admitted that religion has some points in its favour... [S]omething must be done to prevent believers and non-believers spending another century talking past each other'.[17]

Alain de Botton, also an atheist, devotes an entire book to what he calls 'A non-believer's guide to the uses of religion'.[18]

Meanwhile, agnostics remain unsure about what grounds there may be for believing or not believing what are in reality pre-scientific and outdated religious concepts, on which in fact little or nothing hinges, and on which agnostics would do well to waste no more time or brainpower. Baby is being thrown out with the bathwater. It is important to emphasise in passing that that is not the same as saying that because something is not literally true there is no truth or value in it.

Humanists make an important point, when thinking of religion in human terms. But this is not the exclusive preserve of secular humanists. It has long been argued by theologians and other scholars; and today, increasing numbers of Christians—not only lay people, but clergy and bishops as well—are finding themselves 'in exile', less and less able to accept the church's traditional, supernatural dogma. Some leave the church. Others remain because they still find solace there.

Many, no longer able to conceive of God as a supernatural being 'up there' or 'out there', find it more liberating to believe in

> God [as] the sum of our values, representing to us their ideal unity, their claims upon us, and their creative power.[19]

Given that those values do have claims upon us, and that they have creative power, we will do well to identify what the claims are, and in what ways they have creative power. Here will be a new way for us to think and speak about 'God', as the creative energy of love and compassion, forgiveness and reconciliation, mercy and humility, is demonstrated and experienced.

At long last, honest radical rethinking of this kind is set to facilitate the removal of age-old differences between 'believers' and 'non-believers' — many of those differences being more imagined than real — thus freeing men and women to come together to work towards the creation of the fulfilment society.

* * *

Here, then, are a few clues about a range of possibilities when discussing spiritual or religious values, and when searching for a meaning of the 'Other-than-oneself'. The proposition now is that there is a need to invite into the embryonic fulfilment society all or any who wish to think about — and, better still, take action on — the relevance of spiritual values in remaking the world.

It is likely that, at one level or another, those accepting the invitation will have an interest in spirituality, or in religion in a broad sense, but not necessarily in theistic religion, that is, a religion with an objective, realist God. Perhaps their interest is in Christianity in particular, whether or not they call themselves Christian, whether or not they would consider themselves to be religious, whether or not they are church-goers, but especially if they are among those who find themselves unable to believe the church's traditional, supernatural teachings. Even today, far too many people inside the church remain unaware that it is permissible let alone essential to ask these questions. It is equally certain that far and away more people *outside* the church, people who have rejected the church's doctrines or who have never believed them, are unaware that these questions are already being asked. So there is a place in the fulfilment society for all seekers or searchers—the atheists, the agnostics, the church-goers, those who feel exiled from the church and those who have never had any time for the church.

It is to be hoped that the discussion will also be of interest and relevance to those of other faiths, even though the starting point is with a Christian church in decline. Other authors have looked at the wider picture and at some of the issues which world faiths may need to consider and deal with.[20] However, the concept of the fulfilment society is an all-inclusive one, not only universally relevant and applicable, but also positively requiring the participation of all. Here is an opportunity to play a part in promoting religious understanding and tolerance, first within local communities, then throughout Britain, and eventually between countries, so fostering international peace.

Clarifying and sharing our values and beliefs, then, establishing their relevance, and finding ways of tapping into and applying them, is an important and urgent issue, the issue upon which enquiring readers are now invited to concentrate and hopefully take action.

* * *

It is important at the outset to emphasise that, while in large measure this is a 'how-to' book, it is a how-to book with a difference. Authors of how-to books can customarily be relied upon to pass on to you their knowledge or expertise or wisdom. They set out to teach you how to achieve something: how to transform or at least improve some supposedly less than satisfactory aspect of your life in a mere thirty days, perhaps, or even ninety minutes. Or they tell you how to undertake a do-it-yourself project which previously you would have hesitated even to contemplate, but which now, thanks to the expertise of the how-to author, you are going to be able not only to begin but also complete, without shedding tears of frustration or rage. Thus, the conventional how-to approach is about *teaching*.

This book, by contrast, is about *learning*. It devotes little space to telling you how to do anything. The hope is that you are going to feel encouraged and enabled to make some discoveries for yourself, taking action, and learning in the process. That is to say, it asks the question, How to?

Conventional how-to books are about sharing knowledge. This one (replacing How-to! with How to?) is about sharing ignorance, in the strict meaning of *not knowing*. It is for you to start asking questions, challenging your assumptions and long-held beliefs, possibly discovering gaps in your own knowledge, do some thinking and share your thoughts with others—at the same time, sharing doubts and uncertainty—and together begin what can be called opportunity search. In that sense, the book is incomplete: the authors will be you and others who will recognise the benefit of coming together to collaborate as a learning community. This is not a book merely to be read, therefore; it is a book to be used.

Taking this questioning approach, acknowledging (if not welcoming) ambiguity and flux, may not satisfy some teachers, the guardians of the official version, those who possess and propagate a body of knowledge. One teacher took me to task for using this style in my earlier book, *Jesus and the Trojan War*,[21] her criticism being that I 'reject the language of assertion and certainty [and so] sidestep debate'.[22] Present readers can be the judges of which approach is more likely to engender enquiry and learning: these open questions, or the teacher's requirement for 'the language of assertion and certainty'. We shall return to this topic. In effect, it is the very essence of the present book's discussion. For my part, though, I am content to borrow the words of the Cambridge theologian Alec Vidler: 'I am more interested in other people's thoughts than in my own. I regard my proper role as an editorial one, or as that of a midwife.'[23]

* * *

Now for an invitation, not only to give thought to what might be meant by spiritual values, but also to rethink religious values and belief, no longer in accord with obsolete, pre-scientific supernatural dogma but in the language of the here-and-now. The invitation is to join a new enterprise, reconstructing the traditional but worn-out ways of thinking about God and religion and Christianity, and developing a new vocabulary to replace the old, outmoded language, and identifying practical applications for these restated values. But this must be no comfortable talking shop: the fulfilment society will be essentially a proactive society committed to making a cultural shift to equality and opportunity, 'co-operating in worthwhile projects... meditation and withdrawal... self-development and unselfish action'.

In essence, then, this book is intended for all who are prepared to join a quest, and follow it wherever it may lead. But here is a caution: the quest will be characterised by ambiguity and uncertainty and discomfort, as the old ways are challenged and even rejected, and new ways are sought and found, tried and modified, shaped and reshaped. That will demand preparedness in all to learn.

The book has three parts. The remaining chapters of this first part begin with an outline of the Christian church in Britain and how it came to be where it is today. This has been chosen as the starting point simply because it is still a commonplace that Britain is a Christian country. For many, words such as 'belief' and 'believers' have specific religious meanings, and for our purposes these concepts have to be remodelled and broadened far beyond the narrow confines of the church's traditions. Moreover, it is this traditional and orthodox theistic Christianity about which agnostics are uncertain, and against which atheists rage. The time has come for the reducing numbers of people who attend a church in decline to recognise the reasons why church-going is going.

The discussion continues with the observation that while historically the church has been a *teaching* organisation, the relevance of that teaching is being questioned and challenged. Arguments are put forward for the need for reconstruction through *learning*. There is a reminder that learning is significantly different from teaching; and it is proposed that one of the qualities of the fulfilment society, the new enterprise, will be a shift from teaching to learning, with seekers and searchers collaborating in learning communities. Thought is given to what a learning community might be; and that is followed by ideas about ways in which diverse groups can collaborate and learn together.

The book's second part provides a framework within which individuals and communities of learners can rethink what it means to believe. The model used here for deconstructing traditional supernatural concepts is the Apostles' Creed (agnostics and atheists, please be patient). While this provides a structure for examining outdated ideas, it also challenges the reader to make some decisions. But this is only a beginning, enabling the decks to be cleared. Or (to use another metaphor) it is pump-priming for further thought. It has been observed that sceptics and cynics never built anything, and the task here therefore is to decide what one does believe rather than what one does not believe. In seeking to define what spiritual values might be, there will be a need to move on to ethics. Other models might include the Sermon on the Mount,[24] or Plato, or Aristotle, or the Meditations of Aurelius. You can create your own list of sources.

I neither wish nor expect to convert the atheists. But I do want them to know, if they do not know already, that they are not the only ones rejecting supernatural or superstitious beliefs, and it is possible that they have chosen the wrong targets for their attacks. Their insights are essential to this new enterprise.

I am not setting out to convince the agnostics. On the contrary, I invite agnostics to consider it possible that while it is fine to say 'I don't know' or 'I'm not sure', that is an unnecessarily uncomfortable place in which to remain. Better to decide how to go about discovering answers to the questions.

And to believers-in-exile I say, We are in the same place, you and I, and I want to journey with you in a quest for new meanings for belief and faith.

Social construction, the theme of the book's final part, not only means building a new society, but also refers to the constructs that we put on 'society' and those within society whom we may perceive to be different from ourselves. It considers the role of the fulfilment society, and suggests an agenda to which learning communities within the society can apply themselves, to put their thinking and beliefs into practice, and to give meaning in our time to the words of a text from nearly thirty centuries ago:

> He has showed you, O man, what is good. And what does the LORD require of you? To act justly and to love mercy and to walk humbly with your God.[25]

* * *

Ernst Bloch and T.S. Eliot had the same insight as each other, and expressed it in the same words: that the discoveries can begin once our explorations come to an end, and that the end is where we start from. Bloch proposed that once we use our creativity to rethink the 'facts' and give them a new shape, we can at last hope to 'come home', to the place we have known all along as the place where we belong.[26] It was Eliot's discovery that, when our wanderings are at an end, we find ourselves where we began, and for the first time are able to recognise the place.[27]

The journey to our 'homeland' is ultimately what this book is about. I believe that understanding and collaboration between humanists—whether atheist or agnostic, religious or secular—and radical Christians, and others who wear no labels, can give rise to a vision for rethinking the 'facts' and so give them a new shape, and with these values harnessed as a force for social reconstruction, that vision will become socially liberating.

In effect, then, this picks up at the point where I ended *Jesus and the Trojan War*, saying that we have come not to an end, but to a beginning:

> We may have come home, but we have not come home to stay. Now there is a journey to make, a quest to pursue—'For here we do not have an enduring city, but we are looking for the city that is to come'.[28]

As we set out, we may catch something of the Old Testament prophet's vision, a vision of re-birth and renewal: 'Behold, I will create new heavens and a new earth. The former things will not be remembered, nor will they come to mind.'[29]

So, as we set out, we need to do what all journey planners need to do: having defined our destination, we now need to check where it is we are starting from.

- What issues or questions has this chapter raised for me?
- What have I learned?

---

1   Mary Warnock writing in *The Guardian*, 10 April 2014.
2   Genesis 12:1, 12:5–6, 13:14–17, 15:18, Deuteronomy 34:1–4.
3   George Fox writing to Friends in 1656. George Fox, *Journal*.
4   Rabbi Jonathan Sacks, speaking on BBC Radio 2, 29 April 2013.
5   Boublil and Schönberg musical, *Les Misérables*.
6   From 'Advices and queries' in *Quaker Faith and Practice*, published by the Religious Society of Friends.
7   Richard Holloway, *Looking in the Distance*.

8   *The Guardian*, 4 February 2013 and 29 April 2014.
9   Julian Huxley, 'The Coming New Religion of Humanism' in *The Humanist* magazine, January/February 1962.
10 Two examples from a survey carried out by Ipsos MORI for the Richard Dawkins Foundation in the week after the 2011 census: (i) Of the adults who said they were recorded as Christian in the census, more than a third had never or almost never prayed outside a church service, with a further six per cent saying they prayed from choice less than once a year; (ii) The majority (sixty per cent) had not read any part of the Bible independently and from choice, for at least a year. See richarddawkinsfoundation.org.
11 Bonhoeffer's tantalising and possibly barely understood phrase has become something of a cliché. It is perhaps too readily used as shorthand for undefined radical ideas. Dietrich Bonhoeffer, *Letters and Papers from Prison*.
12 Discussions about faith and belief will have philosophical and theological bases, of course. Now a legal opinion needs to be added to the pot when thinking about the meaning of words and phrases such as religion, belief systems and worship. Rather than incorporate a lengthy summary of the Supreme Court judgment within the main text, however, it is included at appendix 1.
13 For discussions of metaphysics, see E. Honderich (ed.), *The Oxford Companion to Philosophy*.
14 It has proved difficult at times to be consistent or clear in my use of a capital G or a small g when writing about God, and about gods in general. The principle I have attempted to adopt is to use a small g for god as a common noun, and a capital G when God is a proper noun, that is to say, when using the name of the Judaeo/Christian god.
15 A.C. Grayling, *The God Argument: The Case against Religion and for Humanism*.
16 Richard Dawkins, *The God Delusion*.
17 Douglas Murray writing in *The Spectator*, 9 February 2013.
18 Alain de Botton, *Religion for Atheists*.
19 Don Cupitt, *The Sea of Faith*.
20 See, for example, Karen Armstrong, *A History of God*. Also of specific relevance is 'Christianity and Islam' in John Hick, *Who or What is God?*
21 Michael Horan, *Jesus and the Trojan War: Myth and meaning for today*.
22 Kathleen McPhilemy, *Sofia* No. 84 (journal of The Sea of Faith Network), July 2007.
23 Alec R. Vidler, *20th Century Defenders of the Faith*.
24 Matthew 5:1 to 7:29.
25 Micah 6:8 [NIV].
26 Ernst Bloch, *The Principle of Hope*.
27 'Little Gidding', T.S. Eliot, *Collected Poems*.
28 Hebrews 13:14 [NIV].
29 Isaiah 65:17 [NIV].

Chapter 2

Closing down: Everything must go!

Little more than a century had passed since the mid-Victorians embarked on their truly astonishing church building programme when Philip Larkin's poem 'Church Going' asked what churches would be turned into, once they are no longer used, no longer needed.[1]

One answer to Larkin's question would have been that while it was to become trendy to add a mezzanine floor to disused rural chapels and so convert them into desirable residences, that would not so often be the destiny of redundant churches in towns and cities. True, some disused urban church buildings were to be born again to serve as theatres or community centres or libraries. None the less, the estate agents' boards were going up, advertising *Church buildings for sale*, only to be replaced by bold, brightly-painted fascias, announcing the imminent reopening of the premises. A welcome was extended to everyone to come along, on Sundays certainly but also on all the other days of the week, to buy tyres, batteries and exhausts at unrepeatable discounts, or to browse among carpets at unbeatable bargain prices, with the screamer 'Everything must go!'

This modern-day Cromwellian desecration, this spoliation of once-revered sanctuaries, would not have escaped the notice of Philip Larkin's friend John Betjeman, champion of Victorian architecture and British heritage. The Anglo-Catholic Betjeman, one of those 'who remember the Faith, the grey-headed ones', can be visualised crafting the melancholy theme of a new poem, not only regretting the church's decline, as he reminisced that 'those were the waking days /

When Faith was taught and fanned to a golden blaze'[2] but also expressing once again his dismay at twentieth-century urban vulgarity and vandalism.

The church's demise was foreseen by Larkin, a still less religious man than Betjeman,[3] but one who even so called himself an Anglican agnostic. In his poem, Larkin recalls visiting a church, but having looked around, thinks it has not been worth the visit. And yet, he realises, he *did* stop and go in. As he wonders what churches will be used for, once they are no longer needed, the possibility occurs to him that in fact they will never become wholly redundant, since there may always be a few people whose memory will be stirred, and who as a result will return to the church, even though the church is literally surrounded by the dead. Elsewhere, churches have been described as 'enormous stone memorials' to a dead religion.[4]

What is the explanation for this dramatic and rapid decline in the church's place in British society, from an unquestionably unparalleled mid-nineteenth-century expansion, when in the space of a few decades perhaps ten thousand new buildings went up, to a mid-twentieth-century poet's agnostic musings about an obsolescent church, reflecting a national apathy?

With the benefit of hindsight, there is little reason to conclude that the Victorians' scramble to build churches was anything other than misplaced or misguided, even if sincere, enthusiasm. The statistical evidence provided by the first-ever census of religion in 1851 shocked the prosperous, respectable church-going middle classes into understanding just how low was the level of church attendance at that time —although, at something around half the population, that was an infinitely higher proportion than it is today. Intent on providing places for the absentee artisans, in the mistaken belief that it was a lack of pew space that kept them away from church, and competing to secure the adherence of the seemingly apostate masses of the working classes to their discrete brand of Christianity, the various denominations set about building thousands upon thousands of new churches and chapels, restoring and repairing countless others, and recruiting thousands of clergy.

It needs to be understood that this astounding expansion did not have a purely religious or evangelising motive. For thirty or more years following the end of the Napoleonic wars in 1815, waves of revolution rolled through continental Europe. Victorian Britain dreaded a similar fate. If revolution came, respectable Victorians feared, it would be initiated, as elsewhere, by the vast underclass of labouring men. The 'Peterloo' massacre in Manchester in 1819, when 80,000 people marched on the city and eleven people were killed in a cavalry charge, had been a disaster that no one wished to see repeated. The threat to social stability was believed to lie with the 'apostate' working classes. Make these people mindful of their religious obligations, it was argued, and in this way social unrest would be pre-empted.

For all that, these politically motivated church-building efforts were in vain. From 1851 onwards, church attendance figures continued to decline: the fifty per cent or so in that year had dwindled to twenty per cent a hundred years later, continued to drop for another twenty years, and then seemed to level out at something well below ten per cent. There is evidence, however, that the decline has far from ended.

A survey undertaken in 2005 by Christian Research, an organisation with a commitment 'to encourage change in Christian culture so that by 2010 more churches are growing' — and which might therefore be expected to paint an optimistic picture of progress being achieved — gave an indication of the extent to which attendance in Britain's churches had declined since 1990.[5] The figures may not be wholly reliable, such statistics seldom are, but they suggest falling attendance in the churches of the main denominations of between a half and a third.

It was only in the emergent Pentecostal churches that increases were to be found, with growth of up to twenty per cent; and these increasing numbers lifted those new churches into third position behind the two largest and oldest denominations, the Anglican and the Roman Catholic churches. It is estimated that in the second half of the twentieth century as many as five hundred of these new religious movements were established outside the mainstream in Britain. However, although much is known about them, thanks to the interest taken by sociologists, 'we know much less about the beliefs of committed church goers — still less about the "silent majority" in Britain, who, according to surveys, continue to believe in God but are happily unspecific about the nature and implications of such belief'.[6]

The Christian Research survey concluded that perhaps three million adults attended church at all regularly in 2005, that is, about five per cent of the population. Whatever the figures may in fact be today, whether an optimistic but dubious ten per cent or a more likely five per cent, or possibly something in between, there can be no question that only a small minority of Britons attend church, and evidence suggests that the numbers continue to fall. Clearly there are some exceptions, and in places individual churches thrive, with large and growing congregations. For those who are keen to emphasise that, the most frequently quoted example is the Anglican Holy Trinity church, Brompton, London, home of the fundamentalist evangelical Alpha course. However, this can be considered to be an anomaly. Growth has been especially evident in the cross-denominational charismatic movement and in urban, black, mainly Pentecostal churches, which in some measure are the same thing. There have also been reports of an influx of Polish communicants to the Roman Catholic church, reminiscent of the mid-Victorian Irish immigration, although today's newcomers are far fewer. The arrival of eastern Europeans may have slowed the decline but it has not generated growth.

In the overall picture, however, these random or unrelated growth points are not typical. A 'Decade of Evangelism' promoted by Anglican bishops in the closing years of the twentieth century was not simply a damp squib; statistics showed that by the end of the decade, numbers were lower than they had been at the beginning. In 2013 John Sentamu, Archbishop of York, expressed his dismay at the church's failure to reach a wider population, and issued a bold call for a campaign of renewal and the 're-evangelisation of England' that would follow in the tradition of the great northern saints who spread Christianity in Britain in Anglo-Saxon times. The church synod's barely active response to this ambitious challenge, this clarion call to mobilise and motivate the church's resources, was to set up a committee.[7]

It is possible that the Alpha courses organised at local level by evangelical churches in a number of the main denominations may make some small differences to church attendance; but if the results replicate those of the 'crusade decade' of the mid-1940s to mid-1950s —exemplified by the mass crusade assemblies led by the American

Closing down: Everything must go! 17

evangelist Billy Graham—they will not 'translate into significant church growth... Graham's work did nothing to arrest the imminent commencement of rapid secularisation'.[8] The verdict of an archbishop of Canterbury was that Billy Graham's 'crusades' had had minimal continuing impact on life in Britain, and that there was little to show for the massive evangelistic effort.[9]

What can be expected, however, is that any who do join the church *and remain* (a significant but uncertain factor), as a result of attending an Alpha evangelical recruiting mission, will form a new generation of believers in the church's traditional supernatural and dogmatic teaching, thus perpetuating acceptance of its outdated concepts. Even so, such endeavours have thus far been unable to apply the brakes firmly enough to slow or stop a continuing downhill slide.

A reminder or clarification is not out of place here: I am of course talking about the church in Britain. In the developing world, certainly in Africa, the picture is of a quite different nature. Churches in developing countries have yet to encounter the kind of issues with which western churches are familiar—the place of women is one example, homosexuality is another. As those issues arise in the future, and as living standards rise (possibly a contributing factor in the growth of secularisation), it may be that those developing churches will also experience a slowing in growth, followed by decline.

It is possible that changes are taking place in Britain's churches which are not reflected in the statistics. Be that as it may, to continue to propagate teachings which had their origins in an ancient, pre-Copernican, pre-scientific world, and to maintain a dogmatic doctrine which takes little account either of scientific discoveries or of developments in theological and philosophical scholarship, appears to suggest a lack of intellectual integrity, if not dishonesty. There can surely be no surprise that this outdated imagery and language finds no place in the lives of people in a modern or post-modern age.

It must be acknowledged, and very readily acknowledged, too—and this should not be forgotten nor its importance minimized—that churches and church agencies have long played and continue to play an active and effective role in many aspects of voluntary and charitable work, locally, nationally and on an international scale. Outstanding results have been achieved, quite out of proportion to the limited resources involved, and it is a strength which must be built upon. It is relevant, too, to add that major, effective voluntary and charitable work is at least equally found in secular organisations.

One tactic adopted by the Victorians in their vain attempts to draw the absentee masses into their churches was to introduce into their Sunday services hymns with catchy tunes and easily-learnt words, which they thought would appeal to the unschooled working classes. Present-day evangelicals have attempted a similar approach, in the belief that composing songs in a modern and simple idiom, and accompanying them with guitars or drums and trombones, will demonstrate to modern outsiders, especially young people, that the church is up to date and that church-going is 'cool'. There is no evidence that these tactics have had a measurable effect in drawing a new generation into the churches.

The continued use of the Jacobean English of Cranmer's 1662 *Book of Common Prayer*, beautiful as that language unquestionably is, did nothing to attract late twentieth-century people to active participation in the Church of England, either, and in 1980 the modern-language *Alternative Service Book* was introduced. One reviewer at the time observed that the new book had already raised more 'hysterical objections' than all previous prayer books put together.[10] It is probable that this so-called modern prayer book made no more sense to twentieth-century people than had its predecessor. Families continued, of course, to use the church's good offices for the 'hatches-matches-dispatches' rituals; but it is unlikely in the extreme that they could in conscience say that they believed (even if they could understand) the language of the service of baptism of infants. They were

> fobbed off instead with pathetic substitutes:
> *The Alternative Service Book* contains a feeble, half-baked service of 'Thanksgiving for the Birth of a Child' — which, where they are used, frequently become yet another occasion for a clergyman or clergywoman to get at people not involved in the church's life, instead of serving as an opportunity to rejoice with them.[11]

Looking at the *Alternative Service Book* now, it is easy to understand why it should be thought that the church 'had exchanged the glorious language of Cranmer for a deadness and a dullness which suggest that the compilers... had cloth ears'.[12] It is easy, too, to see why the Prayer Book Society was formed, 'to promote and preserve the use of the Book of Common Prayer [which] contains the church's historic beliefs'. The Society laments that 'the Book of Common Prayer is increasingly endangered by indifference and undermined by neglect. In many churches, it is not used at all... and most younger church-goers and newcomers to the church have barely even heard of it'.[13]

In the year 2000, the Church of England published *Common Worship*, which appears to an outsider looking in (I speak for myself, with my dissenter's bias) to be a mixture of the 'vernacular' and the old, traditional language, including the ancient creeds. Cranmer's 1662 prayer book, with its majestic but archaic language, enshrined the church's historical (supernatural) beliefs. Naturally, it also contained seventeenth-century expressions of those beliefs, concepts which have now long been obsolete. However, those supernatural concepts have been retained in the prayer book's successors. One example from *Common Worship* will illustrate this: in the service of baptism, the infant's parents or those bringing the child to the priest are asked, 'Do you reject the devil and all rebellion against God?' The required response, not surprisingly, is 'I do'.

Ironically, of course, people today can honestly and unhesitatingly answer 'I do'. That is not because they are now making a commitment to reject the works of a devil in whom (or in which) they believe, but rather because they have already rejected the literal *idea* of a devil, or did not believe in a devil in the first place, or in any of the other supernatural teachings of the church, for that matter. So, not a great deal of progress was being made by these attempts to bring the church up to date.

Today, the use of seventeenth-century prayers, or even some present-day versions of them, requires a kind of quick-reference mental phrase-book, to provide an interpretation of outdated, supernatural language. They can hardly be expected to make sense to people in the twenty-first century.

It is, then, a mistaken view that such changes enhance the perception of the church's relevance to the modern world. The large majority outside the church can doubtless see through these attempts, assuming that they have even noticed the attempts being made, and they remain outside.

* * *

Was there ever a time, though, when the churches were full? The answer may well be that we shall never know. What is known, of course, is that Britain has been a 'Christian' country for many centuries, at least in this sense: within a hundred years or so of the Roman legions' withdrawal from the remote province of Britannia early in the fifth century, a new wave of Christian missionaries arrived in these remote, offshore islands, reintroducing the faith to post-Roman Britain. Native kings and chieftains converted to the new religion, some choosing to call themselves Christian for political or other pragmatic purposes, and so their subjects were no longer deemed to be a pagan people. Over time, church and state became synonymous and Christendom was born. As a result the nation's culture could justifiably be labelled Christian. But because of its close links with the court, the church was more an organisation of political power and privilege than a place of personal piety. Moreover, Christianity was the religion of the learned and the literate; the democratisation of belief was still far away in the future.

Churches were built, then, not by the ordinary folk, but by the rich and the powerful, the men who had built the castles and the cathedrals. Within a few miles of my home in the High Weald of Sussex, for example, stands the surprisingly large and impressive Saxon church at Worth. When it was built at some point early in the tenth century, possibly before that, this imposing church stood in what was then no more than a clearing in the dense and dangerous forests of Andredsweald. When the Romans built their roads, they had tended to avoid this impenetrable and dangerous expanse of forest, which for many centuries afterwards continued to isolate Sussex from the surrounding country. Worth had no neighbours: there was only one other tiny settlement within literally dozens of miles in any direction. It is thought possible that the church was built by orders of the king or his family, or perhaps by a wealthy abbey some twenty-five miles distant.[14] Clearly, the splendid Worth church was not built by the local Saxon foresters. But who worshipped there and what were their beliefs?

It is correctly pointed out that surviving artefacts provide some evidence of Christian faith and practice in earlier ages, but they bear witness more to an establishment dogma, an orthodox body of teaching, than to individual conviction or personal faith. Early sixteenth-century books of hours which survive, produced by the then new technology of printing, include the owners' handwritten devotional additions; but these entries appear to be expressive of a pragmatic piety, with prayers for good weather for the crops, health for the farm animals, and protection from all harm. The religion of remote rural communities, which meant the greatest part of the realm until the time of the eighteenth- and nineteenth-century industrial revolution and even later, was a religion of holy wells and a cult of saints, a religion intertwined with ancient rural rites, and with pagan beliefs never far away. Officially, this may have been the Roman Christianity; in practice it seems more to have resembled the Celtic Christianity of Ireland and the Scottish isles, where, even in living memory, prayers were still said to the moon, and an ancient tradition of addressing the planets was not unknown.[15]

Whatever form personal piety may have taken, in public the common people found it prudent to observe and practise the monarch's religion. For example, under the Roman Catholic Queen Mary, the people — at least, those not attracted to the idea of being burnt at the stake — observed the Catholic rites. When Mary's sister, the Protestant Queen Elizabeth, came to the throne, the people discovered loyalties which matched the monarch's. Elizabeth was succeeded by Mary's son James and, with his actively Protestant sympathies, Catholicism came under pressure once more, putting incendiary notions into Guy Fawkes' head. The common sense of switching religious allegiance in line with the monarch's beliefs was immortalised in the traditional song, 'And this is law I will maintain / Until my dying day, sir, / That whatsoever King shall reign, / I'll still be Vicar of Bray, sir.'

Taking a view of British Christianity as, at worst, an imposed religious regime, and at best a tacit acceptance of a cultural norm, it cannot be known at this distance in time what personal belief or faith the common people may in fact have held, even if there is evidence of what they practised.

By the seventeenth century, dissenters broke away from the Church of England, forming new denominations which demonstrated doctrinal dissatisfaction with the established church's teaching and practices. The Wesleyan revival of the mid-eighteenth century most assuredly brought about large numbers of personal conversions, and increasing literacy among the common people almost certainly contributed to a growth in individuals' faith.

Even if we cannot know what Christian beliefs individuals were committed to, we do know what the church had been teaching all across those centuries. From earliest times, the church believed that the Bible—a collection of initially unrelated ancient documents written in different styles by different authors in different ages and in different parts of the Middle East—was literally the word of God. Supernatural doctrines, by definition from a pre-scientific era, derived from that belief and were enshrined in the creeds. Even today, the same doctrines continue to be taught as essential orthodoxy, with varying denominational interpretations and emphases, and the ancient creeds continue to be recited. While not all denominations are by any means formally creedal churches, virtually all would say 'yes' to the beliefs affirmed by the Apostles' Creed. Furthermore, many individual Christians in many denominations today continue not only to say 'yes' but also to maintain a literal belief in the supernatural content and imagery contained within the creed.[16]

It is possible that the man and woman in the street encountered this creed while at school, for example, and to varying degrees be familiar with, or at least be aware of, parts of the Bible. However, for one reason or another, but most likely because they simply cannot reconcile these supernatural teachings with the world that they experience or recognise any relevance in them, they have been unable to accept them, any more than they have a literal belief in (say) unicorns, ghosts or Father Christmas. So it is clear that many, or most, reject concepts such as a creator and an omnipotent and omniscient god 'up' in heaven (although that is something to which we shall return later), cannot accept that a virgin gave birth to the god-man Jesus (with a 'holy ghost' involved in the process in some way), do not believe that Jesus literally and physically returned to life three days after his death, or that he then 'ascended' to be with God. And while there is some ambivalence about life after death, it is safe to say that there is no widespread belief in the teaching that Jesus will be coming back to our world in time for 'Judgment Day'.

* * *

Closing down? *Everything* must go? Well, while that may be something of an exaggeration, it will at least serve as a metaphor. The evidence is that the church is in decline, and the practices of traditional faith are dying. If what remains of the church were to survive—and it may well be that the hands on the clock have all but reached midnight—it would have to change radically beyond naïve attempts to appear relevant by introducing jazzed-up hymn tunes, or by camouflaging its supernatural teachings with modern-day language. If a fading church continues to teach belief in the supernatural, as no doubt it will, the outsider will remain on the outside. It is also likely that more and more believers will become uneasy with the mismatch between a literal belief in the church's teaching and the world that they experience from day to day, and become believers-in-exile. Dwindling numbers of church attenders will prove insufficient to justify the buildings' continued use. And the 'For Sale' notices will go up.[17]

The church in Britain, then, continues to decline as congregations fall away. It seems to be inevitable that, as those numbers continue to fall, churches will close, and the remnants of local congregations will merge. What will be demanding, of course, will be for those congregations and the different denominations to agree the basis on which closures are to be effected. A merging of denominations or the removal of denominational differences would doubtless be a powerful contributor to resolving this problem, although there would remain the need to develop a realistic understanding of 'unity in diversity', that still-elusive and perhaps unattainable ecumenical ideal.

Almost certainly, this shaking of the foundations, this collapse of the familiar, will be denied by many or considered to be unjustifiable scaremongering. After all, for hundreds of years there have been those who thought they could see the beginning of the end of the church. Even before Victoria came to the throne, Dr Thomas Arnold, the headmaster of Rugby, had declared that no human power could save the church as things then stood. In more recent times, a not dissimilar view has been taken by a former archbishop of Canterbury, who has warned that the Church of England could be 'one generation away from extinction' unless it can attract young people into membership.[18] Unfortunately, simply replacing older members with younger ones, without making the most radical of changes to church teaching, would not in itself solve the problems of an outdated and irrelevant church, but merely postpone the demise of a moribund organisation.

On the other hand, a more positive view is entirely plausible. These turbulent times, this age of discontinuity in which we live, may be recognised as a time of renaissance. This may very well be the era of renewal for which John Sentamu was calling. Perhaps we are seeing the emergence of what Dietrich Bonhoeffer may have meant by 'religionless Christianity', a time when 'God is teaching us that we must live as [those] who can get along very well without him'.[19] It may be that we are moving toward the realisation of a dream, 'the dream of a post-religious religion... a form of radical Christian humanism'.[20]

An understanding that religion is a human creation, and that spiritual values are a part of being human and not the exclusive arcane property of 'believers' and their teachers within religious organisations, will be liberating for many: for those who have doubts or who have never believed, as well as for those who are no longer at home with the church's traditional teachings, or have even rejected them. Here is a place to which they can at last come, and say 'yes!' with honest conviction. Considering what form the new enterprise might take is the question to which we now turn.

- What issues or questions has this chapter raised for me?

- What have I learned?

---

1   Philip Larkin wrote 'Church Going' in 1954. He pointed out that while this poem was not an attack on the church, it was not a religious poem, either. He said that he 'felt the decline of Christianity in our century as tangibly as gooseflesh'. *Philip Larkin: The Complete Poems*.
2   'Anglo-Catholic Congresses' in *John Betjeman's Collected Poems*.
3   Stephen Games has suggested that while the public Betjeman was a professing member of the Church of England, in private he was very unclear and uncomfortable about what he should make of Christian belief and the validity of the church's doctrine. John Betjeman, *Sweet Songs of Zion: Selected Radio Talks*.
4   Graham Greene observed that whenever Christianity featured in the stories of Walter de la Mare, it was as a dead religion to which the churches were like massive stone memorials. Graham Greene, *Complete Essays*.

5   Christian Research (2005): http://www.equip.org.
6   Gerald Parsons (ed.), *The Growth of Religious Diversity*.
7   Reported in *The Telegraph* (London), 19 November 2013.
8   Callum G. Brown, *Religion and Society in Twentieth-Century Britain*.
9   Archbishop of Canterbury Geoffrey Fisher, cited in David Aikman, *Billy Graham: His Life and Influence*. The archbishop's verdict may well have held good for the remainder of the twentieth century: Billy Graham returned to Britain at least six times between 1961 and 1985.
10 A.N. Wilson in *The Spectator*, 29 November 1980.
11 Hugh Dawes, *Freeing the Faith: A Credible Christianity for Today*.
12 Monica Furlong, *C of E: The State It's In*.
13 The Prayer Book Society: http://www.pbs.org.uk.
14 E.A.Fisher, *The Saxon Churches of Sussex*.
15 Oliver Davies and Fiona Bowie, *Celtic Spirituality: Medieval and Modern*.
16 The eleven sets of 'sketches' which follow Chapter 6 look at the Apostles' Creed in detail. The author makes the assumption that this series of notes encapsulates what few people today believe to be literally true, and what many or most people reject. But the point is made that the creed can be used, as it is here, as a model for individuals to rethink what they do indeed believe, rather than what they do not; and as a result give thought to new ways of expressing what ultimate reality means to them.
17 At the time of writing, the Church of England is closing churches at the rate of twenty a year, and has a website listing 'Closed churches available for disposal'.
18 Former Archbishop of Canterbury, George Carey, in *The Telegraph*, 19 November 2013.
19 Dietrich Bonhoeffer, *Letters and Papers from Prison*.
20 Don Cupitt, *The Sea of Faith*.

Chapter 3

Opening shortly: A new enterprise

Increasing secularisation in Britain can be co-related to the fact that fewer and fewer people are attending church. It has already been noted that reliable statistics for church attendance are hard to come by, but clearly, even if numbers were to double overnight, those going to church would remain as a minority. If, on the other hand, the numbers continue to fall, as there is good reason to believe they will (some evidence for these falling numbers is presented later in this chapter), then Britain may in truth be on its way to becoming a secular society, with apparently little time for institutional religion.

In this context, I am taking secularisation to mean the process by which religious organisations (that is to say, the churches; but this may also be true of synagogues, I do not know) and the practices associated with them, and their teaching and awareness of them, are gradually losing their social relevance and significance. That loss, some argue, is a function of our exponentially increasing knowledge, which is gained through continuing scientific advances and is replacing religious belief. While some contrast science with religion, as though they are mutually exclusive (not a position held by all scientists by any means), and argue that scientific knowledge has replaced religious belief in the supernatural, it would not be true to claim that science has replaced religious belief *per se*.

The sociological argument is not a closed one. Others take the position that church attendance statistics are not the only indicator, or may not be the most reliable indicator, of the presence or absence of religion in society, or the extent to which there is an interest in religion. For those taking this view, Malcolm Hamilton points out, 'religion is seen as very much on the agenda and part of modern society, if in very altered, diverse and unfamiliar forms'.[1]

One altered or unfamiliar form of religion or religious belief, introduced earlier, is Christian humanism, which has a key part to play in the fulfilment society, our new enterprise. Given that religion is 'very much on the agenda', Christian humanism merits a place high on that agenda, presenting as it does new opportunities for those who, for whatever reason, have either rejected or never believed the church's supernatural teaching. Equally, secular humanism has a vital role in a world envisaged by Julian Huxley and which

> will see the birth of a new religion based on evolutionary humanism...
> it is clear that a humanism of this sort can provide powerful religious, moral and practical motivation for life.[2]

Without doubt it is true that religious institutions are losing their social significance; but it is certainly to be questioned whether there is at the same time a loss in religious consciousness.

* * *

To what extent, then, have I been justified in thinking or labelling the majority of Britons as 'outsiders', as I have done so far, simply because they are not to be found regularly or literally inside church buildings, perceived to be the home of religious belief? The world could more rationally be looked at the other way around, with church-goers (the minority) seen to be outside the social norm. Increasing secularisation may result in declining church attendance, but it does not necessarily indicate a decline in religion, or at least in religious or spiritual beliefs or values, which in some measure are held by the majority.

Emile Durkheim defined religion as 'a unified system of beliefs and practices relative to sacred things... which unite [all those who adhere to them] into one single moral community'.[3] Durkheim's definition has three main elements: beliefs, practices and a community. The evidence presented here, and the evidence observable 'on the ground', suggests that religious practices and church membership are indeed losing their social significance, as argued by the secularists.

What is being challenged, however, is the proposition that religious or spiritual *beliefs and values* are similarly in decline.

In the mid-Victorian era as well as in more recent times, church-going was 'ranked amongst the recognised proprieties of life' and the respectable middle classes were 'eminently distinguished' by their 'strictness of attention to religious services'.[4] A present-day view, though, is that

> church attendance is no longer an indication of respectability [and] absence from church may have nothing to do with a change in... religious beliefs.[5]

The notion of insider/outsider may be thought to imply polarities such as believer/unbeliever, as though there are two distinct, homogeneous populations: with church-goers forming one identifiable group which possesses some arcane truth, and whose values in consequence are held to be 'right', setting them apart from non-attenders; while those outside the churches form another distinct group, which has somehow missed something or lost (or never found) its way, and whose values as a result are seen at best to be misguided or inadequate and at worst to be 'wrong'.

The intention here is to put question marks against ideas about belief and Christianity, beginning to look at the new enterprise in which all comers can play a part, regardless of their belief and irrespective of which side of the church door they stand.

In spite of, or perhaps in face of, the rather depressing image of 'Church for sale' in Chapter 2, occasional polls in recent times have suggested that a majority of British people wish church buildings to be preserved, and even that National Lottery money should be made available as grant-aid to ensure their preservation—not a proposal that would have gone down too well with the nonconformist chapel-goers among whom I grew up sixty or more years ago. This suggests that churches, that is to say, church buildings, are recognised and accepted as a part of our heritage. This may be thought to be especially true in rural communities, and not only by those who live there. The parish church is commonly the largest and most visible building in the village; and it is not without significance that guide books such as the incomparable *The Buildings of England*[6] devote the greatest amount of space to detailed descriptions of church buildings.

What is not clear, however (as Philip Larkin asked), is what the buildings are to be preserved for: are they to act as some kind of monument or memorial, or become religious museums, perhaps? And who will pay? There are 16,000 of them, and that does not include the churches and chapels of the other denominations. Will they become a national asset? Will we be prepared to pay for their upkeep through taxation?

It is not unusual for those who are by no means regular churchgoers to comment that they 'feel something' whenever they do go into a church, not necessarily to attend a service but perhaps simply to look around. It seems to be difficult to enter a church building without having this sense of atmosphere. Quite how that atmosphere would be defined by the visitor is not easy to summarise, though. The response is almost certainly going to vary according to the type of church, from the simplicity of an unadorned Quaker meeting house, for example, to the splendour of a Baroque Roman Catholic cathedral; but it may well include words such as tranquillity, peace, restfulness, tradition, history, as well as an awareness of an intangible and undefined 'otherness', a presence even. Something, somewhere stirs, as Larkin suggested it would.

This 'otherness' is what Albert Einstein, who did not believe in a personal God, gave as the basis for calling himself a 'deeply religious unbeliever' and for ranking himself 'among profoundly religious men'. Einstein's argument was this:

> To know that what is impenetrable for us really exists and manifests itself as the highest wisdom and the most radiant beauty, whose gross forms alone are intelligible to our poor faculties—this knowledge, this feeling... that is the core of true religious sentiment.[7]

It is perhaps paradoxical that within the infinity of his mathematical cosmos, Einstein could find a place for the existence of what he called 'the impenetrable', made manifest in wisdom and beauty, for example, and, in his understanding, forming the essence of true religion.

That is perhaps what Wordsworth sensed when he wrote:

> A presence that disturbs me with the joy
> Of elevated thoughts; a sense sublime
> Of something far more deeply interfused,

> Whose dwelling is the light of setting suns,
> And the ocean and the living air
> And the blue sky, and in the mind of man;
> A motion and a spirit that impels
> All thinking things, all objects of all thought,
> And rolls through all things.[8]

In more recent times, the idea of 'otherness' has been expressed in a quite different way:

> Millions of people have it and don't know what it is that they have. God is their guest, but they haven't the faintest idea that he is in the house.[9]

It seems to be possible, then, and it is intrinsic to the argument here, that a sense of the spiritual, an awareness of the 'Other-than-oneself', is an integral part of being human. However, assenting to supernatural notions such as those taught by the church and enshrined in the creeds is clearly not a prerequisite for that spiritual awareness. A belief in transcendent values, for example, may spring from within some kind of cosmic consciousness, of which we are all a part, aware or unaware.

So it is probable that, for most people, church and religion are synonymous, and both would be linked with the spiritual. And yet it is clear that spirituality is not synonymous with the church's supernatural teaching, and Christianity is not to be thought of as the same as, or to be dependent upon, church attendance. These are topics which we need to examine more closely, as we think about learning communities and the fulfilment society, of which they will be a part.

On this account, then, the Christian church can be said to be recognised as both an historical and an historic phenomenon: historical in the sense that it is a factually verifiable institution, having a story traceable across two thousand years, with a great number of its buildings dating from something like half that time; and historic in the sense that without question it has had the greatest imaginable impact, for good and ill, on western civilisation.

In passing, it is fascinating to conjecture in what ways western civilisation would have developed, had not the newly-converted Roman emperor Constantine, whatever his motives, 'exhorted all his subjects to imitate... the example of their sovereign and to embrace the divine truth of Christianity'[10] and Europe had instead continued to worship the old gods. That was in the early years of the fourth century of our era, but the transformation did not come about overnight. Even when, 750 years later, William the Conqueror landed in England, bringing his ecclesiastical architects with him, Christianity in other parts of Europe was still competing with a polytheistic paganism.

So, while it is clear that many Britons believe church buildings to be a part of their heritage—along with Morris dancers and Stonehenge, perhaps—and that historically the institutional church itself has formed a part of that heritage, it seems also to be true that the majority see little if any significant relevance today for the church, that is, for organised or institutional religion.

In the 2001 National Census, nearly three quarters (seventy-two per cent) of the adult population gave Christianity as their religion, but by the time of the 2011 census, the figure had fallen to fifty-nine per cent.[11] Current figures for church attendance, however, whatever their source, are hugely at variance with those findings, as we have already seen. It may therefore be a matter of what Malcolm Hamilton has called 'believing without belonging'.[12] And this is a critical point.

But believing what? Probably not what those inside the church believe, or are expected to believe, at least not in its entirety or in the same way. Not that there is only one way to believe. It is because of the infinite number of ways of using and understanding language, coupled with each individual's life experiences and perceptions, 'that no two individuals ever possess the same Christian faith'.[13]

It has already been noted that the church's traditional role has been that of a teaching organisation. For countless generations, men and women have been trained, qualified and authorised to continue to propagate and so perpetuate a centuries-old orthodox body of beliefs. They were taught by similarly trained, qualified and authorised teachers in approved seminaries and colleges, and the orthodoxy was based on the church authority's interpretation and understanding of the Bible and its ancient biblical creed.

Teaching is a top-down process, and the church's teaching role has been underpinned by the unshakeable sense of authority arrogated by it. In parts of the church, notably the Roman Catholic church, that assumed authority is vested in a powerful and paternalistic hierarchy. Parts of the Anglican communion, in Africa especially, are barely less authoritarian or censorious. Other churches, the nonconformist denominations in particular, invest that authority in the Bible itself. The Evangelical Alliance, for example, to which several thousand individual congregations in mainstream British churches are affiliated (including the Church of England), requires its members to sign up to a belief in 'The divine inspiration and supreme authority of the Old and New Testament Scriptures, which are the written Word of God — fully trustworthy for faith and conduct'.[14]

In Part Three, we will look at ways in which one social group, usually a dominant group, believes its own status or values to be the right or superior ones, and develops and nurtures a view of another, 'different' group of people, whose behaviour or values they consider to be undesirable or possibly wrong. They may even take steps to defend themselves against a perceived threat from them.[15] It has been proposed that this was the process by which the Christian creeds were formulated by the early church councils. The creeds were considered necessary, not as additional teaching, but as a definitive defence for orthodoxy against the challenges of heresy. Thus it was, for example, that the theoretical concept of the Trinity emerged, an unnecessary and puzzling dogma which had not existed in early Christianity.

Charges of heresy are a minimal, indeed negligible, risk for modern-day lay people; but, incredible as it may seem, even today the risk of being hauled over the coals as a heretic remains very real for clergy who depart from the official line. Heresy trials were not left behind in medieval times. In the mid-twentieth century (1966) Lloyd Geering, a minister and professor in the New Zealand Presbyterian church, was tried for heresy, as a result of publishing an article rejecting the supernatural world.[16] In 1993, Anthony Freeman's bishop removed him from his post of priest-in-charge of a Sussex church when he went ahead with publishing a book in which he had the courage to say 'I do not believe in God'.[17] In 2002, Andrew Furlong, Anglican Dean of Clonmacnoise in Ireland, came before a heresy trial for denying the divinity of Jesus.[18] It is known that there are very many members of the clergy who hold beliefs that would be quite unacceptable to the establishment if they were made known

Opening shortly: A new enterprise 33

but, understandably, they do not go public with them. Inevitably, it must be very uncomfortable for them to live in these two worlds.

In large measure this illustrates the problem with asking people if they believe in God, as though there is just one definitive meaning for the word, of which everyone is aware, and with which everyone agrees. Early in 2013, a British Humanist Association press advertisement asked a number of yes/no questions—for example, Do you believe in God? and Do you consider yourself religious? The questions appeared to assume that all respondents would understand the words God and religious in the same way as each other, and that they would know what the words meant definitively to the questioner.

When it comes to the question of what people believe, the data in polls and surveys are interesting, if confusing or inconclusive. The table below is taken from a national survey,[19] comparing the first and last years of the twentieth century's closing decade. The figures are expressed as percentages of the population. Respondents were asked to tick one box to show which statement came closest to expressing what they believed about God.

	1991	2000
[a] I don't believe in God	10	12
[b] I don't know whether there is a God and I don't believe there is any way to find out	14	15
[c] I don't believe in a personal God but I do believe in a Higher Power of some kind	13	12
[d] I find myself believing in God some of the time but not other times	13	13
[e] While I have doubts, I feel that I do believe in God	26	24
[f] I know God really exists and I have no doubts about it	23	21

While we cannot tell from these data which age groups are represented, more recent figures[20] provided some indicators. In 2010, a survey gave comparative figures for religious belief in the years 1983 and 2010. In the earlier year, fifty-five per cent of those aged between eighteen and twenty-seven stated that they had no religion, but that proportion had risen to sixty-five per cent by 2010. When it came to older age groups, there was similarly an increase: in 1983, of those aged more than sixty-five, twelve per cent stated that they had no religion; by 2010, the figure had risen to twenty-four per cent. The survey concluded that the decline in religious affiliation was brought about by generational replacement. Older, more religious generations are replaced by younger, less religious ones. Fewer people are born into families with religious affiliation and lack of 'religiosity' tends to remain with individuals as they get older.

This generational shift may be illustrated by a falling level of interest in once-popular Victorian hymns, taking the BBC television programme *Songs of Praise* as a reference point. When introducing his well-received series of radio talks, which were broadcast throughout the 1970s, John Betjeman observed that 'Even today, when it is assumed that we've all given up religion, millions of people enjoy programmes on the radio and television that consist solely of people singing old familiar hymns'.[21]

His claim still held good more than ten years later: the Christmas 1988 edition of *Songs of Praise* attracted more than eleven million viewers, although that high figure doubtless reflects a continuing widespread affection for Christmas carols (which in itself is an interesting element within this discussion). Twenty years later, however, the programme's average audience was down to 3.4 million; and by 2012 the BBC's audited figures showed that the average age of *Songs of Praise* viewers was sixty-five.[22]

Disraeli is said to have believed that there are three kinds of lie: lies, damned lies and statistics. The statistics in the table can be analysed or interpreted in a number of ways, with different inferences being drawn. For example, some may argue with positive enthusiasm that the great majority, as many as eighty-five per cent, believe in God to one extent or another—anything from certainty to ambivalence—whereas only twelve per cent of the population say they do not [a]. Although the rise over the decade from ten to twelve per cent is an increase of a fifth, it can be said to be relatively small in absolute terms. Others may counter what appears to be a positive position by pointing out that only twenty-one per cent of people now state with conviction that they *do* believe in God, down from twenty-three per cent ten years earlier [f], whereas up to seventy-six per cent now express varying shades of doubt or unbelief [a to e]. If the answers to d, e and f are combined, that is to say, looking at the varying degrees to which Britons do believe in God, there has been a fall from sixty-two to fifty-eight per cent; and by adding [c] and [d] together, it could also be said that there has been a small increase in agnosticism.

Taking the figures as a whole, then, it can be inferred that between 1991 and 2000 there was an overall decline in a belief in God.

However, it cannot be emphasised enough within this discussion that statements such as those used in the tabulated survey findings above are less than satisfactory, in that they make assumptions about the meaning of 'God', making no attempt to define what is meant by the word or the concept. It is only statement [c] which is helpful in this context: 'I don't believe in a personal God but I do believe in a Higher Power of some kind.'

In 1983 Britons were asked with which denomination (if any) they were prepared to identify themselves—not the same thing as saying which church they attend—and forty per cent answered 'Church of England'. That may be no surprise; like the other statistics, this figure may be suspect, since it is a commonplace that when asked questions about religion and church, the English person is likely to side with Parson Thwackham: 'When I mention religion, I mean the Christian religion; and not only the Christian religion, but the Protestant religion; and not only the Protestant religion, but the Church of England.'[23]

Be that as it may, by 1998 the percentage of those identifying with the Church of England had fallen from forty to twenty-seven per cent. In 1983, sixty-two per cent of the population was prepared to be identified with a Christian denomination, but this was down to forty-six per cent by 1998. Those answering 'no religion' rose from thirty-one to forty-four per cent in the same years.[24]

A survey published at the end of 2006[25] did little to clear an already muddied pool. To the question 'Are you religious?' sixty-three per cent of respondents answered 'No', and yet when asked, 'Which religion do you belong to?' sixty-four per cent answered 'Christian'. Fifty-nine per cent said either that they never visit a place of worship, or that they did so once or less often a year.

While hardly conclusive, the findings of this survey add weight to the argument here, that a commonly held view is that 'being religious' is to be equated with church-going; thus, it may be inferred that if one does not go to church, one is not religious. On the other hand, a majority of people who never or very rarely go to church are prepared to call themselves Christian; that is to say, they tacitly acknowledge that they have a religious identity of some kind. It would, of course, be useful to know what the survey meant, or what the respondents understood, by 'visit a place of worship'.

After researching 'religiosity' both 'in terms of religious membership or belief' a study concluded 'extensive international comparison suggests the Church of England is doing no worse than [other] churches'.[26] But what a splendid motto that would make: *We are no worse than anyone else!*

From all this, then, it seems likely that few of my so-called outsiders would wholeheartedly agree with Dylan Thomas's Nogood Boyo, as he gazes up at the sky and says, with all the apathy that he can muster, 'I don't know who's up there and I don't care'.[27] There is clearly far more to it than that.

For my part, I suggest that the figures in the table can be read in this way: to one extent or another, seventy per cent of the population have a belief in what they call 'God' [c, d, e and f], and if those who are 'not sure' [b] are included, that rises to eighty-five per cent. What interests me is the remaining twelve per cent [a]: what do these people mean by the God in whom they say they do not believe? Is it the God of the church, the supernatural God, the God 'out there'? How would they describe this God, to whom, or to which, they are saying no? It is my view, I should add, that there are far fewer thought-through, convinced atheists than any figures or any claims suggest. Might some of those in [a] really belong in [c]? For that matter, how would *any* of the respondents describe the God in whom they say they do or do not believe, little or much?

* * *

These questions of belief are questions with which the nascent fulfilment society will be directly engaged. No longer will the guardians of orthodoxy be the teachers; but working within a community of *learners*, the new enterprise will be tasked first with deconstructing and then reconstructing the meaning and practical relevance of belief, and identifying needs and opportunities for social action.

To reconstruct may entail rebuilding something that is damaged or in need of repair. That is partly what is meant here, although learning communities will have to avoid stitching new patches onto old garments, or pouring new wine into old wineskins. The task is neither to patch up, nor to reorganise existing organisational structures or (necessarily) create new ones.

Essentially, reconstruction is to be understood as giving a new meaning to something. One of the problems with language is that words do not in themselves have a meaning; they are given a meaning.[28] So, before re-construction can begin, there is need for deconstruction. Deconstruction makes an attempt to uncover and identify the ambiguities or oppositions of 'meanings' within the words or text (for which read creed or traditional teaching) and examines ways in which these 'meanings' may have been accorded privilege or legitimacy at the expense of other possible interpretations. The challenge, and it is an extremely difficult one, is the attempt to turn a familiar word or phrase or concept into a thoroughly unfamiliar word or phrase or concept, as though one has never come across it before.

In spite of any appearances to the contrary, neither this chapter nor indeed this book has any wish to prolong the theme of defeat and closure and demolition. Rather, the aim is to look forward to reopening, rediscovery and reconstruction, as the decline of the church continues, and with it its authority and influence, and to see the emergence of a 'fulfilment society'. Among the beginnings of this new movement of the human spirit will be the establishment of a new enterprise, the learning community, tasked with learning and opportunity search, with a vision of a broken world remade. Membership of the learning community is open to everyone, no longer making a distinction between insiders and outsiders. Engagement in opportunity search and input to the work of the new enterprise are required of everyone.

It has been observed in recent times that 'nobody has yet had any lasting success in modernising one of the old faith-traditions [but instead] we have seen an anti-modern, neo-conservative backlash'.[29] Those outside the church and looking in may well have wondered, given that they cared, what hope there may have been for modernisation, as robed and mitred men [sic] literally pontificate and prevaricate over the issues of the day. But learning communities will be concerned not so much with reformation as with reconstruction, rediscovery, even resurrection. Others write and talk about reformation, but that is not sufficiently revolutionary. A greater vision is required.

Community is what the Romans called *communitas*, from their word *communis*, with its meanings of shared, communal, held in common. For Cicero, the *communitas* was a place where people were willing to come together to take counsel and to take action. It is the same concept as the Greek *ekklesia*, about which we will think in Part Two. This will be the dual role of the learning community: first to take counsel together, then to act together. And when we come to look at what it means to learn, it will be clear that this is a continuing process: think... act... review... think again... act again...

The shape that learning communities take will vary from place to place, and their structure, if they have one, must remain fluid or, better still, undefined. Learning communities will bring together diverse individuals from the widest imaginable range of backgrounds (more about diversity in the next chapter), who are prepared to be a part of an enterprise which defies definition. It is possible that the learning community will form and work within a variety of existing structures, as well as independently of any organisation. But the sense of community will be strong, felt both when the members are together and when they are dispersed. Community is not defined by a place: it is defined by common purpose and shared values.

So the emphasis here is not that the learning community should become a formal organisation, quite the opposite. Indeed, it may have been unhelpful of me to refer to this as an 'enterprise'. It will be interesting, as an example, to see how the Sunday assemblies referred to in Chapter 1 develop, since they have already created a formal organisational structure. Perhaps significantly, even at this embryonic stage, their organisation is already reported to be facing the possibility of breakaway groups, through disagreement over a definition of 'atheism'.[30] Avoiding the establishment of the official line (once known as orthodoxy) and maintaining a culture of unity through diversity will be essential characteristics of the learning community.

At the local level, there will be gathered meetings of the learning community, coming together regularly or occasionally.[31] A small number of local learning communities may choose to form an area network, and area networks might conceivably make loose regional links, all within an informal national connection. At all levels, the

Opening shortly: A new enterprise

purpose would be to share concerns and findings, to optimise the use of resources and commit to joint action. In short, to learn together and to work together.

Then again, the learning community's 'shape' may be nothing like that, not least because globalisation, internet connections and social media mean that we are fast becoming accustomed to our ability to communicate instantly and directly with others, whether they are in Peru or Thailand, Namibia or Kazakhstan.

Should the day dawn when the emergence of a formal organisational structure can be discerned, especially if any kind of authority is recognised or a hierarchy established, or if 'big names' in a movement are admired or quoted, then the learning community will most certainly have lost its way.

However, that is still in the future. First there is a need to recruit some learners to the community.

- What issues or questions has this chapter raised for me?
- What have I learned?

---

1. Malcolm Hamilton, 'Secularisation? Now You See it, Now You Don't'.
2. Julian Huxley, 'The Coming New Religion of Humanism' in *The Humanist* magazine, January/February 1962.
3. E. Durkheim, *The Elementary Forms of the Religious Life*.
4. Horace Mann, cited in J.R. Moore (ed.), *Religion in Victorian Britain*.
5. M. Haralambos, *Sociology: Themes and Perspectives*.
6. Nikolaus Pevsner and Ian Nairn, *The Buildings of England*.
7. Albert Einstein, cited in C. Hitchens (ed.), *The Portable Atheist*.
8. William Wordsworth, *Lines written a few miles above Tintern Abbey*, 1798.
9. Bernard Canter in an editorial in *The Friend* vol. 123 (1962).
10. Edward Gibbon, *Decline and Fall of the Roman Empire*.
11. Census figures are Crown copyright and are reproduced by permission of the Controller, HMSO: www.statistics.gov.uk.
12. Malcolm Hamilton, *op.cit.*
13. John Hull, *What Prevents Christian Adults from Learning?*
14. Evangelical Alliance: www.eauk.org.
15. Peter L. Berger and Thomas Luckmann, *The Social Construction of Reality*.
16. Lloyd Geering, *Wrestling With God*.
17. Anthony Freeman, *God in Us: A Case for Christian Humanism*.
18. Andrew Furlong, *Tried for Heresy: A 21st-century Journey of Faith*.
19. British Social Attitudes Survey, National Centre for Social Research.
20. *Ibid.*

[21] John Betjeman, *Sweet Songs of Zion: Selected Radio Talks*.
[22] Aaqil Ahmed, BBC Head of Religious Broadcasting, *The Telegraph*, 25 May 2013.
[23] Henry Fielding, *Tom Jones*.
[24] British Social Attitudes Survey, *op. cit*.
[25] *The Guardian*/ICM December 2006.
[26] N.D. De Graaf and A. Need, 'Losing Faith: Is Britain Alone?'
[27] Dylan Thomas, *Under Milk Wood*.
[28] For a comprehensive discussion of 'meaning' see Terry Eagleton, *Literary Theory*.
[29] Don Cupitt, 'After Religion—What?' in *Sofia* No. 80 (Journal of The Sea of Faith Network), November 2006.
[30] *The Guardian*, 29 April 2014.
[31] In writing this book, I came to realise that in large measure I had been describing the Religious Society of Friends (Quakers). I can see that the Quakers anticipated the fulfilment society by several centuries and have long had it in their hands to reverse the church's decline. My concern, however, would be that the Quakers' focus on quietism would not appeal to everyone. And, in spite of many years' association with Friends, it is still not clear to me how teaching and learning feature in their religious society.

Chapter 4

Learners wanted: Now recruiting

The unambiguous message is there for all to see: as a new supermarket prepares to open yet another out-of-town store, the new site is draped with banners proclaiming in letters so large that none will miss them:

NOW RECRUITING!

So, let it be known to one and all: the fulfilment society is now recruiting to its learning communities. And, to borrow words from recruitment advertisements, with a few more added, this is an equal opportunities enterprise, open to all, regardless of age, religious belief (or none), denominational affiliation, ethnic origin, gender, height or weight, marital status, disability, sexual orientation, colour of eyes, hair or skin, educational achievement, previous experience, present occupation (or none), political views, post code, regional accent, or size of bank balance.

What requirements will be made of those joining the learning community? Few, in fact: but those that are made will be demanding.

The first will be an ability to value diversity, demonstrating a ready acceptance of the 'other' person. This is what Carl Rogers called unconditional positive regard, a readiness to accept the other person 'without reservations, without evaluations'.[1] That will have a special relevance to the community's programme for action, outlined in Part Three, with its focus on the concept of social construction. Social construction is the process by which individuals and groups construct a view of the world, as perceived from their own, possibly privileged, position. Words such as poverty and 'the poor', for example, or single mothers, benefits claimants, immigrants, homosexuals, Roma or Muslims, trigger what are in practice well-rehearsed sets of responses. Recognising and managing those responses will be essential both to the learning community's health and to its effectiveness.

Thus, diversity will be experienced within the community's membership itself, which will be characterised by any combination of those equal opportunities descriptors. I will be required to learn quickly how to collaborate with people 'not like me', just as others will have the need to find ways of working with me. There will be no place for notions such as superiority and inferiority, or better and worse. Different we most certainly will be, but this at least we will have in common: every one of us is 'work in progress', every one of us is still *becoming*. The question for me is the same as the question for every one of my fellows—am I becoming what I am capable of becoming?

It will be questioned whether such inclusivism is possible. Are there to be no boundaries? One criterion would be that members of a learning community pose no threat to others. That members should be law-abiding may be another expectation: but what about those who refuse to pay the portion of their income tax used for armaments? And what of those belonging to a cult, or to an extremist political group? Membership of the learning community will be self-selecting, but even so, these questions already illustrate the effects of social construction.

Is this a naïve expectation, then, that all and everyone will catch this vision and seek to be included in this new enterprise? Certainly. But among the hundreds of shoppers milling about in the supermarket, the thousands of commuters crowding into the Underground train, the tens of thousands of fans cheering at the football match, there will be many who will recognise here an opportunity for looking at and thinking about their beliefs and values in a new way. They may come to see, perhaps for the first time, that here is a space or a place where they can experience personal renewal and spiritual growth, and how they may play a part in rebuilding the world, or at least their small corner of it, not only recognising the opportunity but also responding to it.

An early task for the learning community will be to find ways in which a community rule might be expressed. An amber light may begin to flash at the mention of the word rule; but it is not intended to imply regulations, quite the opposite. Rules and regulations would be limiting and totally at variance with the spirit of creativity and exploration which must remain at the heart of the learning community. Perhaps vision is a better word, an ideal by which community members live and towards which they constantly move. Certainly it is my conviction that these groups will wish to resist creeds and dogma; but on the other hand they will experience greater cohesion and sense of belonging if they have an agreed 'script' which they can rehearse individually and corporately. For example, the Sunday assembly referred to in Chapter 1 has such a vision: 'Live better, help often, wonder more.'

The essentials for that ideal are to be found in a biblical story, told in one of the New Testament gospels, where a member of the religious establishment tried to catch Jesus out by asking, 'Teacher, which is the greatest commandment in the Law?' Jesus was more than a match for the questioner, and wrapped up the Jewish law into just two requirements: 'Love the Lord your God with all your heart and with all your soul and with all your mind' and 'Love your neighbour as yourself'.[2]

Learning communities will do well to build on that expression of the ideal, although it goes without saying that for some there will clearly be a need to adjust the God language. Love is at the centre of the Christian ideal. But of course love has never been Christianity's sole property, nor is love evidenced anything like enough among Christians. It is a universal ideal, though, and one that is far from easy to live up to. As G.K. Chesterton observed, the Christian ideal has not been tried and found wanting: it has not been tried because it was found difficult.

Two other requirements of recruits to the learning community will be that they are comfortable with ambiguity, and that they are and remain open-minded, that is, they are prepared to learn.

In my professional past, there was a penny waiting to drop, but it was a very long time before it finally did so. Then at last it dropped with a loud clatter. Over many years, countless business and management books had been written and published, and seminars and courses had been developed and presented (*taught*, I mean), based on a number of assumptions that there was some kind of body of knowledge, or a right (or at least, a preferred or recommended) way to do things. The long-delayed penny dropped when I came across this:

> In an epoch of change, such as that in which the world now flounders, there is no handicap to exceed the misconception of past experience… the idolisation of successes established in circumstances unlikely to recur is of little help in the fugitive present.[3]

For me, those (at the time) startling words marked a shift from teaching to learning. In a fast-changing world, in 'the fugitive present', there was (is) a need to challenge our assumptions, and even abandon the tried and tested. What once was true, or thought to be true, may no longer be true. Change is here to stay, and the discovery that the once-familiar has been replaced by the unfamiliar inevitably creates ambiguity and uncertainty. Members of the learning community must learn, if not actually to welcome change and ambiguity, at least not to allow uncertainty to divert them from their ideals and their goals within the programme of reconstruction.

Learning the skills of creative thinking will be a priority, although this is not to suggest that there will be no place for logical approaches to opportunity search and problem solving. The originator of 'lateral thinking', Edward de Bono, makes a contrast between what he terms vertical thinking and lateral thinking, though he is at pains to emphasise that the two are complementary. De Bono's vertical thinking is a method many or most of us were taught to use (although de Bono points out and regrets that in fact we are not *taught* to think at all): be sensible, collect the facts, don't make assumptions, build on experience, listen to the experts. Vertical thinking moves on by logical steps, each new step taken once the previous step has been validated.

Lateral thinking, by contrast, or 'thinking outside the box' (in itself an over-worked cliché), uses information to generate new ideas, to escape from the captivity of old ones. De Bono uses the analogy of digging holes: you cannot dig a new hole by digging an existing hole deeper, he points out, that would be vertical thinking. To dig a hole in a different place requires lateral thinking.[4] To go on doing the same thing over and over again and expect a different result has been described as lunacy.[5]

Similarly polarised ways of thinking have been classified by Nobel laureate Daniel Kahneman, who labels them System 1 and System 2. System 1 is instant or intuitive thinking, quick and automatic, with no sense of voluntary control, and it can produce unexpected patterns of idea; whereas the slower System 2 involves or requires effortful mental activity and calculation, and produces thoughts on an orderly step-by-step basis.[6]

Those who have visited a primary school cannot have failed to notice that the classroom walls are decorated with the children's paintings, not just paintings by a few 'artists', though, but every child's painting. However, as children get older, they are nurtured away from a natural, uninhibited freedom of expression and when painting they are encouraged to keep their colours 'inside the lines'. And so their creativity is lost and they give up painting. It is said that while looking at small children's pictures one day Pablo Picasso commented, 'When I was the age of these children I could draw like Raphael; it took me many years to learn how to draw like these children'.[7] Rediscovering and regaining an uncomplicated, child-like freedom of expression will contribute to creative thinking.

As the learning community begins its journey along the road to reconstruction it will be imperative to keep an eye open for side turnings, to use a lateral thinking analogy. Side turnings are fundamental to lateral thinking, but it is essential to be able to identify which turnings to take and which to avoid. Some side turnings may be seductive diversions, yet are in fact roads to perdition. Other turnings may be the ones to take, but they are missed because we are too busy scanning the horizon — which we also need to do — so intent on the road ahead that we lose our way. Then, having lost our way, we retrace our steps, but can no longer find the side turning that we missed.

Open-mindedness means more than simply being prepared to soak up new ideas. It also means actively learning to recognise not what we know or are familiar with (that is, more of the same) but what we do not know, or even the unwelcome, the things we would rather not know!

Learning to learn

What other skills will recruits to the learning community need to develop? This chapter opened with a commercial allusion, and a number of other business references have been made elsewhere. So I want now to proceed with great caution, lest I give the impression that I am writing yet another management manual! On the other hand, I have not the least doubt that the concepts outlined in the remainder of this chapter and in the whole of the next one do indeed belong here, because they have a vital importance and direct relevance to the development of the learning community. However, since I claimed at the outset that this 'how to' book would devote little space to telling you how to do anything, my hope is that what follows will provide ideas for learning communities to explore for themselves, as a part of their development.

One of the tenets of the fulfilment society is that it should offer 'the fullest opportunities... for co-operating in worthwhile projects [and] for self-development'. But it needs to be remembered that the essentials of effectiveness and excellence in working groups—both in communities of learners and in those which are engaged in collaborative social action—do not just happen; they have to be made to happen. Experience leaves little doubt that while groups may be quite capable of concentrating on the *task*, the job to be done, they neglect the *process*, the ways in which the group works and how its members interrelate.

There are, then, two or three reasons for my conviction about the validity of including these models or theories. First, because they are about people, whether those people are in the parent-teacher association, the office, the tennis club, the parish council, the pub, or of course in the family. Secondly, these ideas form a useful structure for thinking about learning and collaborative action, and provide a language or vocabulary for understanding perhaps unfamiliar (even if common sense) concepts. And if the concepts are unfamiliar, then that in itself offers a valuable learning opportunity.

Learning how to work together will require not only an acceptance of our various physical, social, educational, cultural or political differences, and so on, but also an understanding of personality and temperamental diversity. One way in which this diversity is likely to be made manifest is through the different approaches which we take to learning. Some, those among us who take an activist or pragmatic approach, want to get on and do things; while others, those who like to reflect or theorise, need to spend more time thinking and planning before finally rolling up our sleeves. This is a significant enough topic to warrant a discussion all of its own and we will return to it in the next chapter.

It may be helpful here to develop further the proposition that learning is different from teaching. This is an important contrast, one that has already been made when thinking of the church's historical but now outdated role as a place of teaching, and, in contrast, our new enterprise as a place of learning.

Swift and terrible retribution from the headmaster of my old school was guaranteed, should a boy attempt to explain away his ignorance by objecting, 'But, sir, we've only been taught that once!' A common perception may well have been that school was more about teaching than about learning. There were those in authority who possessed a body of knowledge—just as the church did across the centuries—and it was their job to get that knowledge, some of it anyway, into our heads.

If there is a place for teachers within the learning community, and there is, it is in the role of facilitator, providing support and guidance to learners, as they recognise and explore their ignorance and go prospecting for new ideas. It is likely to remain true that there will be those who believe that they have a vocation, that they are called to be teachers. If so, their most effective contribution will no longer be to perpetuate a fixed, unchanging dogma, but to open up limitless opportunities for discovery.

The aim of teaching is to make learning possible. This was one of the church's failings. A consequence of the church's concentrating on its unquestioned, traditional function as an authoritative teaching organisation was its neglect of the learning processes. John Hull has very neatly observed the paradox. The churches which had the clearest sense of community tended to be those which discouraged any challenge to orthodoxy. This strong sense of community should be the ideal foundation for learning to take place; but in fact, by putting so much emphasis on authority, these churches were seen to 'place a low value on adult Christian learning'.[8] By contrast, those churches which did not shy away from or even actively encouraged independent enquiry, and so should have been open to corporate learning and opportunity search, tended to be gatherings of individuals and so lacked the cohesion necessary for a learning community. Either way, it has been proposed that 'religious communities seem to be waging a losing battle for hearts and minds—especially minds'.[9]

The new function of teaching will be not so much to ensure the propagation and perpetuation of what has always been taught, maintaining the unquestioned 'body of knowledge', but in sourcing new concepts and providing a link between the innovators and the seeker-learners. Facilitator-teachers will need to understand their role in providing guidance towards new thinking, as the boundaries continue to be pushed outwards. It is not a new idea. Forty years ago, a future church was glimpsed, which would 'assign appropriately trained representatives to study the various aspects of the society in which it lives and to lead experiments in Christian service to that society'.[10] That opportunity was missed. Now may be the time for the nascent fulfilment society to catch that glimpse again, and turn it into a reality.

Terence Copley has taken the view that indoctrination, both secular and religious, gets in the way of education, questioning and thinking.[11] For at least the past thirty years, schools have become less influential in the teaching/learning process. Pupils and students have access to information and knowledge from such a wide range of sources that teachers' input has reduced in importance. The schools' main task now, according to this argument, is to concentrate on enabling young people to learn.[12] Had it not been too late, the same would have been true for teachers within the church.

Encouraging or enabling adults to engage readily in what they recognise as structured or active learning may be more easily said than done, however. The point has been made already that we are all learning all the time; but when it comes to planned or intentional learning the picture is dramatically different. A survey of adult learning in Britain in 2007[13] found that only two in five adults were currently learning or had engaged in learning during the previous three years, and there was a clear divide between the more affluent and the less well-off. One third of all adults said that they had done no formal learning since leaving full-time education.

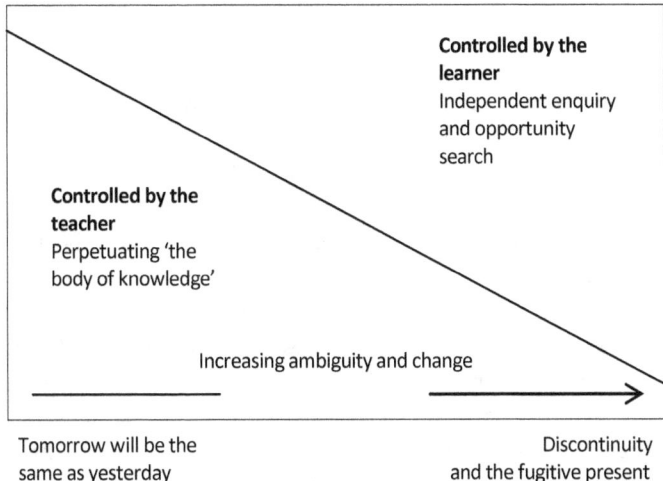

If there is either inertia or resistance to learning, is it possible that this is a leftover from schooldays, when there was a perception (reality?) that being seen as a learner puts one in an inferior position, perhaps even with a sense of being deficient in some way? John Hull observes that, traditionally, teachers have been in control of learning, because pupils/learners were not considered to be in a position to make decisions about what they should be learning or indeed what there was to be learnt. This decision about what is to be learnt, according to Hull, 'is no longer the prerogative of the occasional, strong-minded individual, but it is a necessity confronting [everyone]'.[14]

Like greatness, then, some have had learning thrust upon them, or feel that they have. But while only some are born to be great, we are all born to be learners, and we can all achieve learning. Even if Confucius did not say it, he doubtless thought it:

> Tell me, but I forget.
> Show me, and I may remember.
> Involve me, and I learn.

Working together

In proposing ways in which a learning community may develop and function, there are very good reasons for me to pause, once again, before linking this new collaborative enterprise with that vogue word 'teams', or introducing notions of so-called team-working. The word team and ideas about team-working have long been a managerial fad and a cliché in commercial and industrial parlance. In practice, many organisations use the word team to mean nothing more than a work group. The local men who were once referred to as the bin men now have a vehicle declaring them to be Team Waste (to be fair, they may work as a team for all I know). It is a fad which has spilled over into all our lives: in 2012 no one in Britain could have missed the 'brand' of Team GB.

In spite of that caution, I still believe that many aspects of teamwork and what it is that characterises a winning team will find a valuable place within the learning community. Some of those aspects and characteristics are outlined in Appendix 2. They are offered as a resource for members of the learning community to work through and assess, initially in terms of relevance, and then to determine to what extent they are present in or absent from their working group. But I re-emphasise my caution about an over-use of the word team, and recommend that it is used interchangeably with a term such as 'working group'.

Now, if having looked at Appendix 2 you find any of the ideas or language about working groups rather formal, or too structured and impersonal, perhaps — or if you think 'That is all very well for managers and businesses, but what has it got to do with us in the learning community?' — this is the place to underline an insistence that these concepts are not definitive, immutable laws of some kind. They are ideas presented as the basis for discussion and decision, providing a vocabulary for the learning community's use in determining how it will proceed. The themes can be accepted, rejected, modified, added to. In other words, this is a part of the learning process.

Roles within the working group

A study by Dr Meredith Belbin at Henley management college identified a combination of skills and behaviour demonstrated by winning teams competing in business games. These groupings of skills and behaviour are now referred to as the Belbin Team Roles.[15]

One of the qualities of an effective working group suggested in Appendix 2 is that members are clear on roles and *relationships*. Belbin's team-role analysis can be helpful in increasing individuals' understanding of how other group members feel and behave and interact, and gives insights into how relationships are affected by those feelings and behaviours. Again, this is an aspect of the diversity which learning communities need to be aware of, and manage. These descriptions of team roles also give the learning community a framework for identifying individual strengths, and an appreciation of how its members' various skills can be put to the best use in achieving their objectives.

This team role	contributes to the team in this way	but is not quite as good here…
PLANT	Creative, imaginative, unorthodox. Solves difficult problems.	Ignores incidentals. Too pre-occupied to communicate effectively.
RESOURCE INVESTIGATOR	Extrovert, enthusiastic, communicative. Explores opportunities. Develops contacts.	Over-optimistic. Loses interest once initial enthusiasm has passed.
CO-ORDINATOR	Mature, confident, a good chairperson. Clarifies goals, promotes decision making, delegates well.	Can be seen as manipulative. Offloads personal work.
SHAPER	Challenging, dynamic, thrives on pressure. The drive and courage to overcome obstacles.	Prone to provocation. Offends people's feelings.
MONITOR EVALUATOR	Sober, strategic and discerning. Sees all options. Judges accurately.	Lacks drive and ability to inspire others.
TEAMWORKER	Co-operative, mild, perceptive and diplomatic. Listens, builds, averts friction.	Indecisive in crunch situations.
IMPLEMENTER	Disciplined, reliable, conservative and efficient. Turns ideas into practical actions.	Somewhat inflexible. Slow to respond to new possibilities.
COMPLETER FINISHER	Painstaking, conscientious, anxious. Searches out errors and omissions. Delivers on time.	Inclined to worry unduly. Reluctant to delegate.
SPECIALIST	Single-minded, self-starting, dedicated. Provides knowledge and skills in rare supply.	Contributes on only a narrow front. Dwells on technicalities.

As your learning community moves ahead and as relationships develop, it will probably become clear who occupies which role, and how the various strengths are deployed. However, it may be that an earlier caveat needs to be sounded again: these concepts are being presented here, not in definitive terms, but to provide a vocabulary as an aid to an understanding of self and others. This is all a part of the fulfilment society's concern with the process of self-development. Care must be taken, however, that these labels are not regarded as something that an unknown but omniscient third party is determined to pin on you.

The team-role descriptions suggest that while each role has its strengths it also has a down-side. Working group members should therefore play their strongest role with enthusiasm and confidence, and at the same time gain benefit from working with others whose strength is in areas where they themselves are not as strong. The boundaries are not definitive, of course, and the adjectives used to describe one role may in some cases apply also to another role.

It may need to be noted at this point that it should not be inferred that the working group needs to be made up of nine people. There may be two or more people playing the same role, and one individual may play more than one role, and indeed may change from one role to another in different circumstances. Some of the roles may be absent, and thought may be given to how the missing skills can be developed and the gaps filled.

The roles are complementary, and they can be grouped into three styles: a bias towards *action*, or towards *people*, or towards *brainwork*. The Shaper, Implementer and Completer finisher have a bias towards action; the Co-ordinator, Team worker and Resource investigator have a bias towards people; and the Plant, Monitor evaluator and Specialist have a bias towards brainwork.

Thus, provided that the group has a mix of these three types of role, it should be well-placed for effective working on collaborative tasks. It may be unnecessary to point out that a bias towards action does not exclude an interest in people, any more than a bias towards brainworking excludes taking action.

Knowing me, knowing you

Another characteristic of effective working groups suggested in Appendix 2 is that *Openness is such that relationship issues can always be discussed in a mature way*. Openness requires trust, trust has to be earned, and trust is easily lost. Some people are very ready and willing to be open with those whom they do not yet know well, while others are more private and need time before they feel comfortable

Learners wanted: Now recruiting

with sharing their ideas, disclosing personal thoughts and values, or showing their feelings.

Experience will confirm, however, that when there is openness and trust within a working group, there is an increase in the sense of group identity and cohesion, and a rise in the level of energy, enthusiasm and commitment.

The development of self-awareness and openness between people can be illustrated by reference to a widely-used model known as the Johari Window.[16]

	Known to me	Not known to me
Known to others	1: OPEN TO ALL	2: MY BLIND SPOTS
Not known to others	3: HIDDEN BY ME	4: AS YET UNKNOWN

What are the practical applications of this? Let us take as an example the 'window' that looks in on me. Pane number one in my window is *open to all*. Here are all those things about which I am perfectly happy to be open, things that are known to me as well as being known to others. For example, both you and I know that I have written this book, so that is in pane number one, the open area. I am also ready to tell you that I have a nonconformist background, that I worked as a management consultant and that I live in Sussex. You may have spotted all three pieces of information in earlier pages. And there are many other things about myself that I will readily disclose to any who care to listen!

The second pane represents my *blind spots*. These are things about me that are known to others but not known to me, things of which others are aware but of which I am unaware. An example: some years ago, I was speaking with a group, and after a time noticed one or two people making little bunny-rabbit signs in the air with their fingers. When I enquired why, I was told that I did this whenever I referred to 'so-called' terminology or when I wished to indicate that I was using a quotation. I had been unaware of this irritating mannerism and, thanks to the group's feedback, was able to stop doing it.

Pane number three refers to the things that continue to be *hidden by me*, things that are known to me but not known to others. So there are things which, as I get to know people better and trust them more, I will be increasingly relaxed about opening up and disclosing. On the other hand, there will be other things which I am not prepared to disclose, or see no value in making public—things from my past, perhaps, which are best forgotten. And, of course, I have every right to keep those things hidden.

In the fourth pane are things which are unknown both to me and to others, at present at least. It may be that, as I work within a group, I shall discover things about myself which others may then become aware of too.

Developing openness between myself and others can be achieved in the two ways already touched upon—through *feedback* and *disclosure*. Feedback can be sought from others, or offered by them. I asked my listeners about the bunny-rabbit signs, and they gave me feedback (although they had in fact already been doing so in an indirect and unassertive way). So, in the second diagram, it can be seen that feedback by others pushes back the boundary between pane one and pane two, enlarging the former and reducing the latter. Similarly, when I choose to be open and disclose something previously hidden, the boundary between pane one and pane three is pushed back.

	More is known to me	*Still not known to me*
More is known to others	**FEEDBACK BY OTHERS** → 1: OPEN TO ALL **DISCLOSURE BY ME** ↓	REDUCES MY BLIND SPOTS (2)
Not known to others	REDUCES WHAT IS HIDDEN BY ME (3)	4: AS YET UNKNOWN

Feedback and disclosure enlarge the arena that is 'Open to all'. This does *not* suggest, let it be emphasised, that we are expected to disclose everything about ourselves. Why should we? I have every right to keep some things to myself. On the other hand, when it comes to a question of where I stand on an issue being discussed by my working group, for example, it will not be helpful nor will it contribute positively to the group's progress if I keep my thoughts to myself. Nor indeed are we being asked to give others feedback on everything of which they may be unaware but which are clear to us: there may be things that it would be kinder not to mention.

Assertiveness must not be confused with aggression. Feedback, whether volunteered or in response to a request, should be given confidently, factually, openly and without any sense of aggression in either party. Assertiveness is the mid-point between aggression or attacking someone (I'm OK – you're *not* OK!), and non-assertion or submission to the other person (You're OK – I'm *not* OK!). Being assertive means expressing one's thoughts, feelings and beliefs in a direct, honest and appropriate way, retaining respect both for oneself and for the other person. It means letting others know how we feel, in a way that leaves them with a clear sense that they are not under attack (I'm OK – you're OK!).[17]

Assertiveness is not a particularly British trait. We are rather more prone to behave aggressively: not being violent, necessarily – sarcasm is aggressive, for example, and so are criticising and patronising people. Or we tend to behave submissively or demonstrate non-assertive behaviour, when we ought to make our position clear. If in a situation that is not favourable to me, I fail to make my feelings known, it is likely that I shall feel aggrieved afterwards, because I have lost out in some way or feel victimised. You may believe me if I tell you that I am perfectly capable of apologising to someone who has trodden on *my* toes!

* * *

For now, we can leave the subject of the interpersonal and communication skills which the learning community needs to develop, if it is to ensure productive, effective and enjoyable collaboration. Learners can return to this chapter from time to time, to revisit the topic of communication styles, and perhaps jot down some thoughts in the learning review included as Appendix 3.

One more vital characteristic of groups which collaborate effectively and successfully, already touched upon, is that its *members learn as they work together*. The next chapter is devoted in its entirety to this process.

- What issues or questions has this chapter raised for me?
- What have I learned?

1. Carl R. Rogers, *On Becoming a Person*.
2. Matthew 22:36 [NIV].
3. Dr Reg Revans, professor of industrial management at the University of Manchester. I regret that I no longer know the source. If I have unwittingly infringed copyright, I apologise and would want to rectify matters at an early opportunity.
4. Edward de Bono, *Lateral Thinking*.
5. Commonly attributed to Albert Einstein but I have been unable to find a reliably annotated source.
6. Daniel Kahneman, *Thinking, Fast and Slow*.
7. Pablo Picasso, cited in *The Oxford Dictionary of Quotations*.
8. John Hull, *What Prevents Christian Adults from Learning?*
9. Canon Nick Jowell, writing in *The Guardian*, 15 November 2008.
10. John Hick, *Christianity at the Centre*.
11. Terence Copley, *Indoctrination, Education and God*.
12. Torsten Husén, cited in John Field, *Lifelong Learning and the New Educational Order*.
13. F. Aldridge and A. Tuckett, *The Road to Nowhere?* Published by the National Institute of Adult Continuing Education: www.niace.org.uk. In this survey, learning was defined as practising, studying or reading about something. It was also taken to mean being taught, instructed or coached. The survey gave details of percentages of adults engaged in learning, either currently or in the past three years, by socio-economic groups: 55 per cent of ABs, 48 per cent of C1s, 27 per cent of DEs.
14. John Hull, *op. cit.*
15. I am grateful to Belbin Associates for permission to reproduce the team-role descriptions. For more information on resources available for identifying team roles, see www.belbin.com.
16. The 'Joe-Harry' window was named after its creators, Joseph Luft and Harry Ingham. See J. Luft and H. Ingham, 'The Johari Window: A Graphic Model of Interpersonal Awareness' in *Proceedings of the Western Training Laboratory in Group Development*.
17. See Thomas H. Harris, *I'm OK – You're OK*. The book deals very comprehensively and in a wholly accessible way with aggressive–assertive–submissive communication, using the Parent–Adult–Child model. See also Eric Berne, *Games People Play*.

Chapter 5

In place of teaching: Learning to learn

In contrasting vertical (logical, sequential) thinking with lateral (creative, insightful) thinking, Edward de Bono argues that the established approach to education has gone on assuming that useful ideas can somehow be produced simply by allowing more and more information to collect.[1] The place for the complementary lateral thinking, on the other hand, is exemplified in Professor Revans' image of the fugitive present, where survival requires that 'learning must be equal to or greater than the rate of change'.[2] Yesterday's solutions may be irrelevant or inapplicable to today's problems, and it follows that this continuous process of learning includes unlearning, letting go of old knowledge as well as accumulating new.

Experience must constitute at least one element in the process of learning and problem solving, of course: it would be foolish to disregard it. On the other hand, in a fast-changing world it may be risky to rely too much on what was learnt in the past. Simply because we succeeded in the past does not mean that we shall succeed in the present or the future, since past problems will either not recur, or if they do, they will almost certainly take a different form.

What, then, do we mean by 'learn'? And how do we learn?

We say that we learn when we acquire knowledge that we did not have before. We also say that we learn when we gain the ability to do something that we could not do before, or become better at doing something that we could already do, but did not do especially well. We improve by learning. We can also be said to have learnt when, as the result of a bad experience, we seek to avoid that experience in future; that is what is known as intelligence. It is not especially bright to repeat previously unpleasant or hurtful experiences. By the same token, we learn to repeat good experiences.

Most significantly in the present context, we can be said to learn when we discover that what we once thought or believed to be true is no longer true, or was not true in the first place.

Learning may not be as simple as that, however. Evidence suggests that over time, and through many diverse experiences, each of us develops preferences for the way or ways in which we learn (also in ways that match our individual temperament or personality). For example, some people prefer to learn by listening to a talk or lecture, or by studying a book, or by quietly and carefully watching what someone else is doing, taking the role of observer, or using a *reflective* approach to learning. Others of us, by contrast, quickly become impatient with that approach, preferring instead to learn by getting involved, rolling up our sleeves, taking a hands-on approach, having a go for ourselves, preferring an *active* approach to learning.

Learning theorists[3] describe learning as a cyclical, four-stage process:

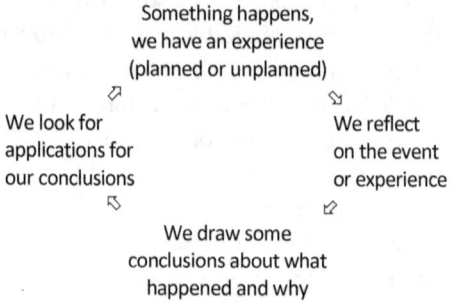

What is proposed here is that there are four principal approaches to learning, four different learning style tendencies, which correspond to those four stages in the learning cycle.[4] This model gives some pointers to the way we all go about learning from our experiences, how we view the world and think about events and people.

What, then, are these four learning styles or tendencies? They can be described as the *Activist, Reflector, Theorist* and *Pragmatist* learning styles. As you read the descriptions, you may recognise yourself

In place of teaching: Learning to learn

under one or more of the headings. However, let it be stressed again, these descriptors do not pretend to define personality, and they must not be seen as some kind of ineluctable branding which you will now be required to bear for all time—rather like those catch-all character descriptions to be found in newspaper horoscope columns. As will be made clear shortly, we have choices, and opportunities to develop strengths in all or any of the four.

The descriptions of the learning styles or tendencies are included here in order to form a framework for thinking about learning, and for becoming more effective learners.

The *Activist* tendency describes those who are keen to get involved in new experiences. They like to have a go: 'I'll try anything once' is their motto. Activists tend to be open-minded and free from scepticism, one of the reasons why they are enthusiastic about trying new experiences. They are inclined, though, to rush in where angels fear to tread, throwing caution to the wind. As their name suggests, Activists' days are full of activity, and it is not unknown for them to be doing more than one thing at a time. They do not avoid crises and, if there isn't a crisis, they may even go looking for one! Once the novelty of one activity is past, they are busy searching for another. New experiences are welcomed as a challenge, but Activists are not at all keen on the routine of implementation. It may be that they start more than they finish. They tend to be sociable people, needing others' company, and they like to be the centre of attention.

The *Reflector* tendency shows a preference for analytical thinking and caution about anything new. Reflectors watch and observe, standing back to give full consideration to a new experience, looking at it from many different angles before voicing an opinion or reaching a conclusion. To do this, they collect information from as wide a range of sources as possible, and spend time digesting it before making a decision. Caution is their watchword, and this leads to delayed decisions. 'Better safe than sorry… look before you leap… you can never be too careful…' are the mottoes of Reflectors. They tend to be quiet people, happy in their own company. In discussions, they are inclined to keep a low profile. They like to observe other people. When others are in discussion, Reflectors prefer to listen before making their contribution (if they make one).

The *Theorist* tendency is towards a logical, step-by-step approach to problem solving and decision making. Theorists are rational people who like to collect the facts and put them together to develop theories which make sense. Like Reflectors, Theorists tend to be perfectionists, not content if things are inconclusive or untidy or if there is a mismatch with their latest theory. Their preference is to explore and analyse, and to ask 'What if...?' Always, though, the answer to that question has to satisfy the next question, 'And how does that fit?' They tend to be wary of unsubstantiated opinions, and focus on evidence and logic. Certainty and objectivity are to be preferred to ambiguity and wooliness. If anything, Theorists tend to be rather detached people, and possibly seen as a little cold. The constant question is, 'Is it logical?' One result is that Theorists are inclined to show impatience with anything flippant or trivial.

The *Pragmatist* tendency is to try out new ideas and techniques, to see if they work in practice. Pragmatists are interested in a theory provided it can be shown to have practical application. So, Pragmatists are seen and like to see themselves as no-nonsense, down-to-earth people who take a practical approach to decision making and problem solving. They welcome new situations and problems as a challenge or, better still, as an opportunity. Pragmatists go out of their way to look for new ways of doing things and cannot wait to see whether or not they will work. They like to get on with things and they act with assurance and focus on ideas that attract them. Pragmatists are impatient with procrastination or indecision, and are frustrated by endless or inconclusive discussions. Their watchword is 'Let's get started...' and their approach is 'There's got to be a better way...'

* * *

Where would you place yourself among those four descriptions? You may recognise your own approach to new situations, problems and opportunities, and you may recognise the approaches taken by others whom you know. It is entirely possible, by the way, that you will identify your preference as a hybrid of a number of these styles. There is nothing wrong with that. In fact, it is to be expected, not least in that it all depends on the seriousness or implications of the new situation,

In place of teaching: Learning to learn

how relevant or important it is to you, who else is involved and many other factors.

What is worth reflecting on (!) is this: the fact that people are different from each other means that when it comes to discussion and opportunity search, it is likely that you and others in your learning community will differ in your ways of thinking and acting, and you may take differing approaches to new situations. The Activists certainly, and to some extent the Pragmatists, will tend to welcome change with open arms; whereas the Reflectors, and to some extent the Theorists, will be more cautious and possibly even resistant to new ideas, at least initially. Moreover, the get-up-and-go Activists or Pragmatists may become impatient with the Reflectors and Theorists, as they continue to give more thought to the situation, while the Reflectors and Theorists may feel the others are being pushy and in too much of a hurry.

It seems to be true, then, that we each have learning style preferences, and there is a possibility that we tend to use one or two of these learning styles at the expense of the others, simply because we have learnt by experience that our preferred style works for us, or it is an approach with which we feel most comfortable. As a result, some learning opportunities may be missed.

The effective learning process follows a number of stages:

1. Something happens—either something that the learner chooses, or something random or accidental—the part that the *Activist* likes.

2. There is then a need to reflect on the event—What happened? Why did it happen in that way?—many other questions that the *Reflector* will ask and want answers to.

3. Following reflection, and by comparing the findings with earlier experiences, or ideas that others may have, the *Theorist* develops some theories and reaches some (tentative) conclusions.

4. Based on those theories or conclusions, a point is reached where the *Pragmatist* asks, How can we use this? How can we put this into practice?

It is possible to develop under-utilised learning preferences, in order to broaden opportunities for learning from experience. It may be that there are some types of behaviour which, if modified, could be more productive, or might bring new insights or experiences. It is also possible in this way to borrow behaviour that will make communication between people of differing styles more empathic and productive, helping to avoid clashes and misunderstanding.

Here are a few thoughts on some of the problems which may be encountered when using unfamiliar styles, and which may therefore not only deter us from using them, but also deprive us of possible benefits; and a few suggestions on how some of the less-used approaches might be practised and developed.

Strengthening your 'Activist'

Difficulties for non-Activists: A fear of failure or of making mistakes, or of being ridiculed when trying something new; anxiety about doing something unfamiliar; having a preference for planning things carefully and in detail; perhaps taking oneself too seriously.

Opportunities for non-Activists: Identify an activity that is not threatening but which will put you—briefly, in the first place—in the limelight; practise starting a conversation; volunteer to chair a discussion group; or offer to speak on a subject that is familiar to you.

Strengthening your 'Reflector'

Difficulties for non-Reflectors: Impatience, no time to spend on thinking or planning, a wish to move on to the next thing; disinclination to listen and analyse; relying on memory rather than writing things down.

Opportunities for non-Reflectors: Spend time observing others' behaviour; keep a 'learning journal' (a daily diary, checked each evening, to see what you have learnt during the day: see Appendix 3); write down the pros and cons of a proposed course of action; offer to research a problem and prepare an analytical summary of it.

Strengthening your 'Theorist'

Difficulties for non-Theorists: An inclination to take things at face value; a preference for spontaneity and intuition; resistance to a too-structured approach; putting high value on creativity and fun.

Opportunities for non-Theorists: Spend time on asking the kind of questions that elicit information: What/Why/How/When/Where/Who?; analyse differing news reports or political comment in newspapers to develop your critical skills; prepare agenda for meetings, with clearly-stated purpose and structure.

Strengthening your 'Pragmatist'

Difficulties for non-Pragmatists: Thinking that others' solutions or experiences do not apply in your situation; preference for further thought before putting something into practice; suspicion of new and untried ideas; concentrating on developing ideal rather than practical or expedient solutions.

Opportunities for non-Pragmatists: Look for opportunities to experiment; prepare and use action plans, including time scales; watch out for and try out new methods and techniques; emulate the successes of others.

* * *

One or two final words on learning to learn before we move on. Remember that these 'labels' have not been presented here as some kind of pseudo-scientific or definitive statements about people and their personalities or temperaments (the Theorists will love the concepts, of course, and the Pragmatists will be dying to see how they work in practice). The purpose is simply to provide a vocabulary which hopefully will give some insights into the different ways in which people (you and I) think and learn, and how people (you and I) respond to problems and new situations.

You will be familiar with the following truisms. 'You learn something new every day'; well, you do, you cannot help it. Or 'You're never too old to learn'; well, you are not. Lifelong learning is not just a political slogan. That is why a personal learning review has been included at Appendix 3. Why not look at it now? It is designed to enable you to take stock of your learning from time to time, not only as you work through Parts Two and Three of this book, but also in other areas of your life. In effect, this is learning about learning.

* * *

Provisionally, the learning community's ideal has been expressed in the two interlinked commandments: love God (substitute here your word or phrase for the 'Beyond' or the 'Other-than-oneself') and love your neighbour. Let us turn now to those two parts of the programme for action: considering first, in Part Two, what it may mean to believe and to love God or that 'Other'; and then, in Part Three, how our belief can be demonstrated in practice, in loving our neighbour and being committed to building a better world for all people.

- What issues or questions has this chapter raised for me?
- What have I learned?

[1] Edward de Bono, *Lateral Thinking*.
[2] Reg Revans, *ABC of Action Learning*.
[3] Notably David Kolb and Peter Honey.
[4] Here I have drawn extensively on the work of Dr Peter Honey. I am indebted not only to Dr Honey but also to the Pearson TalentLens Division of Pearson Education for their agreement for me to do so. For more information on Peter Honey's learning-to-learn material, visit www.peterhoney.com.

Part Two

Chapter 6

But that *I can't believe*

Now to return to questions of belief. The argument has been made already that spiritual values are held by us all to some extent, little or much, aware or unaware, higher or lower in our consciousness. Thus, the argument continues, since fewer and fewer Britons attend church, it follows that spiritual values and beliefs are held quite independently of religious affiliation. That is to say, the continuing decline in church attendance is not to be equated with a decline in spiritual values or belief.

For our inclusive project to progress, then, there is a need to explore what those values and beliefs might be. It has already been conceded that the creation of one universally accepted list is unlikely. What is possible, however, is a consensus, even though the language and modes of expression will vary widely, including 'religious' words and phrases. Acceptance of this potential outcome is an imperative for a community which values diversity.

It was noted earlier that some atheist attacks on what are imagined to be universally held religious beliefs are in effect misdirected effort. For example, many non-theist Christians share the atheists' conviction that there is no Being 'out there', nor do they believe the literal truth of biblical creation stories or accounts of divine intervention in the affairs of humankind (to take just two examples). More and more people within the church—and this includes bishops and members of the clergy—are taking that position, understanding and accepting that religion and its attributes are human creations.

Agnostic thinkers, for their part, continue to be unconvinced, uncertain about what can or cannot be believed, remaining unnecessarily doubtful about outdated religious doctrines on which in fact nothing hinges, doctrines which are about the unknowable and are left-overs from an ancient, pre-scientific Middle Eastern culture.

'Believers in exile', who know what it is that they no longer believe, have an opportunity here to think through what it is they *can* believe.

And my friends who remain within the church, holding fast to their beliefs, are challenged to find ways of making their message relevant in an increasingly secular, if not hostile, world.

Meanwhile, for the vast majority of people, those outside the church, little or no thought is given to these matters, even though to one extent or another they are aware of the church and have some conception of 'religion', however incomplete or vague or even inaccurate.

It is for every one of these groups that the next part of the book has been designed, using a Christian creed as the starting point for discussion (atheists, please continue to be patient: your input is important to us).

For many centuries, the Apostles' Creed has been the touchstone for Christian orthodoxy.[1] This creed continues to be recited corporately and regularly as an affirmation of belief, for example within the Church of England. In the non-creedal churches (in very broad terms, the nonconformist denominations) the creed is not formally recited, but its content could still be said to constitute a checklist of beliefs tacitly accepted by their members. For readers who are not church-goers, awareness of the creed, or indeed their attitude to it, may lie anywhere on a scale from unfamiliarity, to indifference, to antipathy or even hostility. However, the creed's content does at least have the virtue of affording a neat and useful summary of orthodoxy in religious belief, as it encapsulates the church's traditional teaching. That is the reason for its being used here as the framework for the book's second part, and it is intended as a prompt for de-constructing the language of supernatural and outdated belief and reinterpreting faith for today and tomorrow.

Earlier, we looked briefly at the concept of 'otherness', and how, when a so-called deviant group departs from the norm, another, perhaps dominant, group is provoked into taking action to protect its own 'rightness' against potential threat. We also noted the theory that it was in this way that a new dogma, that of the Trinity, which had not existed in earliest Christian times, resulted from the church's perceived need to defend its orthodoxy against the challenges of heresy.

It would be a nonsense, of course, to suggest that this trinitarian creed, expressing a belief in a three-in-one God, is the sole foundation on which the Christian faith is built. The creed itself is based on verses to be found in the Christian New Testament, although it is pointed out in the sections which follow that from time to time biblical sources for the creedal statements are rather few and far between. Furthermore, both Bible and creed were written when the earth was still flat, or was thought to be. But that primordial flat-earth epoch has long been superseded, of course, by an age in which a progression of scientific discoveries and developments and scholarly research have given good reason for no longer accepting the world-view or supernatural images contained within those ancient formularies. In spite of that, literally thousands of churches within mainstream Christianity in Britain continue to uphold 'the divine inspiration and supreme authority' of the Bible, which is held to be 'the written Word of God'; and members of those churches appear to be able to maintain and propagate literal belief in the outdated supernatural content of both the Bible and the creed. That was the rock on which the church was built.

However, rocks can be either good news or bad news, depending on whether you are a builder or a sailor. The proposition made here is that this body of pre-scientific teaching, the rock on which the church was founded, has become a rock on which the church has foundered. That is to say, the mismatch between the supernatural, outdated teachings which the church continues to propagate, and the language and experience of twenty-first-century men and women, significantly contributes to the majority's choice to remain outside the church.

So, a question: is it—or was it ever—rational to accept that the words of the creed (or of the Bible itself, for that matter) enshrine an immutable body of knowledge, literally true for all time, past, present and future, to be understood in one and only one way? The answer, clearly enough, is no, it is not.

When the mathematics teacher introduces her pupils to the notion $2 + 2 = 4$, she can be confident that there is one and only one correct way for that to be understood; and that has always been true, and will always be true, for all maths teachers and all pupils everywhere. Having listened to the teacher, her pupils discover that two plus two does indeed equal four because it can be demonstrated and proved to be true. Any who reject the idea, deciding instead that 2 + 2 = 5, are likely to come up against problems sooner or later.

This once-and-for-all, universally true category of teaching is clearly quite different from the centuries-old teaching of the church (admittedly, it is also different from teaching some other kinds of school subjects—history, for example). Even if, in some abstract sense, the church does indeed have access to an unchanging body of knowledge, there will be as many ways of understanding its meaning as there are believers. As we have already noted, 'no two individuals ever possess the same Christian faith'.

In the pages which follow, that diversity of belief will become abundantly clear, as lexical leakage gives clues to some of the denominational teachings, beliefs and emphases (prejudices?) which I soaked up in the first half of my life, and which I am still endeavouring to unlearn, or at least reinterpret.

Many readers will doubtless declare, with varying degrees of amazement, 'But I've *never* believed *that*!' Good. That is really what this second part of the discussion is attempting to do: to get underneath or behind the language and images, the interpretations, half-truths and misconceptions, take them apart, and see in what ways they can be reconstructed or reassembled so as to give meaning, relevance and value to people in the twenty-first century. Even if there is as little unanimity on new meanings as there was on the old, let us at least make an attempt to discover new and liberating expressions for our belief.

There is a gospel story about two men who built houses.[2] One man built his house on sandy ground, and the other built his house on rock. When the storms and floods came, the first house collapsed, but the second man's house remained standing. The most significant difference between the two house-builders was that the latter had taken the time and trouble not only to choose firm ground for his building site but more importantly to *dig foundations* before he did anything else. For centuries, the church stood firmly on its rock, protected by power and privilege, perpetuating the teaching of unquestioned doctrine. But now the foundations have been shaken.

The time has come to excavate them, first to uncover their origins, and then to lay down some new footings on which a new enterprise, the fulfilment society, can be established. This is not a matter of patching up, but of reconstruction.

The Apostles' Creed provides a framework for learning communities to begin their work: first, deconstruction, uncovering the origins, examining the pieces, and then reconstruction, putting the pieces back together but in a completely new way. The creed is presented here as no more than a collection of sketches or exploratory notes and themes, intended for you and others to think about, challenge, argue with, develop, add to or reject. Each of the sections begins with a creedal statement and ends with a question, intended to focus your mind on what it is that you do in fact believe.

Biblical quotations, from the *New International Version* [*NIV*], are included to illustrate points, but hopefully it will be clear that the intention is not to present them as proof texts. Should I appear to break this rule, I trust that the reader will go and search the scriptures for a text that at least puts a question mark against the one that I have quoted. Usually, that is not difficult.

In writing for a widely diverse readership, I have this obvious difficulty: on one hand, I might assume readers' familiarity with biblical texts, and as a result provide a minimum of notes; on the other hand, I might think it possible that the references are unfamiliar, and therefore over-do the notes, thus running the risk of sounding patronising. In the event, I have chosen to annotate the text fully, as an aid to those who may find it useful from time to time to check my sources. (Even so, the words grandmother and eggs come to mind.) In fact, to those for whom the references are familiar, I make this suggestion: *look them up anyway*! Attempt to see the words as though for the first time.

- What issues or questions has this chapter raised for me?

- What have I learned?

1   There are three creeds in the Church of England's Book of Common Prayer. The Apostles' Creed is used here because it may be the most familiar of the

three, and it is the shortest, which makes for ease of reference. The Nicene Creed is a good deal longer, and although it affirms the same series of beliefs, it does so with fuller attributes. The third, the Athanasian Creed, takes a quite different form from the first two and is longer than the two combined.

2   Matthew 7:24–27 and Luke 6:48–49.

Sketch 1: The gods and God

As we take this very first step in the process of deconstructing 'religious' language, with the creed's opening line, 'I believe in God the Father Almighty, Maker of heaven and earth', the atheist reader will declare without hesitation, 'No, I do not!' The agnostic will hesitate, with 'Well, I can't be sure about that'. And the believer-in-exile may say something along the lines of 'It depends on what you mean by God'.

I am with all three.

The purpose here is to begin defining or redefining words in ways that best work for each of us in finding expression for the 'Other-than-oneself'.

To believe that there is a god, or at least to have some sense of the 'Other-than-oneself', may be the most fundamental meaning of being religious. But as we go on, I want that idea to become wider and deeper, with a suggestion that humankind has always sought, and continues to seek, to be a part of what might be termed 'the eternal', some kind of cosmic wholeness.

(In thinking of humanity as a whole, the discussion ought to include other religious traditions. However, since our starting point was with a Christian church in decline, and in the interest of brevity and familiarity, these jottings are limited to Christianity and the Judaism out of which it grew. Having said that, it is of course right that any who wish to include other traditions should do so.)

So, to begin with the Apostles' Creed: it does not say 'I believe that there *is* a god'. That is a given. Rather, it begins with a declaration of a *belief in* — a belief *in* a deity whose name is God. Moreover, in using the name 'God' in this way, there is the unquestioning implication, 'And you know which god I am talking about'. This is not just any god; and lest there should be any doubt, the believed-in god is given three defining attributes: he is the almighty god, he is the father and he is the maker of heaven and earth.

This particular manifestation of the 'divine' is first met in the Hebrew Bible, where the name God takes a number of forms. For example, in an ancient story about an encounter between God and Moses, at least three forms are used:

> God [*Elohim*] also said to Moses, 'I am the LORD [*Yahweh* or *Adonai*]. I appeared to Abraham, to Isaac and to Jacob as God Almighty [*El-Shaddai*], but by my name the LORD [*Yahweh* or *Adonai*] I did not make myself known to them.'[1]

In the Hebrew Bible, God is usually named *Elohim*. *Yahweh* (Jehovah) was a later transliteration of the ancient tetragrammaton YHWH, a holy name too sacred to utter and rarely used, with the name *Adonai* (LORD) often substituted for it. It was as the Canaanite god *El-Shaddai* that God revealed himself as the Almighty One, first to Abraham and then to Moses, according to the biblical narrative.

Bible stories tell how this almighty god gave to Moses the first commandment: 'You shall have no other gods before me.'[2] This mandate made clear that there were other gods, but that the Israelites must avoid choosing them. Indeed the Bible names a number of them: Ba'al, Astarte, Dagon, Moloch, Marduk, Chemosh, and El the Bull-god. So *El Shaddai* was one god among many. The concept of monotheism, the worship of one god, may ultimately have been discovered by the Jews during their exile among the Persians in Babylon during the sixth century BCE. By the beginning of our present era, the belief in one god had not only long been essential to Judaism but was also fundamental to Christianity, the religion which was to emerge from it, and later to Islam.

This Old Testament god, sometimes a warrior god, a god of anger and terrible vengeance, a god who at times turned his back on his chosen people, seldom appears in these guises in the New Testament.[3]

How is this ferocious Old Testament god, a god who has been blackened as perhaps the most unpleasant character in the whole of fiction,[4] a god who seemed to blow hot and cold, arbitrarily punishing and rewarding men and women in the same way as did the Greeks' god-of-gods Zeus—how is such a god to be reconciled with the New Testament god, 'who does not change like shifting shadows'?[5]

Reference to the fatherhood of God in the Old Testament is expressed in terms of the fatherhood of the nation.[6] Individuals do not address God directly as father, although by the second century BCE there is evidence that it was becoming acceptable for individuals to do so.[7]

To think of this god as father is emphatically a New Testament notion, and hence a Christian one. Paul and other New Testament writers frequently used the term 'father' as an attribute of their god, largely to underline their belief in Jesus as God's son. Throughout the gospels Jesus addresses God or refers to him as father, and he clearly expected his listeners also to have an understanding of him as their 'heavenly father'.[8] The familiar prayer which, according to the gospels, Jesus taught his disciples, and still known as the 'Lord's prayer', begins by addressing 'our father'. However, it is possible that in this respect Jesus was not as much of an innovator as he is sometimes presented: by his time, prayers were in common use which addressed God as father, including one which began 'Our father, who art in heaven'.[9] Today, although the most common form of address in Jewish prayer is the majestic 'King of the universe', many prayers address God as father—at *Bar mitzvah*, for example, and when lighting the Sabbath eve candles.[10]

This creator god, believed literally to be the maker of heaven and earth, is also frequently encountered throughout the Hebrew Bible (Old Testament), not only in the creation stories in the first book, *Genesis*, but elsewhere too, most notably in the psalms.[11] He appears less often in the Christian New Testament, although Paul, devout Hasid that he was, does occasionally refer to his god as creator.[12] This god is believed to have made the whole of creation, and by his hand 'the heavens and the earth were completed in all vast array'.[13]

* * *

That, then, is just a glimpse of the ways in which the Jewish god was portrayed. It was perfectly natural that this god would be adopted by those who were to become known as the Christians. The first adherents of the Jesus sect were Jews who took their god with them as their new religion began to evolve from the ancient traditions of Judaism. He was the god of history, the god who since the beginning of time was believed to have intervened in the lives of men and women, and even to have entered into a covenant or contract with them.¹⁴

But what does it mean to believe? The first word of the Latin creed, *credo*, translates as 'I believe'; and yet the Latin had at least as many shades of meaning as does our English. There are many different ways in which we use the word in our everyday speech: I believe that it will rain tomorrow, I believe that this blue is prettier than that one, I believe that we last met two years ago. Often it is no more than a synonym for 'I think'.

The prime meaning of *credo*, though, was to trust, to put faith in. This is what we mean when we say we believe *in*; it is a deeper meaning than believing *that*. If someone tells you that she believes *in* you, she is expressing emotions such as trust, loyalty, confidence, feeling certain that you can be relied upon.

However, it is not possible to express a belief *in* a personal god without first believing *that* there is a personal god. But what grounds can there be for this 'belief that'? Where can such an assurance come from, on what can it be based, how can it be tested? How is it possible to *know* that there is a personal god, a god as a being?

When the first-century Christian missionary Paul arrived in Athens, 'he was greatly distressed to see that the city was full of idols', and he spotted an altar inscribed *Agnosto theo – To an unknown god*. The Greek word *agnostos* meant not only 'unknown' but also 'unknowable'. Paul declared to the Athenians, 'The god who made the world and everything in it... does not live in temples built by hands', and went on to contrast their 'unknowable' so-called god with the true, living, creator god in whom he believed. One can picture the logically-minded Greeks listening, mystified as Paul preached his sermon – for they 'spent their time doing nothing but talking about and listening to the latest idea'¹⁵ – as they wondered what evidence he might have for claiming to 'know' this unseen god of his. At least they were clear about the grounds for their own agnosticism.

Latter-day missionaries were to continue in Paul's footsteps, as they exported the Christian god to Africa, India and China, and to other 'benighted' lands, in their attempt to eradicate the superstitious worship of gods 'made by human hands':

> The heathen, in his blindness,
> Bows down to wood and stone.¹⁶

Sketch 1: The gods and God

And yet, while Christianity itself is by no means unfamiliar with images and statuary, its god remains unseen, not able to be touched or experienced with any human sense. In that way, this god is like the Athenians' god, *agnostos*, unknowable. It is possible to address a believed-in god as

> Immortal, invisible, God only wise,
> In light inaccessible hid from our eyes[17]

but the hymn's words in effect acknowledge that it is not possible to *know* whether there is a god 'out there' or not. Another hymn uses the same contradictory imagery:

> Thou, Who art beyond the furthest
> Mortal eyes can scan,
> Can it be that Thou regardest
> Songs of sinful men?
> Can we know that Thou art near us
> And wilt hear us?

—questions which the hymn-writer unhesitatingly answers with an astonishing but unjustifiable assurance, 'Yea we can'.[18]

In reality, humankind has created images and concepts of a god as he ought to be, an almighty god, omnipotent, omniscient, omnipresent, as well as creator and father. Thus, both God and the religion constructed around him over many centuries are a human creation.

But in saying that, we have not disposed of God. The probability has already been considered that a majority of Britons believe in God, or some idea of a god, although we have no evidence of how they would define the god in whom (in which?) they say they believe. Do the majority of people literally believe in a *supernatural* god? Do they believe in a god who is a super-person, a 'being' out there or up there or somewhere outside or beyond themselves? Do they believe in a god who is keeping a critical eye on them, ready to catch them out and punish them? Or a god to whom they can make their requests known ('Grant us fine weather for the church fête tomorrow, Lord, if it is your will')? Do the majority think that, if they believe at all, they are required to believe in that kind of god? That, at least, is in large measure what they will have been taught.

It is proposed here that what is now a well-documented, far from new but decidedly radical approach to belief in God, the non-realist position, which some describe as Christian humanism, has much to say to modern men and women. When we acknowledge that religion is man-made, and that God is a human creation, we find that we have at last begun to do without the old superstitious (I should have written supernatural) 'beliefs'.

Now we are being freed to consider each of the other outdated beliefs in turn, to seek and find new language and meanings and relevance for concepts that change individuals and societies. It is most likely that in the process some of these concepts will be abandoned altogether.

It was argued in Chapter 1 that religious values are more widely held than is commonly supposed. It was suggested above that the most fundamental meaning of being religious is to believe that there is a 'god'. It has also been proposed that being religious is to have a 'yearning for what lasts'. It is necessary to give further thought to the place of the 'Other-than-oneself' and to seek an understanding of that 'yearning for what lasts'.

So, here is another priority for individuals and their learning community: to consider the implications of this belief, quoted earlier, and worth repeating:

> God (and this is a definition) is the sum of our values, representing to us their ideal unity, their claims upon us and their creative power.[19]

What are these values? And what are the claims that they make upon us?

- <u>That</u> I can't believe!

- But what I <u>do</u> believe is this:

---

1. Exodus 6:2–3 [NIV].
2. Exodus 20:3 [NIV].
3. Revelation 1:8 is one example.
4. Richard Dawkins, *The God Delusion*.
5. James 1:17 [NIV].

6   Exodus 4:22; Deuteronomy 14:1 and 32:6; Isaiah 1:2, 63:16 and 64:8; Jeremiah 31:9; Hosea 11:1; Malachi 2:10.
7   Ecclesiasticus 23:1 and 4.
8   Matthew 5:16 and 45, and 6:9; Luke 11:2.
9   Dr Israel Abrahams, *Studies in Pharisaism and the Gospels*, cited in William W. Simpson, *Jewish Prayer and Worship*.
10 See Joseph H. Hertz, *Authorized Daily Prayer Book*.
11 For example, Psalms 8, 104, 136, 148.
12 For example, Romans 1:25, and Colossians 1:16.
13 Genesis 2:1 [NIV].
14 God's covenant with Israel, and the foundations of the Jewish law, the *Torah*, are the themes of the first five books of the Bible.
15 Acts 17:16–33 [NIV].
16 Reginald Heber, hymn, 'From Greenland's icy mountains' (1820).
17 Walter Chalmers Smith, hymn, 'Immortal, invisible, God only wise' (1876).
18 Francis Pott, hymn, 'Angel voices ever singing' (1861).
19 Don Cupitt, *The Sea of Faith*.

Sketch 2:
Jesus, the man from Galilee

Having declared a belief in God the father, the creed continues with a belief 'in Jesus Christ his only Son our Lord'.

Jesus was a man who was born, lived and died in the early decades of the first century of our era, in the region roughly equating to modern-day Israel, which was at that time a part of the Roman Empire. According to the stories that are told about Jesus in the four New Testament gospels, for no more than three years he travelled about as an itinerant teacher and healer in the area between Galilee in the north and Jerusalem and Judæa in the south. We have no independent record of the life of Jesus. The creed does not state (or require) a belief in his teaching or the miracles that he is said to have performed — in short, anything between the facts of his birth and death.

Let us, then, take a look at this article of the creed, and the belief that it does affirm. The second article derives from or is dependent on the first, that is to say, a belief in a god-son requires a belief in a god-father. As they moved on to compile this second article, the creed's authors again gave expression to a belief *in*, as well as implying a belief *that*: a belief that there was a man named Jesus, but also much more — a belief *in* this man's divine attributes: he is glorified as the Christ, as the unique son of God, and as the lord of those who believe in him.

Where are the sources for these three titles, and what do or did they signify? The primary evidence for what the early followers of Jesus believed him to be is found in the first-century writings collected in the Christian New Testament: that is to say, in the four gospels, the book of *Acts of the Apostles*, the letters from the apostle Paul and others, and in *Revelation*.[1] These writings include references to as many as forty different titles ascribed to Jesus by early believers, but at the top of the most significant ones is the New Testament Greek title *ho christos*, the christ.

In this creedal statement of belief, however, the title Christ has been combined with Jesus to form what appears to be a name, Jesus Christ. Even a cursory reading of the gospels, though, makes it very clear that far and away the most frequently used name for Jesus is simply that, *Iesous*, a name which appears many hundreds of times.[2] *Iesous* was a Greek transliteration of the traditional Hebrew name *Yeshu'a*, which had become very common in the first century of our era. Near-contemporary records (for example, the histories of Flavius Josephus) indicate just how common was the name Jesus. Recent excavation of burial chambers in Jerusalem has identified at least seventy tombs inscribed with the name. Two or three other men named Jesus appear in the New Testament.[3] One of them, the bandit Bar-Abbas, whom Pontius Pilatus is said to have released to placate the crowd in place of the imprisoned Jesus, is named Jesus in some manuscripts of Matthew's gospel, and in some modern translations. However, this is a variant reading, and may be symbolic rather than historical: it is interesting to note that the name *Bar-Abbas* translates as 'son of the father'.

The meaning of the Hebrew name *Yeshu'a* was 'God saves'. In the gospel story, it was the name which God instructed Joseph the carpenter of Nazareth to give to the son who was to be born to Mary, 'because he will save his people from their sins'.[4] In a number of places, gospel writers explain the meaning or equivalent of a Greek or Aramaic name, word or phrase.[5] Had they explained the meaning of the Hebrew origins of the name *Iesous*, they would probably have used the word *soter*, the Greek for deliverer or saviour. Saviour has become Christianity's most revered title for Jesus, of course; but in the New Testament itself, *soter* is used in that way very rarely indeed. It appears only once in the first three gospels: in Luke's nativity narrative, angels appear to some shepherds and declare, 'Today in the town of David a Saviour [*soter*] is born to you; he is Christ the Lord'.[6] In one incident in the fourth gospel, Jesus is recognised as saviour, not by his fellow Jews, interestingly enough, but by the hated Samaritans.[7] The word *soter* appears a dozen times in Paul's epistles and in other, later, New Testament letters. For the Jews, saviour or 'deliverer' was an attribute of the Lord God, King of the Universe. So here, according to the angels' message and the New Testament writers, it seems to be clear that Jesus was being identified with God himself.

While *Iesous* is the name generally used throughout the Greek gospels, the title *christos* appears far less frequently there. Although it was one of the most important titles ascribed to Jesus in early writings, there are no more than twenty or so references to Christ in the first three gospels;[8] and in two places in the fourth, John explains that the word *christos* is synonymous with the Hebrew word for messiah.[9] The root meaning of both words is 'the anointed one'.

Looking back over their history and through familiarity with their scriptures, the Jews associated the rite of anointing with oil with the consecration of prophets, priests and kings. Ever since the golden age of their great king David, the Jews had dreamt of the coming of the messiah (and indeed await him still), a great king who would re-establish God's kingdom of peace and prosperity. At first, the dream was of a king in the house and lineage of David. Over the centuries, this evolved into an expectation that God would intervene, with the coming of a divine messiah, himself a deliverer or saviour. By the time of Jesus, messianic expectation had long reached such heights that there was talk of those being the last days, when God's messiah would appear, as God's vice-regent who would combine the three anointed roles of prophet, priest and king.

However, this pairing of *Iesous* with the title *christos*, to form the name Jesus Christ, occurs fewer than half a dozen times in the gospels.[10] This suggests that, at the time of their being written, it had not yet become established as a part of the narrative formula. Its more frequent use in the letters of Paul, however, gives evidence of early Christian creedal affirmations, as they declared *kurios Iesous christos*, Jesus Christ is Lord.[11] Even so, since all of Paul's letters pre-date the gospels, it seems entirely possible that this oft-repeated formula was a part of the development of his own doctrine and teaching.

That early creedal declaration, that Jesus Christ is Lord, was eventually incorporated as the second article of the Apostles' Creed. The common Greek word *kurios* had a wide range of meanings or applications. It was used as a title of respect when addressing the head of the household, a rabbi, or a landowner, when it might translate simply as sir or master. And it was used to address the emperor or one of the gods, when it would translate as the more

Sketch 2: Jesus, the man from Galilee

honorific title 'Lord'. Always it indicated respect for status and authority. In the New Testament, the word *kurios* (or *kurie*, the vocative form used when addressing another person) appears over and over again: it is used, for example, by a son speaking obediently to his father, by farm workers discussing harvest problems with their employer, by a slave grovelling to a ruthless master, by the Jewish leaders currying favour with Pontius Pilatus, addressing him as 'Your Excellency', and by Mary imploring the 'gardener' (as she supposed) to tell her where he had moved the body of Jesus.[12] When Jesus read in the synagogue 'The Spirit of the Lord is on me', the Greek word for Lord (God) in the text is *kurios*.[13]

So, simply because it was a standard courtesy, Jesus is addressed in all his day-to-day encounters as *kurie*, and is referred to as *kurios*. That translates in mundane terms as master or sir, and as a teacher or rabbi he would have accepted that courtesy. However, this common, human form of address changes dramatically after the resurrection: Jesus now becomes *ho kurios*, the Lord — a divine attribution — and it is in this way that the apostle Paul speaks of the risen Christ, literally hundreds of times in his letters to the Christian assemblies.

To speak of Jesus Christ as Lord leads on to the creed's stated belief in Jesus as the only son of God; but from a reading of the gospel narratives, it is by no means a straightforward quest to determine to what extent, if at all, Jesus claimed this title for himself.

At one point, when Jesus asks Simon Peter, 'Who do you say I am?', Peter declares, 'You are the Christ, the Son of the living God'. Jesus responds by saying, 'This was not revealed this to you by man, but my Father in heaven'.[14] When later the arrested Jesus is taken before Caiaphas the high priest, he is asked, 'Tell us if you are the Christ, the Son of God'.[15] In the Greek text, Jesus's reply to the high priest is in a quite deliberately emphatic form — *Su eipas*, '*You* said that... your words, not mine'. During the interrogation, Jesus refers to himself as the 'son of man'; but the gospels make many references to his doing so throughout his ministry. Both this and the title son of God were messianic titles.

The concept of sons of a god or of the gods was an ancient one and still familiar at that time, not only within the Hellenistic culture, but also within the traditions of the Hebrew scriptures. There, the sons of gods father 'the heroes that were of old, warriors of renown';

the sons of God all shout for joy at the creation; God called the people of Israel 'my firstborn son'; and Adam is called son of God.[16]

John's gospel places great emphasis on Jesus as the son, perhaps the most familiar reference being the evangelicals' favourite text: 'For God so loved the world that he gave his one and only Son.'[17] In this gospel in particular, Jesus makes frequent reference to God as father; but he also makes clear to his disciples that his father god was also their father god[18] and in another place he admonishes his followers, 'Do not call anyone on earth "father", for you have one Father, and he is in heaven'.[19]

What does seem to be clear is that, whether or not Jesus claimed to be the son of God, it was the charge which led to a demand for his crucifixion.[20] In the years after his death, some degree of belief in the divinity of Jesus began to develop, as seems abundantly evident in New Testament writings. The first verse of Mark's gospel, the earliest to be written, reads 'The beginning of the gospel about Jesus Christ, the Son of God';[21] and the story of the encounter between the apostle Philip and an Ethiopian eunuch in *Acts* tells how the convert declares 'I believe that Jesus Christ is the Son of God'.[22] The letters of Paul and of other later writers refer many times to Jesus the son of God. This doctrine, enshrined in the creed, remained fundamental to the Christian religion.

* * *

Here, then, is some background to the ways in which Jesus was seen by those who had known him, those who first wrote about him, and those who then formulated these early, orthodox statements of belief.

We have caught glimpses of Jesus, said to be the son of God, a man who was crucified by his country's Roman occupiers. Jesus's followers believed that God had somehow raised him from death into his presence, where Jesus lives forever and one day will call believers to be with him for eternity.

However, in thinking about these titles which were ascribed to Jesus in the middle years of the first century—the christos/messiah, saviour, lord, the son of God—it is important to remember that their creators were men of their time. The language and imagery employed in their writing were those of their world, which was not our world.

Sketch 2: Jesus, the man from Galilee

Most significantly, theirs was a world where men and women eagerly awaited the coming of a redeeming messiah, who, after centuries of oppression, slavery, conflict, exile and occupation, would be sent by God to establish the Kingdom of Heaven. So when the gospel writers recalled and recorded their memories of the words and works of Jesus, they had already come to recognise him as the messiah, and their message was 'Jesus is Lord!'

What are we to make of this today? The meaning and relevance of these first-century images and concepts need to be re-examined, and expressed in new ways to which men and women in the twenty-first century can respond with a 'Yes!' As we have already noted, when Jesus asked his disciples, 'Who do you say that I am?',[23] Peter was ready with an instant answer. He had no doubts.

What can we say to that question today? This, at least: in the man Jesus we can see how God, as 'the sum of our values', can be seen in a human being, and in Jesus we can see how fully men and women may respond to their God.

- <u>That</u> I can't believe!

- But what I <u>do</u> believe is this:

---

1. On the whole, and for ease of reference, the New Testament canon is used here as source material. It has to be remembered, however, that there are other, non-canonical sources. Interested readers are referred to (for example) R. Cameron (ed.), *The Other Gospels: Non-Canonical Gospel Texts*.
2. To identify the frequency of use of some New Testament words and names, I have relied on a number of commentaries, as well as footnotes in (for example) *The Jerusalem Bible* and the *New Revised Standard Version* of the Bible, in addition to my own reading of the Greek texts. Of especial value for variant readings is B.H. Throckmorton, *Gospel Parallels: A Comparison of the Synoptic Gospels*.
3. Matthew 27:16; Acts 13:6; Colossians 4:11.
4. Matthew 1:21 [NIV].
5. Matthew 1:23; Mark 5:41, 15:22 and 15:34; John 1:38, 1:41 and 1:42, 19:13.
6. Luke 2:11 [NIV].
7. John 4:42.
8. In discussing the occurrence and the usage of the words messiah and Christ in the New Testament, I am attaching no significance to differentiating one from the other, since the two words have the same meaning. The *New Revised Standard Version* of the Bible, for example, frequently translates the Greek

christos as messiah, where many other translations print Christ. I am here using a standard Greek New Testament as my source.
9   John 1:41 and 4:25.
10 Five gospel references are Matthew 1:1 and 18; Mark 1:1; John 1:17 and 17:3.
11 For example, Philippians 2:11.
12 Matthew 21:30, Matthew 13:27, 25:24 and 27:63, John 20:15.
13 Luke 4:18 [NIV].
14 Matthew 16:15–17 [NIV].
15 Matthew 26:63 [NIV].
16 Genesis 6:4 (Nephilim); Job 38:7 (sons of God sing for joy); Exodus 4:22 and Hosea 11:1 (Israel as son); Luke 3:38 (Adam as son of God).
17 John 3:16 [NIV].
18 John 20:17.
19 Matthew 23:9 [NIV].
20 Matthew 26:65–66; Mark 14:63–64; Luke 22:71; John 19:7.
21 Mark 1:1 [NIV]. The phrase 'son of God' was not in all New Testament manuscripts.
22 Acts 8:37 [NIV footnote]. This verse is not included in all New Testament translations, but is shown in a footnote as a variant reading.
23 Matthew 16:13 and 16:15; Mark 8:27 and 8:29; Luke 9:18 and 9:20.

Sketch 3:
A young woman shall give birth

Of all the clauses in the creed, the one which for some will stretch credulity the furthest is the assertion that Jesus 'was conceived by the Holy Ghost, born of the Virgin Mary'. After all, we know that virgins do not conceive and give birth. So what may have been be the meaning of this article of belief, and what were its origins?

As the story of Jesus's birth is told briefly in only two of the four New Testament gospels, *Matthew* and *Luke*,[1] this immediately raises questions of its importance or significance in the early development of Christianity. While the two narratives take different forms, and to some extent tell of different events with different *dramatis personae*, they seem to agree on this one major doctrinal point: Jesus was conceived by Mary through the power of God's spirit, and Mary was a virgin.[2]

In the Hebrew tradition, the spirit of God — by whose power Jesus was conceived, according to these accounts — pre-existed the creation of time and space. The very first verse of the very first book of the Hebrew Bible reads:

> In the beginning God created the heavens and the earth. Now the earth was formless and empty, darkness was over the surface of the deep, and the Spirit of God was hovering over the waters.[3]

The Hebrew word for the spirit of God was *ruach*, literally meaning wind or breath. When God created Adam, he 'breathed into his nostrils the breath of life; and the man became a living being'.[4] This God-given breath-soul was *ruach*. The spirit of God, sometimes translated as 'holy spirit',[5] is active throughout the Old Testament, from the creation narrative in *Genesis*, to the last book, *Malachi*, when the prophet is inspired (breathing in the spirit) to utter the word of the Lord. Many Old Testament references tell of men being filled with the spirit of God, or having the spirit of God descend upon them.[6] Some commentators suggest that angelic visitations were manifestations of the spirit of God.

In the New Testament, the Greek word *pneuma* has the same range of meaning as the Hebrew, wind or breath, hence spirit, the life-giving force. In one of the post-resurrection stories in John's gospel, Jesus met the disciples and 'breathed on them and said, "Receive the Holy Spirit"'.[7] A little later, at the feast of Pentecost, the disciples were together when

> a sound like the blowing of a violent wind came from heaven and filled the whole house where they were sitting... All of them were filled with the Holy Spirit.[8]

Here the Greek word for wind is *pnoe*, which also meant breath: like *pneuma*, its root was the verb *pneo*, I breathe.

It is Luke's gospel which tells the story of the annunciation:

> God sent the angel Gabriel to Nazareth, a town in Galilee, to a virgin pledged to be married to a man named Joseph, a descendant of David. The virgin's name was Mary.[9]

The message that God's angel brings to Mary is that she will conceive and give birth to a son, the son of the Most High. 'How will this be,' the understandably troubled Mary asks, 'since I am a virgin?' Gabriel answers,

> The Holy Spirit will come upon you, and the power of the Most High will overshadow you. So the holy one to be born will be called the Son of God.[10]

Although he was the only gentile gospel author, Luke seems to have been familiar with the standard image of the 'overshadowing' cloud of God, which appears many times in the Hebrew Bible,[11] and considered it wholly appropriate to use it in his version of what he believed to be the most significant and dramatic moment of divine intervention.

Matthew's gospel tells the story differently. An 'angel of the Lord' appears to Joseph 'son of David' in a dream, telling him that 'the child conceived in [Mary] is from the Holy Spirit'.[12] As he crafted his nativity narrative, Matthew was at pains to incorporate a number of key points from the traditional, prophetic Hebrew scriptures, to ensure that his account would unmistakably match the elements within the then current messianic expectations. According to

Sketch 3: A young woman shall give birth 89

Matthew, Jesus was born in Bethlehem, he was in the family line of the great king David, and (quoting a dubious source) his mother was a virgin.[13]

There is certainly, and predictably, considerable ambiguity and debate about the use of the word virgin in the New Testament nativity narrative. Matthew drew on an ancient biblical source, quoting from *Isaiah*:

> Therefore the Lord himself will give you a sign: The virgin will be with child and will give birth to a son, and will call him Immanuel.[14]

That, at least, is the customary rendering of the text in English translations. In the Hebrew text of that verse, however, the word is not virgin, but young woman, *almah*.

When the Hebrew Bible was translated for Greek-speaking Jews in the second century BCE (the version which became known as the Septuagint), *almah* was incorrectly translated as the Greek *parthenos*, virgin. Matthew most probably wrote his gospel in Greek, although that is questioned,[15] and would doubtless have been familiar with the Greek translation of the Hebrew Bible. Be that as it may, it is said that the Septuagint's Greek *parthenos* is 'an important witness to an early Jewish interpretation'[16] and it is that interpretation, albeit a mistaken interpretation, which found its way into Matthew's account. A century and a half after Matthew, Theodotion's translation of the Bible correctly rendered the Hebrew *almah* into the Greek *neanis*, maiden.[17]

A number of the ancient heroes and great figures in the Hebrew biblical narrative were born following angelic visitations, some in 'miraculous' circumstances: both Ishmael and Isaac were born to an aged mother, with an even older father. Both Samson and Samuel were born to mothers who were barren.[18] In the New Testament, John the Baptist's mother Elizabeth was both aged and barren.[19] According to the second century non-canonical *Protevangelium of James*, Mary herself was born to a barren mother, following an angel's visit.[20] Uniquely among these unlikely mothers, however, Mary is said by the two New Testament evangelists to have been a virgin.

Other than these two gospel sources for the virgin birth tradition, the origin of the veneration accorded to Mary is not clear. The letters attributed to the apostle Paul, the earliest of the canonical New Testament writings, mention neither Mary nor a virgin birth, although he does make one brief reference to Jesus being 'born of a woman'.[21] Neither Mark's gospel nor John's includes a nativity narrative, and so appear to attach no importance to circumstances surrounding Jesus's birth. Apart from the nativity stories in *Matthew* and *Luke*, the gospels rarely speak of Mary again. In one incident, bemused critics of Jesus refer to him as Mary's son.[22] Otherwise, the gospels neither accord special status to her, nor use her name, but simply refer to her as the mother of Jesus. When the missing twelve-year-old Jesus is eventually found in the temple in Jerusalem, it is his anxious mother who scolds him.[23] She is present at two events in *John*, the marriage at Cana and the crucifixion, and on one other occasion in the three synoptic gospels, she and Jesus's brothers come looking for him.[24]

In large measure, the text of both *Matthew* and *Luke* follows that of the earlier *Mark*, on which the two writers modelled their gospels and from which they drew very extensively for their material. The main text of all three gospels begins with the story of John the Baptist — as does the fourth, the gospel of John, after its unique and mystical prologue. However, a major departure from Mark's gospel is the inclusion by Matthew and Luke of what can be seen as stand-alone, nativity prologues. And while the two evangelists' main texts otherwise closely resemble each other (as might be expected, given their common sources), the style of their nativity prologues differs noticeably, not only from the main text itself, but also from each other. This suggests that the prologues may have been added later, as the story, myth or tradition began to evolve. Their differing content also suggests not only different traditions but also that Matthew and Luke were unaware of each other's work.

It is interesting to note that the concept of a virgin birth was not universally believed among the early Christians, as evidenced by the *Gospel of the Ebionites*, a second-century Greek-language gospel used by a Jewish Christian sect.[25] The Ebionites' belief in Jesus as the son of God was based not on any teaching about a virgin birth, which they rejected, but on the gift of the Holy Spirit which Jesus received at his baptism.[26]

Both Matthew and Luke include a genealogy for Jesus, to authenticate their claim that he was the messiah. It was necessary to show that Jesus was descended from the great king David, whose golden

Sketch 3: A young woman shall give birth

age the expected messiah would restore. In fact, both family trees stretch back far beyond David. Matthew's list of Jesus's ancestors begins with the greatest of the patriarchs, Abraham. Luke on the other hand was far more ambitious, and his compilation goes all the way back to Adam 'son of God'. Although Luke adds that Jesus was 'the son, so it was thought, of Joseph',[27] neither of the two gospel writers attempts to explain how Jesus could be a genetic descendant of David if Joseph was not his biological father. In the *Protevangelium of James*, Joseph, the husband of the young Mary, is portrayed as an elderly widower, with other sons from an earlier marriage.[28]

The omniscient narrator Luke tells how Mary, on hearing the angel's miraculous announcement, begins reciting the Hebrew scriptures, singing out the collection of verses which were to become known as the *Magnificat*:

> My soul glorifies the Lord
> and my spirit rejoices in God my Saviour,
> for he has been mindful of the humble state of his servant.[29]

The Blessed Virgin Mary, mother of Jesus, is revered by the Roman Catholic church and given a special place in Catholic devotions. In 1854 a pope 'infallibly' (as accepted by Roman Catholicism) defined the dogma of the Immaculate Conception, holding that Mary was conceived free from the 'original sin' to which mankind has been heir since God drove Adam and Eve out of Eden.[30] In 1950, a second Marian belief was defined by a pope as an article of faith, Mary's 'Assumption'. This dogma teaches that, on her death, Mary was carried into heaven, with body and soul united. By contrast, the Protestant churches' teaching contents itself with the simplicity of the gospel narrative, expressed in this article of the creed.

* * *

The church's teaching that Jesus was both God and man is encapsulated in this creedal statement of belief: that he was conceived through the power of the Holy Spirit, and was born of a virgin, human mother. Used in this way (and disregarding the academic argument in favour of a textual mistranslation) the language is clearly metaphorical, depicting a mystery in mythic imagery. Nothing hinges on whether or not Mary was literally and physically still a virgin at the time of Jesus's conception. A belief in the virginity of Mary is not essential to Christian faith; indeed, the argument above would say that such a belief would be an error. But what is to be made of the teaching that the spirit of God was somehow the source of that conception, and that in Jesus we may see God?

We shall return to think more about a holy spirit; but now the creed moves on, leaping across the decades, from the time of the birth of Jesus to the time of his death.

- <u>That</u> I can't believe!

- But what I <u>do</u> believe is this

1. Matthew 1:18 to 2:23 and Luke 1:26 to 2:52.
2. Matthew 1:18–23; Luke 1:26–35.
3. Genesis 1:1–2 [NIV].
4. Genesis 2:7 [NIV].
5. For example, Psalm 51:11; Isaiah 63:10.
6. Genesis 41:38; Exodus 31:3; Numbers 24:2; Judges 3:10; 1 Samuel 10:10, 11:6 and 19:23.
7. John 20:22 [NIV].
8. Acts 2:2 and 2:4 [NIV].
9. Luke 1:27 [NIV].
10. Luke 1:34–35 [NIV].
11. For example, Exodus 24:15; Leviticus 16:2; 1 Kings 8:10; Ezekiel 10:4.
12. Matthew 1:20 [NIV].
13. Born in Bethlehem, Micah 5:2; the house of David, Isaiah 9:7; a virgin mother, Isaiah 7:14.
14. Isaiah 7.14 [NIV].
15. A.E. Harvey, *The New English Bible: Companion to the New Testament*, and A.H. McNeile, *An Introduction to the Study of the New Testament*.
16. Footnote to Isaiah 7:14 in *The Jerusalem Bible*.
17. A. Souter, *A Pocket Lexicon to the Greek New Testament*.
18. Genesis 16:7–16; Genesis 18:9–14 and 21:1–3; 1 Samuel 1:5 and 19–20; Judges 13:2–3.
19. Luke 1:18.
20. R. Cameron (ed.), *The Other Gospels: Non-Canonical Gospel Texts*.
21. Galatians 4:4.
22. Matthew 13:55 and Mark 6:3.
23. Luke 2:48.
24. John 2:1 and 19:25; Matthew 12:46; Mark 3:31; Luke 8:19.
25. Burton H. Throckmorton, *Gospel Parallels: A Comparison of the Synoptic Gospels*.
26. Matthew 3:36; Mark 1:20; Luke 3:22; John 1:32.

27 Luke 3:23.
28 R. Cameron, *The Other Gospels, op. cit.*
29 Luke 1:46–48. The first lines are quoted from Isaiah 1:10. Other verses in the *Magnificat* are quotations or paraphrases of texts from the Psalms and books of the prophets.
30 Genesis 3:23–24.

Sketch 4: The death of Jesus

With the statement that Jesus 'Suffered under Pontius Pilate, was crucified, dead, and buried', the tone and style of the creed change. This article differs from the first three in a remarkable way: with one giant stride, it steps out of the creed's supernatural world—opening as it does with statements of belief in an all-powerful, creator father-god and in his god-man son, who was conceived through the power of a divine spirit and born to a virgin mother—straight into a world which has every appearance of being independently verifiable, with a named historical secular figure, Pontius Pilatus. So, for a while, we enter what can be taken to be the world of an historical Jesus.

It is very clear from the gospel narrative that Jesus was becoming a serious embarrassment to the Jewish religious authorities in Jerusalem and 'the chief priests and the teachers of the law were looking for some sly way to arrest Jesus and kill him'.[1] And that is exactly what they did, according to the gospels. Late at night, after he had shared the Passover meal with twelve of his closest companions, Jesus was seized by an armed mob sent by the authorities, and dragged before the Sanhedrin, the Jewish council. They 'were looking for evidence against Jesus so that they could put him to death, but they did not find any'.[2] Eventually, under interrogation by the high priest, Jesus seemed to give the council what they were looking for, sufficient excuse to judge him guilty of blasphemy, and so deserving death.

The gospel stories differ in their detail and the order in which they place events; but they are agreed that Jesus was taken to the Roman procurator, Pontius Pilatus, who alone could authorise execution. Unable to find any fault in Jesus, certainly none deserving the death penalty, Pilate made some effort to release him. Luke adds that Pilate referred Jesus to the puppet king, Herod, perhaps in the vain hope that the Jewish Herod could make sense of the priests' claims.[3] The book of *Acts* tells how, following what they believed to be Jesus's resurrection and ascension, the newly-emboldened apostles saw this 'conspiracy' between Pilate and Herod as a fulfilment of an ancient prophecy:

Sketch 4: The death of Jesus

> The kings of the earth take their stand
> and the rulers gather together against the Lord
> and against his Anointed One.[4]

In this part of the gospel narrative, Pontius Pilatus is portrayed as indecisive and craven, although elsewhere a picture of a more forceful and ruthless man emerges.[5] Be that as it may, in spite of his belief that Jesus was innocent, Pilate was quick to accede to the crowd's demands when he became unnerved by their shouted taunts: 'If you let this man go, you are no friend of Caesar. Anyone who claims to be a king opposes Caesar.'[6] So Pilate literally washed his hands of Jesus — why should he care about yet another Jewish troublemaker? — and after having him flogged, sent him away for execution. After cruel humiliation and abuse by the Roman soldiers, Jesus was hauled away to a place called Golgotha, and there he was crucified between two thieves. As Jesus died the death of a criminal, nailed alive to a wooden cross, there was an earthquake and it became unnaturally dark, and it is said that

> the tombs broke open and the bodies of many holy people who had died were raised to life. They came out of the tombs and after Jesus' resurrection they went into the holy city and appeared to many people.[7]

An Arimathæan named Joseph, a respected member of the Sanhedrin, asked Pilate for the body of Jesus. The gospel hints that Joseph was a secret disciple of Jesus, and had not been party to the Sanhedrin's plan.[8] The body of Jesus was placed in a tomb provided by Joseph, the tomb's entrance was sealed with a great stone, and Joseph went away.[9]

* * *

In expressing a belief that Jesus 'suffered under Pontius Pilate', the Apostles' Creed puts down an historical marker, placing the man Jesus at a specific point in history by naming the Roman who condemned him to death. The gospels themselves include very few dates. Luke, for example, sets the date of Jesus's baptism at the fifteenth year of the emperor Tiberius (14–37 CE), that is, 29 CE.[10] Given that Jesus was crucified two or three years later, then he would indeed have been arraigned before Pontius Pilatus, who was procurator or prefect of Judæa from 26 to 36 CE. However, so far we have no verifiable, independent record to authenticate the gospel story of Pilate condemning Jesus to death—that is to say, if there was a record it has not survived, or if it has survived it has not been found. A brief reference was made by the Jewish Roman chronicler Flavius Josephus, although it is thought that this may be a later, inauthentic insertion to his histories. Early rabbinic writings record that a false teacher and sorcerer, Yeshu'a of Nazareth, was hanged by the Roman occupiers. But we know no more.

Pontius Pilatus himself is something of a shadowy figure. He was referred to by the first century Roman historian Tacitus and by the Jewish philosopher Philo of Alexandria, and in the fourth century by the theologian Eusebius. Many other stories were told about Pilate over the years. The second-century non-canonical *Gospel of Peter*, for example, exonerates Pilate from responsibility for Jesus's death, shifting the blame to the Jewish authorities; and the third-century *Acts of Pilate* portrays Pontius Pilatus as a witness of the resurrection of Jesus, and therefore to the truth of Christian belief. This document also states that Joseph of Arimathæa was a friend of Pilate and made his request for the body of Jesus prior to the crucifixion.[11] The *Acts of Pilate* includes a story also found in one of the gospels, in which Pilate's wife advises him to have nothing to do with the innocent Jesus, having been given that warning in dream.[12]

That much and not a great deal more can be said about the stories of Pontius Pilatus which are told in the gospels of the Christian canon, and in a number of apocryphal writings, all or some of which may or may not be historically authentic.

What we can be certain of, however, is that Pontius Pilatus was an historical figure. In 1961, excavation at the Roman site of Caesarea in Israel unearthed a stone, dedicating a building, possibly a temple, to the emperor Tiberius and inscribed with the name of Pontius Pilatus, Prefect of Judæa.[13] The stone has been authenticated by archaeologists, and is the only known artefact bearing Pilate's name. Thus, paradoxically, we have more tangible historical evidence for Pontius Pilatus than we have for Jesus of Nazareth.

Of course, confirming verifiable historical detail was not what the creed's authors were setting out to do, nor was that the aim of the

Sketch 4: The death of Jesus 97

gospel writers. Their purpose was to declare their belief in Jesus as Lord. Moreover, in presenting a suffering Jesus, they were once again affirming a belief in Jesus as the messiah. A number of New Testament texts allude to the ancient prophecies concerning a suffering messiah, and how Jesus fulfilled those prophecies. All three synoptic gospels record Jesus telling his disciples

> that he must go to Jerusalem and suffer many things... and that he must be killed and on the third day be raised to life.[14]

This may be an example of the evangelists writing back into their gospels the beliefs about Jesus which developed in later years. It is interesting to note the extent to which they drew on the images of the 'Suffering servant' found in their ancient Hebrew scriptures, as they wrote their account of the trial, suffering and death of Jesus, most specifically the prophecy of Isaiah, hundreds of years earlier:

> He was pierced for our transgressions... He was oppressed and afflicted, yet he did not open his mouth... By oppression and judgment he was taken away... for the transgression of my people he was stricken... He was assigned a grave with the wicked, and with the rich in his death... though he had done no violence, nor was any deceit in his mouth.[15]

The early Christian writers identified the suffering Jesus with the suffering messiah, and as a result came to believe the suffering of a crucified Jesus to be a redemptive act. The apostle Peter declared that

> This is how God fulfilled what he had foretold through all the prophets, Saying that his Christ would suffer. Repent, then, and turn to God, so that your sins may be wiped out.[16]

The redemptive and vicarious nature of Jesus's suffering, and suffering as the redeeming messiah, is further alluded to in a letter attributed to Peter:

> Christ suffered for you... by his wounds you have been healed.[17]

Once again, a Jewish writer was referring back to the tradition of the Hebrew scriptures, and the messianic expectations.

* * *

This, then, is the creed's statement of belief. Like the gospels, from which it derives, it is not as an affirmation of historical fact but a proclamation that the son of God, the suffering messiah, was crucified as a saviour. That is one way of thinking about these words: Suffered under Pontius Pilate, was crucified, dead, and buried—that is, think of them in the orthodox, 'religious' way.

There are other ways of thinking about these words, though. I began by suggesting that this article was different from the other parts of the creed in that it steps out of the realms of the supernatural into the world of matter-of-fact history. As we have seen, Pontius Pilatus was an historical figure; and although we have very little to go on historically, there can be no reason to doubt that the man Jesus was also an historical figure. If, as the gospel narrative makes so clear, he was a thorn in the side of the Jewish authorities, then it is most likely that he was indeed arraigned before Pilate, and suffered the hideous slow death by Roman crucifixion. Having died, he was buried, as dead men are buried. Joseph of Arimathæa is said to have provided the tomb, which he sealed.

So we may be on firm enough ground to say 'I believe *that*' these events actually happened. But what more are we prepared to say: what do we believe *in*? One choice is to say that we believe in a fully-human Jesus, the man from Galilee, whose words 'proclaim freedom for the prisoners and recovery of sight for the blind'.[18] The words of this Jesus can liberate men and women from those things that imprison them, guilt perhaps, or defeat, or addictive enslavement. His words can restore the sight of men and women, giving them new ways of looking at their world.

- <u>That</u> I can't believe!

- But what I <u>do</u> believe is this:

---

1   Mark 14:1 [NIV]. Also Matthew 26:3–4 and Luke 22:2.
2   Mark 14:55 [NIV].
3   Luke 23:6–12.
4   Acts of the Apostles 4:26 [NIV]. See also Psalm 2:1–2.
5   Luke 13:1. See *Acts of Pilate* in R. Cameron (ed.), *The Other Gospels: Non-Canonical Gospel Texts*.

6 John 19:12 [NIV].
7 Matthew 27:52-53 [NIV].
8 Matthew 27:57; Luke 23:51; John 19:38.
9 Matthew 26:47-27:60; Mark 14:43-15:46; Luke 22:47-23:53; John 18:1-19:42.
10 Luke 3:1.
11 R. Cameron, *The Other Gospels, op. cit.*
12 Matthew 27:19.
13 Illustrated and described at www.english.imjnet.org.il.
14 Matthew 16:21. See also Mark 8:31 and Luke 9:22.
15 Isaiah 53:5-9 [NIV]. See also the remainder of Isaiah 53.
16 The Acts of the Apostles 3:18-19 [NIV].
17 1 Peter 2:21 and 2:24 [NIV]. See also Isaiah 53:5.
18 Luke 4:18.

Sketch 5: Resurrection

In the previous section we saw how the creed's authors momentarily entered history, or at least the world of the here-and-now, as they assembled their statements of belief. They return now to the supernatural with the statement that Jesus 'descended into hell; the third day he rose again from the dead'.

A belief that there was literally a place to which the dead descended featured in the culture of many ancient civilisations, and continued well beyond the time of the creed's composition. The domain of the departed was in the lowest layer of a three-tiered universe. High above the earth inhabited by men and women were the heavens, where a god or gods dwelt, while far beneath the earth there was the underworld, a drear place to which all people went at the moment of their death.

For the Greeks, this was Hades, the kingdom of Aïdes, lord of the dead, the inescapable final destination of all humankind. Still more terrible was Tartaros, the pit of perdition. This was thought to be so far beneath the earth that, if a bronze anvil were to fall, it would be nine days and nine nights before it landed in Tartaros.[1] The Roman dead too were destined to go down to the underworld, to wander forever in the infernal regions of Elysium or Erebus.

In essence, then, just as the living dwelt on earth, so the underworld was where the dead dwelt, although being there did not necessarily involve suffering or punishment.

In the same way, the Greek and Roman gods came down to earth from their realm above, intervened in the lives of men and women, and returned to the heavens. Similarly, they were free to visit the underworld, coming and going at will. For human beings, though, there was a one-way ticket for the journey down into this 'undiscover'd country, from whose bourn no traveller returns'.[2]

Both Greeks and Romans told stories of gods and sons of gods visiting the underworld and returning safely. Persephone, goddess wife of the Greek god Aïdes (Proserpina and Pluto in the Roman pantheon), spent part of her time on earth and part in the land of the dead. Homer's Odysseus, progeny of Zeus, visited Hades, where he met the shades of Achilleus and his former warrior companions among the gibbering ghosts, before resuming his homeward wanderings. Virgil's Aenaeas, Trojan prince and son of Venus, travelled to the underworld to find the spirit of his father Anchises, and lived to tell the tale. Two thousand years after Homer, Dante Alighieri was to be conducted by Virgil on a tour of the underworld, a medieval *Inferno* reserved for the punishment of wrongdoers.

The underworld of the Hebrew Bible was known as Sheol.[3] Like the Greek and Roman domain of the dead, Sheol was a place of shadows to which every man and woman was destined one day to descend:

> he who goes down to Sheol does not return.
> He will never come to his house again;
> his place will know him no more.[4]

In time, Sheol came to be seen not only as the inescapable resting place of all the dead, but also as the place where wrongdoers would suffer, more specifically suffer in hell-fire.[5] A gospel parable tells of a selfish and inconsiderate rich man who, having died, is in torment in the underworld. He pleads with Abraham to send the poor man Lazarus, whom he had abused during his lifetime, 'to dip the tip of his finger in water and cool my tongue, because I am in agony in this fire'. Abraham replies that this cannot be, because

> between us and you a great chasm has been fixed, so that those who want to go from here to you cannot, nor can anyone cross over from there to us.[6]

Impaled on a Roman cross, Jesus cried out, 'My God, my God, why have you forsaken me?',[7] and it was into this hell, into this separation from God, that the dying Jesus now knew he must descend. For the gospel writers, and for the creed's authors, it was an accepted, natural belief that, having died, Jesus would descend to Sheol or 'Hell'. According to the gospels, however, Jesus had told his disciples before that final, fateful Passover that 'the Son of Man will be three days and three nights in the heart of the earth', indicating that he expected his sojourn in the underworld to be a temporary one.[8]

Both in the Christian canon and in apocryphal writings there is some evidence of a tradition that in those three days 'in the heart of the earth' Jesus preached to 'the imprisoned spirits'.[9] According to a letter written towards the end of the first century and attributed to Peter, these spirits were believed to be those of people drowned in the great flood at the time of Noah.[10] Some commentators have suggested that the imprisoned spirits to which Jesus is said to have preached were those of the 'fallen angels', whom God had consigned to the dark pits of hell, held there in chains until the day of judgment.[11]

* * *

For the followers of Jesus, his death and descent into the underworld was not to be the end of the story, however. It is not possible to say with any certainty what happened after the crucifixion. The gospel narrative tells how understandably frightened the disciples were, following the arrest and execution of Jesus, terrified perhaps that they would be implicated in the troublemaking of which he had been accused, and suffer the same hideous and shameful fate.[12] But however they spent the next few days, it seems to be clear that they were not expectantly watching for his reappearance, in spite of having been told by Jesus on a number of occasions (according to the gospels) that after his death he would 'rise again' on the third day.[13] They had not understood what he had meant by that and were afraid to ask.[14]

The New Testament gospel writers, each in his different way, describe not how Jesus rose from the dead, but how it was discovered that he had. When the faithful women went to the tomb where they knew Joseph of Arimathæa had buried Jesus, their purpose seems to have been to embalm the body, obviously unnecessary if Jesus was expected somehow to return. As in so many of the gospel stories, the detail varies; but Matthew writes

> there was a violent earthquake, for an angel of the Lord came down from heaven and, going to the tomb, rolled back the stone and sat on it. His appearance was like lightning, and his clothes were white as snow.[15]

The angel tells the women that Jesus is not in the tomb because he has been raised from the dead, as he said he would be. Luke adds that the women hurried back to bring this astonishing news to the apostles, but the women's story was thought to be nonsense, and the apostles

Sketch 5: Resurrection 103

would not believe them.[16] Hardly the response of men who expected Jesus to return!

A short passage in the first-century *Gospel of Peter* describes the moment when Jesus actually emerged from the tomb. Although this gospel was not included in the Christian canon, it is believed by some scholars to have been produced and circulated with the authority of the apostle Peter.[17] At dawn, according to Roman soldier witnesses, a loud voice rang out and, as the heavens opened, two men descended in a brilliant light. The stone sealing the tomb began to roll away of its own accord, and the two men went in. Then, as the soldiers watched, the two men reappeared accompanied by a third man, whom they supported as they walked.

Perhaps not surprisingly, none of this detail found its way into any of the canonical gospels. Curiously, too, some of the most ancient manuscripts of *Mark*, which was the first gospel to be written and on which Matthew and Luke drew for their narratives, have quite different endings.[18] Some conclude with the crucifixion, and the centurion's declaration, 'This man must have been the son of God'. Others end with a report of the women's discovery of an empty tomb, but suddenly finish with 'They said nothing to anyone, because they were afraid'.[19]

* * *

Quite apart from the resurrection narrative, there are many biblical references to the belief that the dead could return to life. In the Old Testament, there are the twinned stories of the prophet Elijah restoring the son of the widow of Zarephath, and Elisha bringing back to life the son of the Shunammite woman.[20] After Elisha's death, a dead man is restored to life when his body is hastily dumped in the prophet's grave and falls on Elisha's bones, which were buried there.[21] The writer of a letter preserved in the New Testament argues that when in the old days 'Women received back their dead, raised to life again', it was one of many signs that their faith had won God's approval.[22] Jesus wanted the imprisoned John the Baptist to know that among the messianic expectations being fulfilled by his ministry was the sight of the dead being raised to life.[23] Three times the gospels tell of Jesus restoring dead people to life.[24] Matthew notes that, at the time of Jesus's death, the saints were raised from their graves and were seen in Jerusalem.[25] Both Peter and Paul are said to have returned the dead to life.[26]

Against such a background, then, and within such a tradition, the idea of a resurrected Jesus, literally risen from the dead, was far from being considered an impossibility. It was perfectly feasible for people in the first century of our era—people whose understanding of their world was that it lay far beneath heaven and far above an underworld—to believe, speak and write about the son of their god, who not only 'came down' from heaven to earth, but also 'descended' into hell, and after three days 'rose' and 'ascended' to heaven again.

A crucified but risen Christ was absolutely fundamental to Paul's teaching. But in his preserved writings, he made no mention of an empty tomb. Did Paul believe in the literal, bodily return from the dead? Or did he mean something else? What is clear is that today several thousand churches (certainly those associated with the Evangelical Alliance, for example), and presumably therefore many thousands of Christians, sign up to a belief in 'the bodily resurrection of Christ [and] his ascension to the Father'.[27]

One is hard put to find a theologian who is able to write about the 'resurrection' of Jesus without obfuscation, preferring instead to wrap up his thinking in all manner of abstract language. Where is the theologian who will answer this question, in simple layman's terms and without dissimulation, 'Do you believe that Jesus's resurrection was literally a factual, historical, physical event?' David Jenkins, when Bishop of Durham, preached a much-publicised sermon at Easter 1988, referring to the resurrection as 'an extremely mysterious and unlikely event';[28] and, while he was widely quoted as suggesting the crucifixion may have been some kind of 'conjuring trick with bones',[29] he did not add anything that made clear just what he *did* believe about this 'unlikely event'. What became of the bones of Jesus? Do they lie somewhere in the land of Israel—or to ask Geoffrey Lampe's question, 'where else may they be?'[30]

What are we to make of ideas about an underworld, whether or not it involves punishment and suffering? Has hell gone out of fashion? According to press reports, a pope has asked that very question in recent times: Why don't we talk about hell anymore?[31] And for the evangelicals there remains the expectation that Jesus will

Sketch 5: Resurrection   105

return, to raise the dead to judgment, with eternal life for the saved and eternal condemnation for the lost.[32]
We shall return to think more about the concept of an afterlife.

- That I can't believe!

- But what I do believe is this:

[1] Hesiod, *Theogony*, Stanley Lombardo (trs.).
[2] William Shakespeare, *Hamlet*, Act 3 Scene 1.
[3] See Numbers 16:31–33 and 2 Samuel 28:8–14 for two dramatic stories concerning Sheol. See also Psalm 16:10.
[4] Job 7:9 [NIV].
[5] For example, Matthew 5:22 and 10:28; Mark 9:47; Luke 10:15.
[6] Luke 16:24 and 16:26 [NIV].
[7] Matthew 27:46 and Mark 15:34 [NIV].
[8] Matthew 12:40 [NIV].
[9] For example, First letter of Peter in the New Testament, and the non-canonical *Gospel of Peter* (R. Cameron).
[10] 1 Peter 3:19–20.
[11] Jude 6 and 2 Peter 2:4–10.
[12] Matthew 26:69–75; Mark 14:66–72; Luke 22:55–62.
[13] Matthew 20:19; Mark 9:31 and 10:34; Luke 18:33 and 24:7.
[14] Mark 9:10 and 9:32.
[15] Matthew 28:2–3 [NIV].
[16] Luke 24:11.
[17] R. Cameron (ed.), *The Other Gospels: Non-Canonical Gospel Texts*.
[18] B.H. Throckmorton, *Gospel Parallels: A Comparison of the Synoptic Gospels*.
[19] Mark 16:8 [NIV].
[20] 1 Kings 17:17ff and 2 Kings 4:25ff.
[21] 2 Kings 13:21.
[22] Hebrews 11:35 and 11:39 [NIV].
[23] Matthew 11:5.
[24] John 11:43 (Lazarus); Matthew 9:18, Mark 5:41 and Luke 8:41 (Jairus's daughter); Luke 7:14 (son of the widow at Nain).
[25] Matthew 27:52.
[26] Acts 9:37ff (Peter and Dorcas); Acts 20:7ff (Paul and Eutychus).
[27] Evangelical Alliance: http://www.eauk.org.
[28] Cited in Hugh Dawes, *Freeing the Faith*.
[29] This was later reported again in a profile of the bishop in *The Independent* on 5 February 1994.
[30] G. Lampe, 'The Essence of Christianity'.
[31] *The Guardian* London, 27 March 2007.
[32] Evangelical Alliance, *op. cit.*

Sketch 6: Ascending to heaven

Although the creed's stated belief is that Jesus 'ascended into heaven, and sitteth on the right hand of God the Father Almighty', the gospel narratives themselves make scant reference to the 'ascension' of Jesus. There is just one short phrase in a verse at the very end of Luke's gospel (although it is omitted from some ancient manuscripts): Jesus accompanied his disciples as far as Bethany, where he blessed them and 'was taken up into heaven'.[1]

Otherwise, none of the gospels comes to a very clear ending. *Matthew* closes with Jesus saying to his disciples 'Surely I am with you always, to the very end of the age'.[2] *John* leaves Jesus talking with Peter and the other disciples over breakfast on the sea shore. Manuscripts of *Mark*, as we have already seen, have different and inconclusive endings, none of them referring to 'ascension'.

It is in the book of *Acts*, thought to be the work of the gospel writer Luke, that we find the brief story of the ascension.[3] The book's opening chapter states that for forty days after his resurrection Jesus met with the apostles on a number of occasions, and 'he showed himself to these men and gave many convincing proofs that he was alive'.[4] At the end of that time, according to the author of *Acts*, Jesus went with them to the Mount of Olives, just outside Jerusalem, and taking his leave of them, 'he was taken up before their very eyes, and a cloud hid him from their sight'.[5] As the apostles stood staring into the cloud, the story continues, two men in white suddenly appeared at their side. They asked the apostles why they were looking up into the sky, and said, 'This same Jesus, who has been taken into heaven, will come back in the same way as you have seen him go into heaven'.[6]

Once again, both narrative and creed speak of a supernatural 'event', believed to have taken place within the three-tier universe in which the writer of *Acts* and the creed's compilers believed they lived.

Stories of dramatic departures from earth to heaven were well-known for centuries before Luke was writing his narrative. Within the tradition of the ancient Hebrew scriptures, for example, there

Sketch 6: Ascending to heaven

were the stories of Enoch and Elijah, two men who were said not to have died but to have gone to be with God in heaven. The means of Enoch's 'translation' was briefly told very early in the Bible's first book: at the ripe old age of three hundred and sixty-five years, 'Enoch walked with God; then he was no more, because God took him away'.[7] The description of Elijah's departure was more colourful and dramatic: as Elijah and Elisha walked together, 'a chariot of fire and horses of fire appeared and separated the two of them, and Elijah went up to heaven in a whirlwind'.[8]

As we have already noted, the gospels make negligible mention of the 'event' of Jesus's ascension. The three synoptic gospels contain parallel passages which draw on a prophetic vision concerning the End of Days (the subject of the next section), when 'men will see the Son of Man coming in clouds with great power and glory';[9] but they seem to make no direct reference to any prophecy by Jesus concerning his ascension.

John's gospel, by contrast, does. This is congruent with the fourth gospel's generally more mystical and apocalyptic content: for example, the brief prologue of *John* opens with the same words as those of the first verse of the Hebrew Bible's first book, 'In the beginning', presenting Jesus as the *Logos*, the Expression of God, the 'Word' which pre-existed creation itself. It is in *John* that Jesus says to his disciples, 'Go to my brothers and say to them, "I am returning to my Father and your Father, to my God and your God"'.[10] At least three times earlier in John's gospel, Jesus is said to have referred to his ascension,[11] and on another occasion he spoke of the ascension of 'the Son of Man'.[12]

Jesus frequently used the title 'Son of Man' as a synonym for 'I', and it has been described as the 'most personal and most deliberately chosen title for himself'.[13] It appears something like eighty times in the gospels, and once in *Acts*, in the story of the first martyr, Stephen. At his death, Stephen cried out, 'I see heaven open and the Son of Man standing at the right hand of God'.[14]

Here, perhaps, is a clue to the origins of belief in the ascension of the 'Son of Man' and his presence at the right hand of God. For Stephen's generation, the Son of God had come to mean the messiah. While the Hebrew *ben adam*, son of man, had common usage in Old Testament times simply to mean 'man' — it is to be found nearly one hundred times as a form of address in the book of *Ezekiel* alone, for example—by the mid-second century BCE, it was beginning to take on a special meaning, with specific connection with the growing messianic expectations. At that time, the prophet Daniel wrote of his vision of

> one like the son of man coming with the clouds of heaven... He was given authority, glory and sovereign power.[15]

Perhaps a century later, the book of *Enoch* presented the Son of Man as 'a divine pre-existent figure waiting in the heavenly places to be unleashed in vengeance and in judgment upon the world'.[16]

To be on the sovereign's right hand is not to occupy a place but to perform a function, that of the king's right-hand man. The synoptic gospel writers have Jesus using this imagery (about himself?) as he quotes from the Psalms:[17]

> The LORD says to my Lord,
> 'Sit at my right hand until I make your enemies
> a footstool for your feet'.[18]

For Paul (and for the creed's authors) the 'ascended' Jesus was seated at God's right hand,[19] the vice-regent who one day will return to earth to establish the reign of God, King of the universe.

* * *

Those were the beliefs and writings of people who lived in a three-tiered universe (as they thought), where gods descended to earth and returned to their realm above.

What language might twenty-first-century men and women use, what imagery or metaphors would give meaningful expression to the supremacy of Jesus, the man from Galilee, the man in whom we may see the meaning of 'God'?

- <u>That</u> I can't believe!

- But what I <u>do</u> believe is this:

1. Luke 24:51 [NIV]. See B.H. Throckmorton, *Gospel Parallels: A Comparison of the Synoptic Gospels.*
2. Matthew 28:20 [NIV].
3. Acts 1:1–11.
4. Acts 1:3 [NIV].
5. Acts 1:9 [NIV].
6. Acts 1:11 [NIV].
7. Genesis 5:24 [NIV].
8. 2 Kings 2:11 [NIV].
9. Mark 13:26 [NIV]. Also Matthew 24:30 and Luke 21:27.
10. John 20:17 [NIV].
11. John 14:2 and 14:28, 16:5.
12. John 6:62.
13. William Barclay, *Jesus as They Saw Him.*
14. Acts 7:56 [NIV].
15. Daniel 7:13–14 [NIV].
16. William Barclay, *op. cit.*
17. Matthew 22:44, Mark 12:36, Luke 20:42.
18. Psalm 110:1 [NIV].
19. Romans 8:34, Ephesians 1:20, Colossians 3:1.

Sketch 7: Judgment day

The creed's authors paused for one moment in history, at the point where Jesus was crucified and died; but now they have moved on, reaching the highest point of belief in supernatural 'events', with a statement of belief that 'From thence [Heaven] he shall come to judge the quick and the dead'. Jesus had died but was alive again, had ascended to heaven, to sit at the right hand of an almighty god, but now, according to the creed, is to return to earth, to bring judgment both to those still living and those who have died.

In the story of the 'ascension', related in *Acts*, heavenly messengers reassure the understandably astonished apostles that Jesus will return in same way as they have seen him go.[1] This imagery of comings and goings in the skies was typical of expressions of then-current messianic expectations. As we noted in the last section, the prophet Daniel wrote of his vision of 'one like a son of man, coming with the clouds of heaven'.[2] John's gospel has Jesus using the same language: 'You shall see heaven open and the angels of God ascending and descending on the Son of Man.'[3]

In parallel texts in the synoptic gospels, Jesus again quotes the words of Daniel, as he tells his disciples about the End of Days, when their generation will see

> the Son of Man coming on the clouds of the sky, with power and great glory'. And he will send his angels with a loud trumpet call, and they will gather his elect from the four winds, from one end of the heavens to the other.[4]

It is only in *Matthew* that the disciples are bold enough to make the link between Jesus and the prophesied arrival of the messiah, as they ask Jesus what the signs of his 'coming' will be.[5]

The New Testament Greek word for 'coming' is *parousia*. In earlier, classical Greek, *parousia* meant simply presence, the opposite of absence. In Hellenistic Greek (that is, by about the third century BCE) the word had begun to take on a special meaning, referring to a god's visitation, or the arrival of an emperor. In New Testament usage, this later meaning of *parousia* as a royal or divine visit is most

Sketch 7: Judgment day

commonly employed to refer to the second coming of the Christ. For example, Paul's first letter to the Christian communities in Thessalonika, which focuses very much on the expected and imminent return of the ascended Christ, makes frequent reference to his *parousia*.[6]

The themes of judgment and of God as the judge are never very far away in the tradition of the Hebrew scriptures.[7] In a scene wholly reminiscent of Homer's Zeus presiding over the immortals on Mount Olympos, the Hebrew psalmist sang:

> God presides in the great assembly;
> He gives judgment among the 'gods'
> ...
> Rise up, O God, judge the earth,
> for all the nations are your inheritance.[8]

Now, according to John's gospel, the role of judge has been passed by Almighty God to his son, the risen and ascended Christ;[9] he 'is the one whom God has appointed as judge of the living and the dead'.[10] Although it is far from clear how, or if, Jesus saw his messianic role — at least, how he saw it in apocalyptic terms, if he did — the concept of the messiah as judge was already well-established and understood among his contemporaries.[11] In two places in John's gospel Jesus makes what have the appearance of conflicting statements about his role: once, to say that it is for judgment that he has come into the world, and then to say that he has not come into the world as judge but as saviour.[12] However, neither statement seems to make a future, apocalyptic allusion, even though that would have been congruent with the character of John's gospel, in contrast with the three synoptics.

For the people who wrote the first-century letters preserved in the New Testament, and for the people to whom they were writing, the *parousia* was believed to be imminent: 'the Lord's coming is near… The Judge is standing at the door!'[13] But was the expected judgment something to look forward to or to be feared? A judge makes decisions between this position and that: a judge either acquits or passes sentence. Both Peter and Paul had a view. In Peter's vision, the godless will perish on the day of judgment, as the existing heavens and the earth are destroyed by fire.[14] Paul's vision was perhaps more heartening: 'with the voice of the archangel and with the call of the trumpet of God', he wrote, the Christian dead will be the first to rise, followed by those who are still alive, 'caught up together with them in clouds to meet the Lord in the air. And so we will be with the Lord forever'.[15]

Charles Wesley caught something of Paul's vision when in 1746 he wrote his hymn 'Rejoice! The Lord is King'. Two and a half centuries later, a number of the hymn's verses have disappeared from the hymnals and are no longer there to be sung. Perhaps their sentiments have gone out of fashion:

> Rejoice in glorious hope:
> Jesus, the Judge, shall come,
> And take His servants up
> To their eternal home:
> We soon shall hear the archangel's voice;
> The trump of God shall sound, Rejoice![16]

Fashion or no, the visions of both Paul and Peter are preserved in the basis of faith published by the Evangelical Alliance, to which several thousand British churches are affiliated.[17] That document, to which the Alliance's members are required to subscribe, declares a belief that Jesus will return and that all will be raised by him to judgment. The 'redeemed' will be given eternal life, while the 'lost' go to perdition. That is perhaps rather more than the creed declares.

* * *

What then are twenty-first-century men and women to make of these images, images of an archangel's voice and a trumpet call from God? And what is to be made of a teaching that at the 'end of days' all will be raised to judgment? Is it no more than an example of an outdated, supernatural or superstitious dogma? Is it to be swept aside as no more than a typical expression of belief handed down from the culture of an ancient people? Or is it possible that somewhere in the minds of many people today there remains a thought that one day we shall be called to account for our actions during our lifetime?

Sketch 7: Judgment day

Is it not better, though, to focus on words of Jesus, to see how they apply to social action in the here-and-now, rather than await appraisal on an imagined 'judgment day':

> I was hungry and you gave me something to eat, I was thirsty and you gave me something to drink, I was a stranger and you invited me in, I needed clothes and you clothed me, I was sick and you looked after me, I was in prison and you came to visit me.[18]

In that verse there is an agenda for a programme of unselfish action.

- <u>That</u> I can't believe!

- But what I <u>do</u> believe is this:

1. Acts 1:11.
2. Daniel 7:13 [NIV].
3. John 1:51.
4. Matthew 24:30 [NIV]. Also Mark 13:26 and Luke 21:27.
5. Matthew 24:3.
6. 1 Thessalonians 2:19, 3:13, 4:15, 5:23. See also Matthew 24:3, 24:27, 24:37 and 24:39; James 5:7–8; 2 Peter 1:16, 3:4 and 3:12; 1 John 2:28.
7. Examples from Old Testament books are: Genesis 18:25, Deuteronomy 32:36, Judges 11:27, 1 Samuel 24:12, 1 Chronicles 16:33, Job 21:22, Psalm 50:6, Isaiah 33:22, Ezekiel 16:38.
8. Psalm 82:1 and 8 [NIV].
9. John 5:22.
10. Acts of the Apostles 10:42 [NIV]. See also 2 Timothy 4:1 and 1 Peter 4:5.
11. For example, the Psalms of Solomon, dating from the first century BCE. See William Barclay, *Jesus as They Saw Him*.
12. John 9:39 and 12:47.
13. James 5:8–9 [NIV].
14. 2 Peter 3:7. See also Revelation 20:11.
15. 1 Thessalonians 4:17.
16. Charles Wesley, hymn, 'Rejoice! The Lord is King' (1746).
17. Evangelical Alliance: http://www.eauk.org.
18. Matthew 25:35–36 [NIV].

Sketch 8: The spirit of the divine

Just as the creed's second article is dependent on the first—a belief in a god-son requires a belief in a god-father—so this article, the expression of belief in the Holy Spirit, is dependent on a previous one. It affirms a belief in an ascended Christ, since, according to the New Testament narrative, it was only after Jesus had left his apostles that they were filled with the Holy Spirit.[1]

The opening verses of the New Testament introduce the Holy Spirit as giver of life, in the story of the virgin birth.[2] Similarly, the Hebrew Bible's (Old Testament) opening verses speak of the pre-existent, life-giving spirit of God being present at the creation.[3] Because the Holy Spirit features so prominently in the New Testament, it is easy to overlook the extent to which the spirit of God is encountered in the Hebrew Bible, as a life-force and as an enabling power.

In the *Genesis* story of Joseph, the pharaoh appointed him vice-regent, with control of Egypt's administration, because no other man in the land was as full of the spirit of God as Joseph was.[4] During the Israelites' desert wanderings, Bezalel, the craftsman chosen by God to make his tabernacle and the ark, was filled with the spirit of God and was endowed with a wondrous range of skills.[5] When the over-burdened Moses shared his workload with seventy elders, God's spirit settled on them and they were seized with prophetic rapture.[6]

Later, at the time of the 'judges', the great Old Testament heroes Gideon and Samson, each in his day, were suddenly seized by God's spirit, and empowered to achieve epic deeds: Gideon routed whole armies with three small companies of chosen warriors; Samson took a jawbone from a donkey skull and with it slew a thousand of his enemies.[7] When Saul was anointed by Samuel as Israel's first king, the spirit of God suddenly took hold of him, so that he was filled with prophetic ecstasy.[8] Then, from the golden age of David's kingdom, a psalm tells how the great king pleads with God not to take his holy spirit from him, as a punishment for his adultery with Bathsheba.[9]

Many years after David, when the divided kingdoms of Israel and Judah were under attack by the great empires of Assyria and

Babylonia, and their peoples taken into exile, the Holy Spirit is said to have spoken through prophets, men believed to have been inspired by God, having 'breathed in' his holy spirit.[10] Hundreds of years later, it was from the ancient scroll of the prophet Isaiah that Jesus read during a visit to his home town's synagogue, 'The Spirit of the Lord is on me, because he has anointed me to preach good news to the poor'. Jesus surprised and outraged the Nazareth congregation when he added, 'Today this scripture is fulfilled in your hearing'.[11]

Before Jesus's final Passover meal with his disciples, John's gospel tells us, he promised them that following his return to his father, the Holy Spirit would be sent to them by God as a *parakletos*, a helper or comforter.[12] Then, as *Acts* continues the story, the disciples were all together at Pentecost, and God's spirit filled the house and 'Divided tongues, as of fire, appeared among them, and a tongue rested on each of them'.[13] (This image of flame and fire associated with the Holy Spirit occurs a number of times in the New Testament narrative: for example, John the Baptist foretold that while he baptised with water, Jesus would baptise with the Holy Spirit and with fire.[14]) The Holy Spirit filled the gathered apostles and they became changed men; frightened fishermen were transformed into courageous preachers.[15]

The New Testament speaks many times of those who, 'filled with the Holy Spirit', become energised with power and achieve great things.[16] It was the *power* of the spirit that was so remarkable: Paul wrote that it was an act of the Holy Spirit's power that raised Jesus from the dead.[17] The book of *Acts* tells the story of a magician named Simon, who had so enchanted the people of Samaria that they mistook him for the power of God, which was known as the Great Power. When in turn Simon saw the astonishing signs and miracles that were taking place at the hands of the spirit-filled apostles, he was so amazed that he wanted to buy from them the same power, so that he too could perform miracles.[18]

The Holy Spirit was a central theme in the writing and teaching of Paul: indeed of the thirteen of his letters preserved in the New Testament, it is only in his short, personal letter to Philemon that he does not mention the Holy Spirit.[19] He dedicated substantial sections of some of his letters to his thoughts on the spirit of God,[20] and lists some of the characteristics by which those who possess the spirit may be recognised: love, joy, peace, patience, kindness, goodness, faithfulness, gentleness and self-control.[21]

One unexplained warning issued by Paul in one of his letters is 'Do not grieve the Holy Spirit'.[22] Perhaps Paul recalled the words of the prophet Isaiah, who spoke of those whose rebellion against God had grieved his holy spirit, and he had turned against them to punish them.[23] The synoptic gospels record Jesus's teaching that blasphemy against the Holy Spirit was the one sin for which there could be no forgiveness.[24]

* * *

These pages have afforded just a few glimpses of the many ways in which the Bible presents the spirit of God. The books of the Bible and the creed were written in ages when men and women accepted the presence of spirits within their world and within their lives, for good and for ill. Paul believed that

> our struggle is not against flesh and blood, but against the rulers, against the authorities, against the powers of this dark world and against the spiritual forces of evil in the heavenly realms.[25]

Jesus met many who, the gospels say, were possessed by demons or 'unclean spirits' and he exorcised them. One such demon-possessed man screamed at Jesus, 'I know who you are—the Holy One of God!'[26] It has been suggested that the demon could see the Holy Spirit within Jesus, or perhaps even recognised that Jesus was God's spirit.[27]

It is a generally held view that the doctrine of the trinity—that of a three-in-one God, Father, Son and Holy Spirit—is not to be found in the New Testament but developed in later years. As we have already noted, God's holy spirit was at the centre of Paul's teaching, out of which Christianity grew. But while those of his letters which were included in the New Testament consistently opened and closed with greetings in the names of God the Father and Jesus the Christ, in only one did he include the Holy Spirit in such a greeting.[28] If any gospel verse has the appearance of having been written back into the narrative, in light of the development of later beliefs, it is the penultimate verse of Matthew's gospel: there, Jesus is said to have commissioned

Sketch 8: The spirit of the divine

his disciples to baptise in the name of the Father and the Son and the Holy Spirit.[29]

* * *

What then do we mean by spirit, here in the twenty-first century? Would it be true to say that most people nowadays do not believe in ghosts or spirits? Clearly some do, but perhaps such a belief is not to be defended as a healthy one. Indeed, it may well be very sound advice not to dabble in the occult. And if there is an argument for avoiding 'evil' spirits, what is the argument for welcoming 'good' ones?

On the other hand, we are completely comfortable with using the word spirit in an abstract sense: team spirit, public spirit, that's the spirit! My parents' generation spoke of the Dunkirk spirit, when wartime Britons were determined to survive, facing difficulty but not defeat. Today we might refer to the *Zeitgeist*, the spirit of the age. The *Zeitgeist* is the defining spirit, a refining spirit, the *essence*.

What is the spirit of our age? If there is a *Zeitgeist*, are we satisfied with it or could we wish it to be something different or better? This is for the learning community to determine: visualising and clarifying what it is that we mean by the spirit of God or the divine or the 'Other-than-oneself', and seeking to define it and demonstrate it as the spirit of the age.

What is this essence? If 'God' (to use the definition proposed earlier) is the sum of our values, our values must become the highest. In that spirit, the spirit of the divine, our values will be demonstrated in action, so that the world is a better place for our having been here. As Jesus said, 'by their fruit you will recognise them'.[30]

- That I can't believe!

- But what I do believe is this:

1. John 7:39 and 20:22, Acts 2:4.
2. Matthew 1:18.
3. Genesis 1:2.
4. Genesis 41:38.

5   Exodus 31:2–5.
6   Numbers 11:25.
7   Judges 6:34 and 15:15.
8   1 Samuel 10:10.
9   Psalm 51:11.
10 For example Nehemiah 9:20, Isaiah 61:1, Ezekiel 36:27, Joel 2:28, Haggai 2:5, Zechariah 7:12. See also Acts 28:25.
11 Luke 4:18 and 4:21 [NIV]. See Isaiah 61:1.
12 John 14:26.
13 Acts 2:3.
14 Matthew 3:11 and Luke 3:16.
15 Acts 2:14ff.
16 For example, Luke 4:1 and 4:14; Acts 4:8, 11:24 and 13:9.
17 Romans 1:4.
18 Acts 8:18.
19 For example, Romans 15:16, 1 Corinthians 12:1, 2 Corinthians 3:17, Galatians 5:22, Ephesians 2:18, Philippians 2:1, Colossians 1:8, 1 Thessalonians 1:5, 2 Thessalonians 2:13, 1 Timothy 4:1, 2 Timothy 1:14, Titus 3:5
20 Examples are Romans chapter 8, 1 Corinthians chapters 12–14, Galatians chapter 5.
21 Galatians 5:22.
22 Ephesians 4:30.
23 Isaiah 63:10.
24 Matthew 12:31, Mark 3:29, Luke 12:10.
25 Ephesians 6:12 [NIV].
26 Mark 1:24. See also Matthew 12:28.
27 A. Souter, *A Pocket Lexicon to the Greek New Testament*.
28 2 Corinthians 13:14.
29 Matthew 28:19.
30 Matthew 7:20 [NIV].

Sketch 9: The church

Once more, the creed's authors stepped into history, as they did with the crucifixion of Jesus, expressing belief in what is without question an historical phenomenon—'the holy catholic church; the communion of saints'. Significantly, it is not belief in a church (indefinite article), or in churches (plural), but in *the* church (singular, definite article).

In declaring a belief in *the* church, the Apostles' Creed clearly takes for granted its physical existence. The creed's affirmation of a belief *in* rather than a belief *that* concerns itself with what this church is believed to be: that is, holy, catholic and a community of 'saints', people who are sanctified. It is to be noted that it is the Nicene Creed which goes further than the Apostles' Creed, additionally professing belief in a church which is 'one' and 'Apostolic'.

First, let us give some thought to the origins of the church; and then consider what might be meant by 'one holy, catholic, apostolic church, the communion of saints'.

With an Old English root, the modern word church (with its ancient links to 'kirk' and the Greek *kurios*, lord) is the standard translation of the word *ekklesia* in the Greek text of the New Testament. However, what is commonly (even if sometimes mistakenly) understood nowadays by the word church was not the meaning of the Greek. In classical Greek, *ekklesia* was the word for a convened assembly, a meeting of people called together for a specific purpose. When the Hebrew Bible was translated into Greek in the third and second centuries BCE (the version known as the Septuagint), *ekklesia* was the word used to translate its Hebrew equivalent, *qahal*. The word *qahal* appears frequently in the Hebrew Bible, often in the Pentateuch, and quite clearly had nothing to do with 'churches'. It was the standard word for the assembly of Israel, that is to say, the people of God's covenant:

> The LORD spoke to Moses... He said: 'Take a census of the whole Israelite community [*qahal*] by their clans and families.[1]

Identical in transliteration, the Greek *ekklesia* became *ecclesia* in Latin, and the Romans gave the word the same meaning as the Greek. From the Latin came all of the 'ecclesiastical' words in our dictionary, from ecclesial to ecclesiology; and yet these meanings which have become attached to 'church' over the centuries—such as organisational structure, hierarchical authority, law, buildings, liturgy, denominational differences, and so on—are quite at variance with the meaning of the ancient words.

The word *ekklesia* appears rarely in the gospels, and to translate it as 'church' is unsafe and anachronistic. When Jesus described Peter as the rock (Greek *petros*) on which he would build his *ekklesia*,[2] he was surely not speaking of anything faintly resembling what we today would call a church, but rather what has been termed the 'body of Palestinian adherents of the messiah'.[3] Similarly, in his advice to his disciples to take unresolved disputes before the *ekklesia*, it would be getting ahead of events to translate this as 'church'.[4] Jesus and his followers were Jews, attending synagogue, and continuing to live by Jewish law and (largely) within Jewish cultural norms. They were looking forward to the messianic age, not to the beginning of Christendom. This is to argue that Jesus did not found a new religion, and that he did not seek to establish what we now call a church. Modern translations such as 'congregation' or 'community' are perhaps closer to the original meaning.[5]

The book of *Acts* tells how the *ekklesia* in Jerusalem, the Jewish community of those who believed in a risen Christos, began to be persecuted by the religious authorities.[6] Saul, at first a zealous leader of this persecution, became instead Paul, the ardent protagonist of the new movement, chief proselytiser to a new set of beliefs which were eventually to evolve into a new religion.

Whereas the word *ekklesia* appears rarely in the gospels, Paul used it regularly in his teaching and writing, to refer to what was rapidly changing from a local sect into an empire-wide movement. For Paul, *ekklesia* had a range of meanings: sometimes he used it to refer to an identifiable local community in a particular city or region, such as the community at Thessalonika.[7] At other times, he referred to the men and women who were the members of a community as the *ekklesia*.[8] Then there are references to the whole body of this movement, the universal community, the *ekklesia* of God.[9]

Today we can recognise these usages as synonymous with the local church or chapel, or with the people who attend there, or with

Sketch 9: The church 121

all the churches which together make up the world-wide church. There can be little doubt that this rapidly spreading first-century movement was fast becoming 'the church'.

But was there just one church, in those early years? Certainly that was Paul's vision.[10] In reality, however, he was only too aware that division and schism were in evidence.[11] Over the centuries, division and fragmentation were to continue, until the 'body of Christ' had broken into the many churches and denominations which exist today. The most marked division, perhaps, is that between east and west, the centuries-old schism between the Orthodox church (Greek and Russian) and the Roman Catholic church. Each claims to be 'the one true and visible Church of Christ on earth'. Both believe that they have retained an unbroken link with the apostles through a succession of bishops, and Roman Catholic teaching is that their pope is Peter's successor. Although divided from Roman Catholicism, the Protestant Anglican churches share the belief in apostolic succession. The Protestant churches in turn are separated from each other by a multitude of denominational differences: the nonconformist churches, for example, do not recognise the concept of apostolic succession, and invest authority not in the church but in the Bible.

It is likely, however, that all parts of the church, all denominations, would consider the church to be 'catholic' in this sense: in its secular, everyday usage, catholic is understood to mean universal or all-embracing; it is this meaning which can be applied to the church, rather than its limited (and thus misleading) equation with Anglo- or Roman Catholicism. The Christian church is universal in the sense that it is a global organisation, to be found everywhere in the world and open to everyone (although the extent and reality of this 'openness' within the church is clearly a subject for discussion). The all-embracing nature of the church may also be recognised in the near-universal experience of the sacraments, even though these rituals are practised in different ways. (Some denominations, most notably the Quakers, do not observe the 'sacraments' as ritualistic practices, but that need not delay us here.)

For all that, the Roman Catholic church maintains the doctrine that it and it alone is the one true church: the Protestant churches, for example, are deemed by the Vatican to be merely 'ecclesial communities', since they 'lack elements considered essential to the Catholic Church'.[12]

A New Testament letter attributed to Peter quotes the law of Moses, declaring that the church is called upon to be holy, in the same way as God called the *qahal*, the congregation of the people of Israel, to be holy:

> just as he who called you is holy, so be holy in all you do; for it is written: 'Be holy, because I am holy.'[13]

How can the church be said to be holy? Can men and women be holy in the same sense that a perfect 'god' is said to be holy, for example? It is a curious word, and an examination of biblical texts will illustrate a number of shades of what seem to be its elusive meanings, challenging attempts at definition.[14]

The Greek word which the New Testament writers used for holy or sacred was *hagios*, meaning set apart by or for God. To what extent is the church 'set apart'? Well, it can be said to be set apart in the sense that it is dedicated to God; but does its being 'apart' mean that it is somehow separated from the rest of the world, the parts which are not-church?

The New Testament *hagioi* were the holy ones, the sanctified ones, the people of a 'new covenant' with God. An *ekklesia* was a community of people called together, and the New Testament *ekklesia* was the community of those called to be holy, the 'saints'. It is with this community or communion that the church believes it has continuity.

The creed states a belief in the church as the communion of saints. Today, words such as saint and saintly suggest a degree of virtue beyond that of mere mortals; and, used in a critical 'holier-than-thou' sense, the word saint may take on a pejorative quality (He's no saint!). But *hagios* did not have this moral meaning, as though the 'saint' is somehow better than others.

The word used in the New Testament for this communion or fellowship was *koinonia*, a classical Greek word which had the basic meaning of partnership. In secular contexts, it denoted a business partnership—the fishermen apostles James and John, for example, were *koinonoi*, partners, with Simon[15]—or it could signify a marriage, and sometimes it meant one's relationship with a god. Paul used *koinonia* regularly in his writing to describe many aspects of this

Sketch 9: The church

sharing fellowship, which characterised the community of believers, the *ekklesia*. Thus, believers shared the companionship of others, shared with those less fortunate than themselves, shared in the gospel, shared in the eucharist, shared in the Holy Spirit.[16] In Paul's teaching, these and many other aspects of sharing or fellowship were in effect synonymous with *ekklesia*.

* * *

So much for the early history and the origins of what we call the church. In the early chapters of this book, questions were asked about the way 'outsiders' have seen the church, or how they see what it has become, and why they have remained outside. Specific reference was made to what it is the church is thought to be today and what it is thought to stand for. The argument has been made that while there are clearly other factors contributing to the decline of the church — perhaps its terminal decline — the principal source of disaffection has been, and continues to be, the church's inability or unpreparedness to find ways of deconstructing its traditional, pre-scientific supernatural dogma so that the atheist and the agnostics and the believers-in-exile can at last say 'Yes!'

A new home needs to be found for the human spirit. Offering possibilities to meet that need, and so closely congruent with the spirit of the *ekklesia* and *koinonia* described above, is the concept of the Fulfilment Society, introduced in the first part of this book, a society which will be

> organized in such a way as to give the greatest number of people the fullest opportunities of realizing their potentialities — of achievement and enjoyment, morality and community. It will do so by providing opportunities for education, for adventure and achievement, for co-operating in worthwhile projects, for meditation and withdrawal, for self-development and unselfish action.

- That I can't believe!

- But what I do believe is this:

1   Numbers 1:1–2 [NIV]. See also Leviticus 10:17, Deuteronomy 18:16, Judges 20:2.
2   Matthew 16:18.
3   A. Souter, *A Pocket Lexicon to the Greek New Testament*.
4   Matthew 18:17.
5   *The Revised English Bible* and *The Jerusalem Bible* respectively.
6   Acts 8:1.
7   1 Thessalonians 1:1, Galatians 1:2, Romans 16:1.
8   1 Corinthians 11:18.
9   1 Corinthians 10:32 and 12:28, Philippians 3:6.
10 Ephesians 4:3, 1 Corinthians 12:12 and 27.
11 1 Corinthians 1:10ff and 11:18.
12 Cardinal Joseph Ratzinger, *Dominus Iesus*, 2000.
13 1 Peter 1:15–16 [NIV], quoting Leviticus 19:2.
14 For example Exodus 3:5, Leviticus 10:10, Numbers 16:5, 1 Samuel 2:2, Isaiah 58:13, Ezekiel 22:26, Matthew 7:6, 1 Timothy 2:8, Hebrews 3:1.
15 Luke 5:10.
16 Respectively: Acts 2:14, Romans 15:26, Philippians 1:5, 1 Corinthians 10:16, Philippians 2:1.

Sketch 10: Forgiveness

To express a belief in the forgiveness of sins, as does the Apostles' Creed, is first to accept the fact of that good old-fashioned word, sin — or, in no way to water down the idea, wrongdoing. Only then may follow a sense of a need for, and the possibility of, forgiveness.

Who can forgive sins but God alone? That, at least, was the question asked by critics of Jesus;[1] and from a biblical perspective, the creed's affirmation of a belief in the forgiveness of sins means the forgiveness of sin(s) by God.

It was characteristic of ancient religions to believe that the gods could be placated through sacrifice, usually of a slaughtered animal burnt on an altar, but sometimes simply through the offering of gifts. The religion of the people of the Hebrew Bible was no different, and from the beginning their traditional stories told of sacrifices. In the earliest narratives, Adam's sons Cain and Abel brought their offerings to God, but with tragically different results.[2] Having survived God's punitive flood, 'Noah built an altar to the LORD and... sacrificed burnt offerings on it'.[3] God repented and made a covenant with Noah and his descendants after him. In their turn, the patriarchs Abraham, Isaac and Jacob built sacrificial altars, at times when God renewed his covenant with them, promising prosperity in a land which would be theirs for all time.[4] Then, the laws of Moses included many precepts concerning sacrifice, always linked with obedience to God's commandments and atonement for wrongdoing.[5] If the people of the covenant followed God's statutes and kept his commandments, continuing prosperity and peace would be theirs; on the other hand, disobedience would bring the most fearsome retribution:

> I will bring sudden terror upon you... you shall be defeated by your enemies; those who hate you will rule over you... I will punish you for your sins seven times over.[6]

In spite of this dread prospect, God offered a remedy for disobedience: 'if they will confess their sins... I will remember my covenant.'[7]

However, doing the right thing and obeying the law did not necessarily ensure peace and prosperity, if the psalmist's experience was anything to go by. A common theme of the psalms suggests that it is the wrongdoers who prosper, while suffering is the lot of those who do what is right:

> This is what the wicked are like —
> always carefree, they increase in wealth.
> Surely in vain I have kept my heart pure;
> In vain have I washed my hands in innocence.
> All day long I have been plagued;
> I have been punished every morning.[8]

However, the psalmist was able to console himself with the thought that, in the end, the wrongdoers would get their just deserts: 'the Lord laughs at the wicked, for he knows their day is coming.'[9]

By the eighth century BCE, the prophets were speaking out against the religious practices of the time. Although the requisite ritual sacrifices were being observed, moral precepts were being neglected:

> 'The multitude of your sacrifices —
> what are they to me?' says the LORD.
> 'I have more than enough of burnt offerings,
> of rams and the fat of fattened animals.'[10]

What was required by God, the prophet Isaiah declared, was that

> this sinful nation, a people loaded with iniquity [should] stop doing wrong, learn to do right! Seek justice, encourage the oppressed. Defend the cause of the fatherless, plead the case of the widow.[11]

Seven hundred years later, Jesus quoted the prophets to the religious leaders of his day,[12] with a call for compassion, and with a reminder that God is on the side of the weak and the oppressed:

> For I desire mercy, not sacrifice, and acknowledgement of God rather than burnt offerings.[13]

Even so, Jesus accepted that sacrificial offering was an essential part of Jewish orthopraxis, though his Sermon on the Mount taught that its validity depended on mutual or reciprocated forgiveness.[14] 'Forgive us our trespasses as we forgive those that trespass against us', is the petition in the Lord's prayer.

Sketch 10: Forgiveness

Atonement through sacrifice is, of course, one of the principal themes of the New Testament, and it is the basis of the creed's stated belief in the forgiveness of sins. When the creed expresses the belief that Jesus 'suffered under Pontius Pilate, was crucified, dead and buried' it is not, of course, commenting on historical facts, but is focusing on a belief in the atoning death of Jesus, 'the Lamb of God, who takes away the sin of the world'.[15]

The imperative of sacrifice according to the Mosaic law is summed up in one sentence by the first-century Christian writer of a letter to Jewish readers: 'without the shedding of blood there is no forgiveness';[16] but now, sacrifice has taken on a greater and more important meaning:

> The blood of goats and bulls... sprinkled on those who are ceremonially unclean sanctify them so that they are outwardly clean... How much more, then will the blood of Christ... cleanse our conscience![17]

According to the New Testament text, on which the church's teaching is based, God has entered into a new covenant with mankind:

> through Jesus the forgiveness of sins is proclaimed to you. Through him everyone who believes is justified...[18]

* * *

The church's doctrine of original sin holds that all humankind is heir to the 'wrongdoing' of Adam-and-Eve and every generation since has ineluctably inherited their sinful nature.[19] As a result of this mythic 'fall', the church teaches, the state of sin erected a barrier between humankind and God.[20]

It is taken as read here, however, that at no time was there a pristine, complete, perfect creation, free from flaws, as described in the ancient tradition of *Genesis*, a pure, unspoilt creation from which humankind could 'fall'. Evolution has continued, warts and all, across countless ages and continues still. Creation is work in progress.

For all that, can any of us claim to be unaware of self-interest, or self-regard at the expense of others, the things that we choose to do which are selfish and hurtful and wholly lacking in love for others — in short, an inclination to do what is wrong, to commit wrongful *acts*? But to say that we are sinful by nature is to take a negative view of humankind, a negative belief held by the apostle Paul. While we may not agree with him, we do at least share Paul's experience:

> I have the desire to do what is good, but I cannot carry it out. For what I do is not the good I want to do; no, the evil I do not want to do—this I keep on doing.[21]

The Greeks, of course, had a word for it, *akrasia*, meaning lack of self-control or being weak-willed. At this point, I am putting up my hand, and I am not confessing merely to helping myself to the contents of the biscuit barrel.

It may be just as valid to say that 'human nature' is neither inherently good nor bad. We have the capacity for choosing between what is right and what is wrong—God's reason for expelling Adam and Eve from the Garden of Eden:

> 'The man has become like one of us,[22] knowing good and evil. He must not be allowed to reach out his hand and take also from the tree of life and eat, and live forever.' So the LORD God banished him from the Garden of Eden.[23]

In the biblical fable of the Garden of Eden, the father-figure God demands of Adam and Eve, 'What is this that you have done?'[24] Immediately they feel the guilt. And instantly they find someone else to blame: and in the first recorded instance of the evasive response, they say 'It wasn't me!' The man blames the woman. The woman blames the serpent.

The 'Critical Parent'[25] is watching you: What are you up to now? A sense of guilt may be valuable as a deterrent, but it is a negative emotion. The 'Child' (still present in grown men and women) fears this ever-watching, disapproving father-figure God, and agonises, 'How can I appease the wrath of God, how can I attain divine mercy, the forgiveness of sin?'[26] This 'anxiety of guilt and condemnation'[27] leads to loss of self-esteem, to self-rejection, and the habit of believing that we *deserve* punishment. We learn to feel guilty. Practice makes permanent.

There are guilt throwers and guilt catchers. It is the blame game, the familiar 'Now see what you've made me do!' or 'If it wasn't for you, I could have...'[28] Not without reason, it is said that religion is preoccupied with sin. Religion is a guilt thrower. It is doubtless true

Sketch 10: Forgiveness

that we are only too familiar with the sentiment of the prayer book's confession: 'We have left undone those things which we ought to have done; and we have done those things which we ought not to have done.' But might it not be going too far to moan and groan that 'there is no health in us... miserable offenders'?

That is the 'Child' in us, perpetually whining 'I'm sorry... I'M NOT OK... I shouldn't have... ain't it awful...'[29] By contrast, the 'Adult' part of us enables us to recognise our ability to do both good things and bad things and that we have a choice. We are responsible for our decisions and for our actions. Self-affirmation — 'I'm OK' — can replace the self-rejection which flows from the 'anxiety of guilt and condemnation'.

The *acceptance that one is accepted* was perhaps the experience of the woman in John's gospel who was 'caught in the very act of committing adultery', and was brought before Jesus for a judgment. When her accusers had left her alone with Jesus, and he saw that no one had condemned her, he said 'Neither do I condemned you' — and then his vital words, 'Go now, and leave your life of sin'.[30] Jesus did not say 'I forgive you', but the woman knew that she was forgiven, because Jesus had shown his acceptance of her, just as she was.

'Leave your life of sin' had been the message of the prophet centuries before:

> Let the wicked forsake his way
> and the evil man his thoughts.
> Let him turn to the LORD, and he will have mercy on him,
> and to our God, for he will freely pardon.[31]

I can know forgiveness, and this includes forgiving myself, once I recognise that I have done something wrong, admit it, make amends, and leave it behind. This, I believe, is an aspect of the transcendence of the resurrection, making possible the conquest of the negative, deadening emotions of guilt and shame. The New Testament word is *exaleipho*,[32] I wipe out, expunge, not merely cross out, but irreversibly obliterate. I am forgiven when my commitment is never to err in this way again.

* * *

Julian Huxley's vision of the fulfilment society speaks of opportunities for meditation and withdrawal. There is a quiet place where every man and woman can go, a place somewhere inside the head or maybe it is in the heart, a place that no one else can reach. And it is in this quiet place that the calm of forgiveness can be known.

Each of us is able to access that quiet place wherever we are, whatever is happening all around us. Lost in a hostile, far country, the prodigal son yearned to return home.[33] W.B. Yeats borrowed the prodigal's words, 'I will arise and go now', as he longed for the peace that he believed he would find on the lake isle of Innisfree. Even while walking along the dreary city streets, the poet could imagine the sound of water lapping on the shore of the lake, remembering the quiet place in what he called 'the deep heart's core'.[34]

For me, the deep heart's core is to be found in the practice of the presence of God. Others will describe it differently. But it is there, in that quiet place, where we can understand the meaning of forgiveness.

- <u>That</u> I can't believe!

- But what I <u>do</u> believe is this:

1. Mark 2:7 and Luke 5:21.
2. Genesis 4:3ff.
3. Genesis 8:20 [NIV].
4. Genesis 12:7, 26:25, and 35:1.
5. Examples are Exodus 20:24 and 23:18, Leviticus 7:11 and 27:11, Numbers 15:3, Deuteronomy 18:3.
6. Leviticus 26:16-18 [NIV]. See the whole of Leviticus chapter 26.
7. Leviticus 26:40 and 42 [NIV].
8. Psalm 73:12-14 [NIV]. See also Psalms 10 and 37, as examples.
9. Psalm 37:10-13 [NIV]. Among many other examples are Psalms 28, 34, 94.
10. Isaiah 1:11 [NIV]. See the whole of Isaiah chapter 1.
11. Isaiah 1:4, 1:16-17 [NIV].
12. Matthew 9:13 and 12:7.
13. Hosea 6:6 [NIV]. See also Psalm 51:17.
14. Matthew 5:23.
15. John 1:29 [NIV]; 1 Corinthians 5:7, Revelation 7:14.
16. Hebrews 9:22 [NIV].
17. Hebrews 9:13-14 [NIV].
18. Acts 13:38-39 [NIV].

19 Genesis 3:22ff.
20 Isaiah 59:2.
21 Romans 7:18–19 [NIV].
22 In passing, note the plural 'One of us'. There is a similar plural in the creation story: God said, 'Let us make man in our image, in our likeness' — Genesis 1:26 [NIV].
23 Genesis 3:22–23 [NIV].
24 Genesis 3:11–13.
25 The most useful discussion of the 'life positions' of Parent–Adult–Child and the 'transactions' that take place between them is in Thomas H. Harris, *I'm OK – You're OK*. The 'Child' in us feels victimised (not OK) by the 'Critical Parent', who is perceived by the Child to be OK. The 'Adult' in us, by contrast, is able to recognise that life can be changed, so that we are enabled to feel 'I'm OK' and other people are OK too.
26 Paul Tillich, *The Courage to Be*.
27 *Ibid*.
28 A very full exposition of the 'mind games' in which people engage and interact is set out in Eric Berne, *Games People Play*.
29 See Thomas H. Harris *I'm OK – You're OK, op. cit.*
30 John 8:3ff [NIV].
31 Isaiah 55:7 [NIV].
32 Acts 3:18–19, Colossians 2:14, Revelation 7:17 and 21:4.
33 Luke 15:18.
34 W.B. Yeats, 'The Lake Isle of Innisfree' in *Yeats's Poems*.

Sketch 11: An afterlife

Two linked clauses bring us to the end of the creed, with its statement of belief in 'The resurrection of the body, and the life everlasting'.

The first of the two statements expresses a belief not merely in resurrection, but in bodily resurrection. Reference was made earlier to the basis of faith to which thousands of British churches affiliated to the Evangelical Alliance assent as a condition of their membership. That basis of faith includes a belief in the bodily resurrection of Jesus, adding words from one of Paul's letters, that 'Christ has indeed been raised from the dead, the first fruits of those who have fallen asleep'.[1] This implies a belief that those who have died will also be resurrected bodily, although it may be questioned to what extent the tens of thousands of members of those affiliated churches, and indeed other Christians, believe this to be literally true. Be that as it may, here in the creed we have a clear statement of belief 'in the resurrection of the body'.

We have already looked in some detail at the concept of resurrection, and beliefs about resurrection current at the time of Jesus. In the 'resurrection' section of his first letter to the Corinthians, Paul writes that 'flesh and blood cannot inherit the kingdom of God';[2] and he develops this by explaining that 'If there is a natural body, there is also a spiritual body'.[3] In spite of this, it is difficult to determine what it is that Paul had in mind, and it is unclear what the creed's statement means in any definitive terms.

In the first century, at the time of Jesus and of Paul, there were certainly beliefs in immortality, but those beliefs were confused. The Greek concept of the afterlife entailed a belief in the immortality of the soul, whereas Jewish thought had developed into a belief in bodily resurrection. Jesus was a man of his time, and the gospel ascribes words to him which make clear his acceptance of the concept of bodily resurrection.[4] Paul engages in discussion about what form the resurrected body may take; but whereas he is clear about the obvious fact that the human body is perishable, he appears to be unable to go far with his theorising about an imperishable 'spiritual' body.[5]

Sketch 11: An afterlife

While much of the creed's content may be described as metaphysical, any expression of confidence that there is an afterlife may be considered to be the ultimate in metaphysical thinking—for the obvious reason that surely needs no repetition, that death is that 'undiscover'd country from whose bourn no traveller returns'. Of all the creed's beliefs, this is perhaps the most conjectural. But was Paul being literal in expressing a belief in bodily resurrection? After all, in declaring elsewhere, 'I have been crucified with Christ',[6] he appears quite able to be metaphorical in his thinking.

Into what state is the body to be resurrected? The answer, according to the Bible and the creed, is into an eternal existence. The New Testament makes frequent references to eternal life, sometimes as a promise or a reward, sometimes as a warning. In a passage in Matthew's gospel, Jesus speaks of 'the coming of the Son of Man', when those who have neglected to do the right things 'will go away to eternal punishment, but the righteous to eternal life'.[7] A similar promise and warning appear in John's gospel, where Jesus says that

> a time is coming and has now come when the dead will hear the voice of the Son of God... all who are in their graves will hear his voice and will come out—those who have done good will rise to life, and those who have done evil will rise to be condemned.[8]

We looked earlier at beliefs about reward and punishment, 'eternal life to the redeemed and eternal condemnation to the lost'.[9] Paul is clear that 'the wages of sin is death, but the gift of God is eternal life'.[10] So, on this account, the creed's belief in the life everlasting is reserved for those who (in Paul's words) 'have been freed from sin'. In one place, the writer of *Acts* refers to those 'who were appointed for eternal life',[11] a phrase which hints at pre-destination. The *Jerusalem Bible* adds a footnote to this verse, that to be destined for the life of the world to come was a common rabbinic expression, thus suggesting that it would have been familiar to early Jewish believers; but it also comments that within Christian teaching faith in Christ is a condition for such pre-destination. In discussing belief in eternal life, then, there may be a place for considering the concept of pre-destination.

***

The Greek word *aionios*, which appears frequently in the New Testament,[12] meant age-long or unending. Interestingly, though, the word also meant 'having a lasting quality', contrasted with an ephemeral or fleeting quality. Perhaps this gives a clue for belief today, that the 'eternal' quality of our life is not that it continues in some way endlessly after death (it *may*, but there is no way in which we can know, this side of the grave!), but that what we do here and now makes a difference, that the world is and will be a better place for our having been here. The challenge therefore becomes one of reversing the words of Shakespeare's Mark Anthony:

> The evil that men do lives after them;
> The good is oft interred with their bones.[13]

Better that our wrongdoing should be buried with our bones, and that the good which we strive to do in the here-and-now will live after us.

Over the years, I have wondered how frequently in fact clergymen are asked, as they often claim they are, 'Surely there is more to life than this?' or, even more philosophically, 'What is the meaning of it all?' The quest for understanding the meaning of life, the desire for discovering life's purpose (in some kind of metaphysical sense) is likely to prove a chimera. It is without doubt understandable that *in hac lacrimarum valle*, in this vale of tears, or in Cardinal Newman's 'troublous life', men and women might wish to believe that there is a key somewhere which will unlock this mystery, giving access to a better, happier world. Or perhaps boredom and dissatisfaction simply and inevitably give rise to escape attempts, a yearning for something more fulfilling.

But no, this is it!

Or is it? We have choices. We can choose between right and wrong. The decisions are ours to make, the responsibility is ours to take. That is what will give meaning to our lives. The ancient Hebrew scriptures tell how God said to the Israelites

> I have set before you life and death, blessings and curses. Now choose life, so that you and your children may live and that you may love the LORD your God, listen to his voice, and hold fast to him. For the LORD is your life.[14]

Sketch 11: An afterlife

* * *

Now we move on to the third part of the book, *Social construction*. This is in the form of an outline agenda for the learning community's further study and action. A number of social issues are outlined but no solutions provided. The purpose is to form a framework within which the learning community can determine its response to the great commandment: Love your neighbour as yourself.

- That I can't believe!
- But what I do believe is this:

1. 1 Corinthians 15:20 [NIV].
2. 1 Corinthians 15:50 [NIV].
3. 1 Corinthians 15:44 [NIV].
4. Luke 24:37–39.
5. See 1 Corinthians 15:35–55.
6. Galatians 2:20 [NIV].
7. Matthew 25:46 [NIV].
8. John 5:25–29 [NIV].
9. In *Jesus and the Trojan War* (p. 223) I stated incorrectly that the Evangelical Alliance's new, 2005 version of its basis of faith 'appears to have watered down' its earlier statement of belief in judgment, eternal life and eternal damnation. On the contrary: the EA basis of faith retains an explicit belief in the return of Jesus, 'who will raise all people to judgement, bring eternal life to the redeemed and eternal condemnation to the lost'.
10. Romans 6:23 [NIV].
11. Acts 13:48 [NIV].
12. Examples are Matthew 19:29; John 3:16, 4:14 and 12:50; Acts 13:48; Romans 2:7, 5:21 and 6:22–23; Galatians 6:8; Titus 1:2 and 3:7; 1 John 1:2.
13. William Shakespeare, *Julius Caesar* Act III scene II.
14. Deuteronomy 30:19 [NIV].

Part Three

Chapter 7

Social construction

In a New Testament episode, a young lawyer challenged Jesus with what was intended as a trick question: 'What must I do to inherit eternal life?' Jesus had no difficulty in spotting the trap and got the young man to answer his own question: 'Love God and love your neighbour.' But the lawyer was not going to be outdone, and he tried another tack, asking 'But who is my neighbour?' Jesus responded by telling a short story which is known traditionally as the parable of the Good Samaritan.[1]

While on a journey from Jerusalem to Jericho, a Jewish man was mugged by bandits and left for dead. One after another, fellow Jews come along the road and could have helped the victim, but instead they turned a blind eye, crossed the road and kept walking. But eventually a Samaritan, a man from an alien and despised race, came along, stopped and gave first aid to the injured man. He then took him to an inn and paid for him to be looked after until he recovered.

What is significant about the Samaritan in the story is not so much that he was good as that he was the person least likely or the least expected to come to the aid of the injured Jew. Those listening to Jesus's story would have got the point immediately. This was a matter of what today we would call ethnicity or 'race': Jews and Samaritans had no dealings with each other. In the parable, the Jewish victim was not rescued by any of the passers-by from his own culture or community, but by a man from the hated 'deviant' Samaritan culture, against whom he would have had deep-seated and well-rehearsed prejudices, or worse.[2]

In answering the question—Who is my neighbour?—the story challenges us to respect and care about those who in our perception are least like us. We can hardly be unaware of our (natural?) predisposition to associate with people like ourselves, and the tendency to pass by on the other side or turn a blind eye when faced with unpalatable or alien situations, especially those involving people whom we regard as 'them' rather than 'one of us'. One outcome of this way of thinking is the development of notions such as superiority/inferiority or better/worse. Essential to loving my neighbour as myself is the need constantly to take stock of *myself*, honestly appraising whether or not I am becoming what I am capable of becoming. It is not for me to ask that question of my neighbour or to make that judgment; that is for him or her to do.

Experience confirms how readily our thinking and our actions become habitual. Just as when we repeat an action over and again we create a pattern of behaviour (practice makes permanent), so we create thought patterns or values by repeatedly viewing people and situations in a specific way, quite possibly from a privileged position. Given the relevant stimulus, the values and actions embedded in those behavioural and attitudinal patterns replay automatically and without our giving them a second thought.

This has a direct bearing on the present topic of social construction. We saw earlier how members of dominant group A judge the values or behaviour of group B to be 'deviant'; and so group A develop (at best) attitudes or (at worst) defences or action, to shore up their position or convince themselves of their 'rightness', contrasted with B's 'deviance'. Deviance is taken here to relate to 'those situations in which behavior is in a disapproved direction, and of a sufficient degree to exceed the tolerance limit of the community'.[3]

From this, it may be deduced that the behaviour is perceived as deviant only (or specifically) within the community where it takes place, that is to say, it is relative. Deviance is also relative in the sense that behaviour which is not tolerated today may once have been perceived as normal or may be seen as normal at some point in the future.

That is what occupies this part of the book, dealing in turn with a number of social questions, principally as perceived or experienced in Britain in the early years of the twenty-first century. In some cases, these social questions may be more accurately defined as social problems, or even as social *evils*, to borrow the powerful even if unfashionable phrase used in a Joseph Rowntree Foundation project.[4] The

Social construction

headings of the sections which follow may not in themselves define social problems, but social problems are never far away from the main themes.

By the nature of things, between the time of my compiling these jottings and your reading them, some of the issues may have increased in significance or severity, others may have decreased or even disappeared, while new ones may have come into prominence. Some readers may not agree that certain of these themes are social problems, or that they are problems at all. For the moment, let that be accepted: such questions are essential to the processes of deconstruction in which the learning community is to be immersed.

One part of that process will be the necessity to differentiate between what can be defined as personal or private problems on one hand, and social problems on the other. It is principally with social problems that we are concerned here. There is also a need to be aware of differences between people who *have* a problem and those who may be considered to *be* a problem.

An example may help us to get started. A good friend of mine proposed that all those wishing to see their general practitioner should be required to pay ten pounds for each visit. This, he argued, would reduce waiting lists at a stroke and ensure more efficient use of NHS resources. In reply, I wondered whether this might discriminate against poor people, those for whom such an additional expense may prove to be difficult. My friend said he did not know anyone who could not afford ten pounds a visit. I suggested that some poor people's very low income already forces them to decide whether they can pay for either commodity Y or commodity Z, but not for both; and that an additional cost may result in their not seeing their doctor when they should do so. My friend countered with, 'Yes, but what everyone knows about the poor is that they…'

Well, what *does* everyone know about the poor? Who are 'the poor' in the first place? Are they victims of external influences or conditions over which they have little or no control, or have they only themselves to blame? Is there any need for people to be poor in twenty-first century Britain, anyway? And how do people fall into what is termed the poverty trap? Would they climb out of poverty if they could, or do they just not want to be helped? For that matter, do they deserve to be helped? After all, those receiving state benefit do so at the expense of those who provide the money, the better-off taxpayers. Why should those who have been prudent subsidise those who have not?

Where would you say you stand on questions such as these? What would you say it is that 'everyone knows about the poor'? Is poverty a personal problem or is it a social problem? If it is true that just a few people cannot afford the doctor's ten pound fee, for whatever reason, that could be said to be a personal or private problem. On the other hand, if it was found to be true that large numbers of people across the country were prevented through hardship from receiving medical attention, that would have become a social problem.[5]

Let us take another example. How would you say the following statement might be completed: 'The trouble with young people these days is that…'? You will doubtless have come across comments such as these: they don't respect their elders, they have no regard for authority, they do just as they like regardless of the consequences, all they're interested in is drugs and sex, they spend all their time playing computer games or fiddling with their smartphones, what they need is more discipline, bring back National Service, and so on. However, to say 'The trouble with…' or 'What everyone knows about…' suggests that 'young people' (or 'the poor') can all be lumped together into one category; but of course this makes any number of assumptions. And why 'these days'? Compared with when? And in what ways were things different in earlier days (if they were)?

'What everyone knows…' about the poor, or young people, or the homeless, or eastern Europeans, does not constitute a cohesive set of truths which can be summed up in one simple statement. Rather, it is a complex mesh of conflicting or contradictory (and even unsubstantiated) opinions, from which no valid conclusions may be reached. When it comes to what everyone knows about young people, for example, it could just as easily be added that they are more self-confident nowadays, or better educated than they used to be, or that they are more involved in voluntary work than was once the case.

If, in describing some aspects of the problems or issues featured in the following pages as deviant, the word is felt in some way to have sinister overtones, that too illustrates the nature of social construction.

Social construction

Deviant is intended here to mean little more than different from the rest of us, but that alone seems to suggest that 'we' (the majority) are right, and 'they' (the minority) are wrong. The differences between 'them' and 'us' may be perceived as shortcomings or flaws, and one task for the learning community is to examine the origins of these differences, and what validity (if any) there may be in the views expressed within the catch-all 'What everyone knows about...' In short, to see how these issues are socially constructed.

May I suggest at this point that you spend some time looking through the *Personal Check-up* in Appendix 4? You will see that this is headed 'For your eyes only' and its purpose is to enable you to give some preliminary, private thought to the issues listed there. This is not intended as a heavyweight, protracted exercise, but really just as a way of checking some of your own beliefs, values and attitudes, perhaps jotting some notes in your learning journal.

* * *

Back now to the process of deconstruction. By working through the book's second part, you had an opportunity to begin deconstructing a number of fundamental aspects of belief, attempting to look at them as though for the first time, which is likely to be a continuing process. In this third part, similar methods are to be applied to a number of social issues. As we have already noted, deconstruction is to be seen as a positive prerequisite for reconstruction. It means taking apart familiar language, and identifying our assumptions and prejudices, turning the familiar into the unfamiliar, unlearning our knowledge, and looking at all the pieces as if we have never seen them before. Not an easy task.

Intrinsic to this process of deconstruction is the need for understanding our habit of creating stereotypes, on which we base our expectations of the ways in which people will behave, or form views on how they came to be the way they are. Those stereotypes become fixed, so that we make instant judgments: after all, we say to ourselves, that's the kind of people 'they' are!

Some years ago, a Metropolitan Police recruitment poster on the London Underground showed a photograph of a young black man in jeans and leather jacket, running for all he is worth towards the left-hand edge of the poster, with a uniformed policeman hot on his heels. An immediate assumption might be that this was a picture of a London bobby chasing a criminal. The photograph seemed to provide all the necessary clues: a young black male in jeans and leather jacket, running away from a policeman. But that was the poster's intention, to challenge the viewer's assumptions: the two running figures were in fact *both* policemen, one a plain-clothes detective, the other a uniformed officer.

Gender differences afford many examples of stereotyping. We may expect men and women to occupy certain predetermined roles, or demonstrate certain specified behaviours — at work, let us say, or in the home — and we may claim that these are natural gender characteristics. Such assumptions must be questioned rigorously. Similarly, we may have a view of 'the poor' or 'the unemployed' and of what kind of people they are and how they came to be the way they are, or how we perceive or expect them to be.

The ways in which we label individuals or groups, or construct categories of people, will lead us to create norms against which the 'deviant' can be identified or measured. Any deviation from that standard leads to a 'not-like-us' judgment.

In Britain at least, social class is a major source of diversity or division and, to some degree (though not definitively) a source of inequality. In this, affluence tends to be a marker. Those in the 'upper' social classifications are the better-off: they can expect to live longer than those lower on the scale and they are more likely to have access to privileged education. We have already noted the extent to which social class is reflected in adult learning experiences.

Just how these social strata are defined can be seen by reference to government socio-economic classification, which shows that, like other professional and commercial approaches, the official method for defining social class is by occupation.[6] However essential or useful such scales may be for statistical purposes, the creation and use of such hierarchies does suggest superior and inferior status, synonymous with better and worse. There can be little doubt that our competitive culture engenders an admiration for winners; but whatever may be the pros and cons of aspiration, ambition and material success, the coin which reads winner on one side reads loser on the other side. In many aspects of the them-and-us world discussed here, 'they' tend to be the losers, while 'we' come out on top as the winners.

This leads us finally to social exclusion, which can be regarded as an extreme consequence or manifestation of social differences. Our diverse and divided society seems unable to ensure that everyone, regardless of status, is within reach of and has ready access to those resources which might be considered essential to an acceptable standard of living (however that might be defined: more about this later).

There appears to be little consensus on the extent to which those who are socially excluded have excluded themselves or have been excluded by some agency or other set of circumstances. An example is the unemployed: are they job-seekers or are they content to live on benefits? Studies of social exclusion in Britain find, not surprisingly, that the experience of one generation tends to be transmitted to those who follow. Thus, it is thought, children living in a family which is in receipt of social security benefit may see that as the norm, and in their turn grow up to be people who live on benefit. It is with questions and problems of this nature that this third part of the book is concerned.

* * *

These, then, are glimpses of some of the ways in which we create views of society, and how these constructs become a source of power, influence and inequality. Any agenda for building a new society is likely to prove to be a life's work. That is not a reason for not making a start. Eating an elephant is possible, it is suggested, if one takes a mouthful at a time. Our overall purpose has been to explore what our spiritual or religious values or beliefs have to do with issues such as those which follow.

It should be noted that the sequence in which the 'jottings' have been arranged signifies nothing more than alphabetical order. If you and your learning community wish to create your own priorities, that is as good a way to proceed as any. Having looked through the list, you may wish to select your own starting point, although the opening paragraph of jotting number 1, *Children and young people*, might be worth reading first. In any event, it will become apparent very quickly that there are few clear-cut boundaries between the topics, and not only are there blurred edges but also many crossover points: examples are children/poverty/education, and poverty/housing/employment. Further, there will be differing views on the headings under which certain topics ought to be included: for example, are drugs a health issue, or one of crime?

The series of jottings is based on government publications, press reports, various polls, surveys and studies, academic work, the websites of special interest groups, charities and voluntary organisations, and so on. No attempt has been made to reconcile conflicting ideas or evidence, or even to check that the information is accurate (it may not be). Nor is there any claim that the information is up to date (it is not). The jottings are very obviously far from complete. Inconsistency in the length of the sections should not to be thought to indicate their relative importance. The jottings have not been purged of bias or prejudice. The intention is simply to present a random array of data, as a provocation to think, discuss, argue, challenge, research further, and take action.[7]

Each section ends with the question, What action are we planning to take? Taking action is the imperative. There is an urgent need for learning communities to focus on what specifically will be added to the '2020 Vision'. The 2020 Vision is one of a world where moves have at least begun, moves toward building a new social order, the kind of world toward which the fulfilment society will continue to be committed to work. You will find some thoughts on the 2020 Vision in the epilogue.

One last word, a reminder, perhaps: an essential part of making effective plans for action is to set clear goals or objectives. Just as it is true that goal-setting is important for individuals, so it is even more important that working groups share clearly defined objectives. Only in this way can they know that they are all working towards the same, agreed end, it is the only way in which progress can be monitored, and it is only in this way that the group can be certain they have reached a desired endpoint.

- What issues or questions has this chapter raised for me?

- What have I learned?

1   Luke 10:30–37.
2   For the biblical background to the enmity between Jews and Samaritans, see 2 Kings 17.
3   M.B. Clinard, cited in M. Haralambos, *Sociology: Themes and Perspectives*.
4   jrf.org.uk.
5   It is entirely possible that, by the time you read this, my friend's proposal that a visit to one's GP be paid for will have found its way into government legislation. This will serve as an example of the potential for material covered in this part of the book to be overtaken by events. Interestingly, however, a poll taken in the spring of 2014 indicated that twenty-seven per cent of respondents said that they were prepared to pay £10 for a GP visit rather than see their practice closed down, but fifty-six per cent were against doing so.
6   The National Statistics Socio-economic Classification is used for government statistics. The National Readership Survey (nrs.co.uk) uses a somewhat different classification or definition of 'class': A = *upper middle class*, higher managerial, administrative or professional. B = *middle class*, intermediate managerial, administrative or professional. C1 = *lower middle class*, supervisory or clerical and junior managerial, administrative or professional. C2 = *skilled working class*, skilled manual workers. D = *Working class*, semi- and unskilled manual workers. E = *those 'at the lowest levels of subsistence'*, casual or lowest grade workers, pensioners and others depending on the state for their income.
7   As an example, consider the statement '2.4 million households in the UK are in fuel poverty' (defined as having fuel costs above the national average and, were that amount to be spent, the remaining income would be below the official poverty line). This is a government figure relating to the year 2013. It is included in the jottings, not as a definitive statement but in order to generate questions such as: What proportion of that number are pensioners, single parents or unemployed people, with limited ability to generate sufficient income? What are the pros and cons of power generation and supply being in the hands of public companies rather than in public ownership? What are the arguments for and against government policy on renewable energy, and how would the various options affect energy pricing? And so on.

Jottings 1: Children and young people

Issues concerning children and young people may well be the most appropriate place in which to begin, for at least these two reasons: first, because they are the people in whose interest it is — and it is an urgent need — to start building a better world, a task with which they must be inspired to continue. And secondly, because this provides a reminder that 'what everyone knows' about children and young people should include much that is to be celebrated and built upon.

It hardly needs to be said that not all children and young people *are* a problem, by any measure, nor of course do all children and young people *have* a problem. Unfortunately, far too many are and have. So, important as it is to remember and be proud of young people's achievements and progress, it is even more important to focus on issues such as those which concern us here — issues of poverty, crime, abuse, health, education, unemployment, issues which demand remedy.

Children inherit a world that was created (for good or ill) by the generations that went before them. In post-recession Britain, it has been calculated that the next generation will be less well off than their parents, as a result of factors that created a damaging economic downturn. It is a matter for discussion, of course, as to what extent an expectation that living standards will always continue to rise is a foregone conclusion, or that higher and higher living standards are a criterion of well-being and happiness. On the other hand, it would be regrettable if hard-earned past improvements in living standards were allowed to be eroded.

As today's children reach adulthood, they will in their turn either build on successes already achieved, or they will miss opportunities for further developments and squander scarce resources. But until they can become self-determining, our children depend on us, their parents' generation. It is from us that they should be able to expect and enjoy safety and security, and be able to grow up in a caring

Jottings 1: Children and young people

society that affords opportunities for them to become all that they are capable of becoming. To borrow Mencap's vision, the aim may be summarised as

to build a world where all young people are equally valued and able to take up opportunities to achieve their potential.

*

A UNICEF survey of children's well-being placed Britain at the bottom of a 21-nation league table (though absolutely last in only one tenth of the measures used) • Overcrowding at home profoundly affects underachievement at school • In Britain, 33 per cent of children (approaching 4 million) live in poor families: poverty is defined as a household income below 60 per cent of the national average • 27 per cent of young offenders had been in care • It costs £215,000 a year to keep a child in a secure unit • The UK spends 11 times more on putting children into detention than on preventing youth crime • In 2013, 47 per cent of children in Greater Manchester lived in poverty • In 2013, in at least two London boroughs 42 per cent of children lived in poverty — contrasted with 7 per cent in a wealthier borough • 25 per cent of white children live in poverty, contrasted with 74 per cent of Bangladeshi children, 60 per cent of Pakistani children and 56 per cent of black children • 40 per cent of poorest children, and 25 per cent of all children, live in lone-parent households • Compared with those in more affluent families, poor children are more likely to suffer ill-health, underachieve at school, have behavioural problems, become pregnant at an early age, have low work skills and aspirations, be unemployed or in low-pay occupations, become welfare-dependent • Half of the 3.8 million children living in poverty have a parent in paid work — but a low-paid couple can avoid poverty only if both are working • A government objective is to eliminate child poverty by 2020 • Poorer children's development is hindered by missing out on school trips and after-school activities • Poor children living in affluent areas are bullied by their better-off peers • 1 in 4 children has been bullied because of his or her faith • 4 in every 10 children with a disability live in poverty • Children are more aware of obvious signs of affluence (e.g. owning a mobile phone) than of less obvious indicators (e.g. going to school without breakfast) • 30 per cent of British children between 2 and 15 years of age are overweight or obese • Fewer than half of 1 per cent of teenage girls get enough physical exercise; boys are better, but not enough • There is concern over levels of child care and safety in hospitals; 25 per cent of hospitals are rated as good or excellent, the remainder need to improve • In 2006, more than 5,000 children under 16 were admitted to hospital with mental and behavioural disorders as a result of alcohol abuse; more than half were girls • In one year, nearly 42,000 schoolchildren were sent home for alcohol- or drugs-related reasons • Half of the children who had had sexual intercourse, had unprotected sex • 29 per cent of 15 year-olds, and 49 per cent of 16 year-olds say they have lost their virginity, but only half of their parents are aware of that • More British children have had sexual intercourse by their fifteenth birthday, and more 11–15 year-olds have been drunk twice or more often than in any of 21 countries in a UNICEF report • The abortion rate for under-16s has fallen but overall the rate has risen • 21 per cent of children age 11–15 and 9 per cent of pre-teens say they have drunk alcohol in the previous week • 1 in 10 children in the final year of primary school has drunk alcohol in the past week • Average consumption of alcohol by children can be as much as 10 units or more in a week—the equivalent of a pint of beer each day, nearly half the 'recommended' maximum for a man • Problems facing 16 year-old binge drinkers: 60 per cent more likely to be alcoholics by age 30, 40 per cent more likely to be users of illegal drugs, 40 per cent more likely to suffer mental health problems, 60 per cent more likely to be homeless • Nearly half of those likely to engage in antisocial behaviour are under 18 • About 750,000 children each year witness domestic abuse; about half that number have themselves been beaten • 50,000 youngsters are on the child protection register in the UK • Suspects in nearly 3,000 reported crimes were under 10 years of age • More than 1,000 crimes of arson and criminal damage were committed by under-10s • A lack of progress has been made in 10 years in raising the numbers of school leavers achieving basic qualifications • By the age of 3, the social and educational development of children in poorer families lags a year behind that of children from more affluent families • By the age of 7, the least able children of affluent families outperform the most able children from poor families • 1 in 5 14 year-old boys has a reading ability half his age • Each year tens of thousands boys leave school

Jottings 1: Children and young people

without a GCSE qualification • Nearly three quarters of 18 year-olds say internet pornography leads to unrealistic views about sex • Children of unemployed parents are 13 times more likely to die from accidents than children in more affluent families; and children in temporary accommodation are 70 times more likely to die in a fire • Compared with those in more affluent families, poor children are more likely to have low work skills and aspirations, and be unemployed or in low-pay occupations • A survey suggests that 40 per cent of unemployed young people have mental health problems • One in 3 long-term unemployed young people have contemplated suicide • 21 per cent of children in families with at least one disabled member are in poverty • Single parents can rarely earn enough to lift their families out of poverty • 76 per cent of the population disagree that gun crime is only a black youth problem • Compared with white youths, a young black person is 6 times more likely to be stopped and searched, 3 times more likely to be arrested, twice as likely to be detained in custody • Young black people are nearly 3 times more likely to be a victim of violent crime • A cause of high crime levels among young black people is claimed to be social exclusion: being excluded from school, educational underachievement, poor housing and other deprivation • 50 per cent of children of parents with learning disability are removed from their homes • It is estimated that each year 77,000 children under 16 run away from home for the first time • Before they are 16, nearly 10 per cent of children in England spend at least one night absent from home as runaways • Most are running away from family conflict or abuse • Some 30,000 children 'known to be suffering harm' are on child protection registers in the UK • A 2007 study uncovered more than 300 cases of child trafficking; the figures are likely to be far higher • Of the children ringing ChildLine, 20 per cent (21,000) called about physical or sexual abuse or both • 9 out of 10 children who have been sexually abused were abused by men • Women are as likely as men to abuse children physically or emotionally or to neglect them.

▪ As a result of researching and studying the theme of <u>Children and young people</u> introduced by these jottings, what action are we planning to take?

Jottings 2: Crime

Perhaps the most obvious form of deviance is crime, those activities which break the law and are subject to punishment by the courts. There are other forms of deviance, which may be crime-related but are not illegal in themselves: alcohol abuse is an example.

Definitions of crime alter over time. Acts which were once forbidden by law become at least permissible under changing legislation, while new laws forbid acts which once were not subject to penalty. None the less, while the effects of criminal acts are evident enough, with observable results of offences against the person and against property, the causes of crime are by no means as clear.

Some theorists explain the causes of crime either in psychological or in physiological terms, suggesting that individuals offend because of their genetic make-up. Such ideas of a 'flawed' personality will be recognised in 'what everyone knows' about criminals, or in the stereotyping of the 'born' criminal.

Other theorists set the causes of crime within social or sociological contexts. It is said, for example, that deprivation or unequal access to opportunity leads to deviant behaviour.

Another argument proposes that there is evidence of 'a systematic bias in favour of the powerful in the application of the law'.[1] This suggests that the higher the social status of the offenders, the lower is the probability of their being arrested. If they are arrested, though, they are less likely to be prosecuted than offenders from lower social classes; but should they be prosecuted, they are less likely to be found guilty, and if found guilty, they are least likely to be imprisoned.

Such arguments give clues to socially constructed concepts of 'the criminal' or even of a criminal 'class'.

*

In 2014 crime levels were at their lowest for 33 years • In the 10 years to 2012, police recorded crime was down by 38 per cent • However, the accuracy of the police claim has been questioned •In 2011, 1.2 million women in Britain experienced domestic violence • In a national survey, crime was number one in a list of priorities for government action, ahead of health, education and the environment • 80 per cent of women in prison are there for non-violent offences • 6 out of 10 women in prison on short sentences will reoffend • In 2011 there were nearly 9,000 cases of self-harm among women prisoners • The UK spends 11 times more on putting children into detention than on preventing youth crime • It costs £215,000 a year to keep a child in a secure unit • 75 per cent of young people in secure units reoffend • 27 per cent of young offenders have been in care • Britain spends more on public order and safety (2.5 per cent of GDP) than any other of the world's richest nations (OECD) • It is to be questioned whether drugs are a crime problem or a health problem • Home Office and British Crime Survey figures vary; the former show continuing downward trends, the latter show crime levels to be stable • Although crime levels have fallen in recent years, most people believe that crime levels have gone up • A great majority of the population believe that Britain has become less safe • Britain has the highest incidence of burglary in the EU • Violent crime is blamed more on alcohol than on drugs • The chance of being a victim of crime is 30 per cent higher in Britain than in any other EU country • Elderly people have the highest fear of crime, but are the group least likely to become a victim • If they are attacked, older people suffer disproportionately • There may be disagreement on rape statistics, but they are unquestionably too high, the rate of reporting is too low as is the ratio of 'crimed' incidents which are reported, and conviction rates are heavily weighted in favour of the offenders rather than the victims • Antisocial behaviour is increasing: vandalism, rowdiness and drunkenness, litter, noisy neighbours • 80 per cent of Britons believe that a major contributor to crime is family breakdown and lack of discipline in the home • More than 55 per cent of those given an antisocial behaviour order (ASBO) breach its conditions • Most people believe the courts are too lenient • There is a need to increase public confidence in non-custodial (community service) sentences • A majority of people believe that prison sentences are not the answer to crime • The view of 49 per cent of the population is that a custodial sentence makes the prisoner worse, and that imprisonment is not a deterrent to crime • It costs the taxpayer £65,000 a year to keep each prisoner in custody • 80,000 people are being held in a system designed to hold around 50,000 • Nearly 50 per cent of women prisoners and more than 20 per cent of men have attempted suicide at some point • In the UK, there are between 500 and 600 deaths in custody each year • Between 3 and 4 per cent of the prison population are former members of the armed forces • A jail sentence is not a stigma to many offenders • There is an argument that community service sentences help to reduce reoffending, and provide an opportunity for offenders to 'repay' the community • Paying longer-term prisoners for productive work (carried out for external employers) would prepare them for employment on release, contribute to tax, and provide support for their families while still in custody • Restorative cautions (with offenders meeting victims face to face) appear to reduce significantly the likelihood of reoffending • A little more than half of offenders given community sentences reoffend • More than 10 per cent of high risk offenders have been returned to prison for breaking the terms of their release licence • Stable accommodation for ex-offenders reduces the risk of reoffending by one fifth • Penal culture pays little attention to how offenders may change, and reinforces low self-worth and lack of stake in the community • The great majority of prisoners are mentally ill and/or addicted to alcohol and/or illegal drugs • When sentenced to community service, 65 per cent of offenders are not in employment • The risk of reoffending by ex-prisoners who get and keep a job is reduced by one third to a half • Preventing crime means tackling social exclusion and reintegrating those who offend • The most hopeful strategy for reducing youth crime is to identify the main risks within a community and reduce or eliminate them • A call has been made for prison numbers to be reduced from 80,000 to 60,000 within 3 years, and the savings used for programmes of rehabilitation • 1 in 4 15–16 year-olds say they have carried a knife or other weapon in the past year, and 1 in 5 admit to having intended causing another person serious harm • Schools can now require pupils to be screened for weapons • Compared with those in more affluent families, poor children are more likely to have behavioural problems • Almost half of secondary school students admit to having broken the law at some stage • A majority of children fear crime: 95 per cent of 10–15 year-olds have experienced crime at least once • It is thought that users of cocaine are unconcerned about its class A criminal status • Drug treatment is readily available to

Jottings 2: Crime

those committing crimes • Drug-using offenders receive treatment within 5 days, but non-offenders (or those not detected committing crimes) have to wait for up to 3 weeks • A shortcut to treatment may therefore be to commit a petty crime • Something like a third of the population have tried illegal drugs • When a drug user commits a crime, it is readily assumed that drugs were the *cause* of the crime: that is unproven • Nearly half of those likely to engage in antisocial behaviour are under 18 • Suspects in nearly 3,000 reported crimes were under 10 years of age • More than 1,000 crimes of arson and criminal damage were committed by under-10s • 80 per cent of young prisoners reoffend • The incidence of death by dangerous driving is increasing • In one year, more than 2,000 people were found guilty of failing to disclose the driver's identity after a speeding offence • Murder figures may be down, but there is clearly concern about stabbings and gun crime • 76 per cent of the population disagree that gun crime is only a black youth problem • Anti-Muslim crime in the UK increased in 2013, with 500 reported in London alone • Compared with white youths, a young black person is 6 times more likely to be stopped and searched, 3 times more likely to be arrested, and twice as likely to be detained in custody • Young black people are nearly 3 times more likely to be a victim of violent crime • It is claimed that social exclusion is the cause of high levels of crime among young black people—being excluded from school, educational underachievement, poor housing and other deprivation • There is evidence that absentee fathers may be a cause of young people's involvement in gangs, significantly in black communities • In 5 recent years, 1,000 prison officers were found guilty of misconduct, including assault and being drunk at work.

▪ As a result of researching and studying the theme of <u>Crime</u> introduced by these jottings, what action are we planning to take?

[1] This is discussed extensively in M. Haralambos, *Sociology: Themes and Perspectives*.

Jottings 3: Disablement

The category of 'not-able' is socially constructed by the 'able'. The not-able experience a world built and maintained by the able, which to one extent or another excludes them; that is to say, it disables them.

In the view of the able, the 'norm' is that human beings walk on two legs. Any person who has fewer than two legs, or who is unable to use the legs that he or she has, is not included within that norm, and at least in this sense can be considered *not*-normal. However, it can be seen that it is a short step (and 'short step' itself is the language of the fully mobile), a short step from 'not-normal' to *abnormal*. Words such as normal and abnormal carry powerful discriminatory meanings.

From an early age, our storybooks introduce us to baddies with a disability or who are portrayed in stereotypically ugly or frightening images. Long John Silver has one leg, Captain Hook has one hand, Wackford Squeers 'had but one eye… a very sinister appearance… bordered closely on the villainous'. Richard III was 'Deformed, unfinished… so lamely and unfashionable that dogs bark at me'. We early learn that people with a disability are somehow to be avoided, feared, put into a secure place separate from our own, either literally or attitudinally, and there kept at a safe distance from the rest of us.

Medical definitions draw a line around an identifiable set of people, affixing a label to them. The work of disability charities identifies a 'type' of person who is different from 'us'. From time to time, disability takes the interest of the legislators, who prescribe criteria which define whether or not 'they' qualify for welfare provision or special treatment.

'The disabled' are no more a single, identifiable category of people than are golfers (say) or plumbers or blue-eyed people; any of these could be segmented or redefined in a number of different ways. But there are at least two things which people with a disability have in common: one, they are labelled as such; two, they experience disability as social exclusion. On this account, what disables the woman who cannot walk is not the fact that her legs do not function 'normally' but that she is faced by steep steps into her local shop.

Jottings 3: Disablement

Disability may thus more potently be described as *disablement*. The contrast is between the medical model of disability, which focuses on the individual's impairment, and the social model, where disablement results from handicaps created by the world of an able-bodied norm. There are now signs that people with disability, who believe the major source of their disability is not their 'condition' but institutional discrimination, are seeking equality of opportunity—that is, no longer to be subject to a philanthropic but patronising welfare system, but to have the right of self-determination.

*

A government 'vision statement' is that 'By 2025, disabled people in Britain should have full opportunities and choices to improve their quality of life and will be respected and included as equal members of society' • There are over 11 million people with a limiting long-term illness, impairment or disability in the UK • Disability may be physical, sensory, cognitive or mental • Question: what (if anything) differentiates disability, impairment and handicap? • A typical definition of disability is: a physical or mental impairment which has a substantial and long-term adverse effect on a person's ability to carry out normal activities • This and similar definitions place undue negative emphasis on *impairment* and *inability*—that is, implying a flaw, shortcoming or inadequacy—and on *normal*, with the implication of not-normal or even abnormal • The most commonly reported impairments are those that affect mobility, lifting or carrying • The prevalence of disability rises with age • Around 6 per cent of children are disabled, compared to 16 per cent of working-age adults and 45 per cent of pensioners • Recent legislation has been introduced to reduce or eliminate discrimination against people who are disabled, especially at work, in education, on public transport and in housing • Disabled people remain significantly less likely to participate in cultural, leisure and sporting activities than non-disabled people • Around a fifth of disabled people report having difficulties in accessing transport • The concept of 'justifiable' discrimination remains: penalising an autistic child's 'misbehaviour' at school, for example, may be 'justified'; but the school's taking thoughtful preventative steps might have avoided the 'misbehaviour' • It is thought that 1 in 5 people in the nation's workforce qualifies as 'disabled'; but more than half of those do not consider themselves to be disabled • This suggests that the extent of 'disability' cannot be known • There is a need to give people with disability more choice and control over what they do and how they do it • Learning disability (intellectual disability) affects 1.5 million people in the UK • Many receive inadequate health provision and suffer avoidable ill health • 50 per cent of children of parents with learning disability are removed from their homes • 29 per cent of children with a disability live in poverty • Nearly half the population does not recognise schizophrenia, cancer or poor hearing as a disability • Only 19 per cent of British adults would be comfortable with a relative marrying someone with schizophrenia • A slightly bigger minority would be happy with a relative marrying someone with multiple sclerosis • But a small majority would accept the idea of a relative marrying a blind person • Home modifications would allow people with disability to move out of residential care, saving £10 million a year in England alone, and give them greater control of their lives • People with disability are subjected to the 'Does she take sugar?' type of behaviour • People with mental health problems are at greater risk of losing their jobs than people with physical disability • Employers' discrimination against people with disability means they are more likely to be unemployed than able-bodied people, even though (apart from an identifiable disability) they may otherwise have similar abilities or potential • 40 per cent of people who have had psychiatric treatment say that they have been denied jobs because of their medical history • In 2012, 46 per cent of working-age disabled people were in employment compared with 76 per cent of working-age non-disabled people • People with disability tend to be out of work for longer periods than other unemployed people • 90 per cent of unemployed people with mental problems would like to work • When they are employed, people with a disability tend to work in low-pay occupations with comparatively poor working conditions • 19 per cent of individuals in families with at least one disabled member live in relative income poverty • Disabled children and young people do not have access to the same educational opportunities as able-bodied children • Disabled children leave school with fewer qualifications than able-bodied children • Disabled people are around 3 times more likely to have no qualifications • Disabled

Jottings 3: Disablement

people are significantly less likely to live in households with access to the internet • So-called special needs provision may be educationally and socially divisive • Multiple sclerosis is the most common disabling neurological disease among young adults and affects 85,000 people in the UK • MS is most often diagnosed in people between 20 and 40 years of age; and women are twice as likely to develop it as men • There is only a 2 per cent chance of a child developing MS when a parent is affected – a much lower risk than that of developing cancer or heart problems when a parent is affected • In a poll of MS sufferers, 67 per cent were anxious about their ability to manage because of benefits changes • There are 1.5 million people in the UK with learning disability • Every week, 200 babies are born with a learning disability • Of the 15,000 people with Downs syndrome in the workforce, only 16 per cent will have an opportunity to demonstrate their potential • 9 out of 10 people with learning disability are bullied • Disabled people are significantly more likely to be victims of crime than non-disabled people • 29,000 people with learning disability live at home with a carer aged over 70 • 5,000 people in the UK have motor neurone disease • Each year, 150,000 people suffer a stroke in the UK, the largest single cause of severe disability, with a greater disability impact than any other chronic disease • Over 300,000 people in the UK have moderate to severe disabilities as a result of a stroke • It is estimated that there are around 250,000 people in the UK living with aphasia, the communication disability which is usually (but not exclusively) caused by a stroke • About a third of people who have a stroke have aphasia • Osteoarthritis affects 2 million people in Britain and there is no known cure • Studies suggest that 50 per cent of knee osteoarthritis and 60 per cent of hip osteoarthritis is linked to genetic factors • 17,000 blind people use a white stick, and a further 5,000 have a guide dog • Many other blind and partially-sighted people have difficulty to some extent with day-to-day activities • 45 per cent of profoundly deaf people under 60, and 77 per cent of those over 60, have additional (probably physical) disability • Over a quarter of disabled people say that they do not have sufficient choice and control over their daily lives.

- As a result of researching and studying the theme of <u>Disablement</u> introduced by these jottings, what action are we planning to take?

Jottings 4:
Ecology and the environment

Government figures suggest that the UK continues to take action on environmental issues—for example, in reducing greenhouse gas emissions, the country met the Kyoto Protocol target of a 12.5 per cent reduction from 1990 levels and there are plans to meet the legally-binding target of a domestic 20% cut in emissions. By 2010 the amount of industrial and commercial waste disposed in landfill sites had been reduced to 85 per cent of 1998 levels and at least 25 per cent of household waste was being recycled or composted; this is to be increased to 33 per cent by 2015.

In spite of these major improvements, a government report suggested that 25 per cent of the UK population believe that 'It takes too much effort to do things that are environmentally friendly'. In a list of issues which were thought to be priorities for government action, the environment came fourth, after crime, health and education. The figures showed that fewer people saw the environment as a priority for action than six years earlier. Half the population said that they did not think that lifestyle affects climate change. Two thirds of people believed that we are capable of solving the world's environmental problems.

But it is an infinitely more complex issue than simply ensuring that our domestic rubbish goes into the wheelie bin marked 'Recycle'. There remain major concerns about (for example) so-called fracking, sources of renewable energy, fresh water supplies and flood control, air quality, airport expansion, and endangered species. The agenda remains unimaginably diverse and challenging, for us and for our children.

*

71 per cent of households are recycling more and say they intend to go on doing so · Two thirds of local authorities meet or exceed their recycling targets · It is argued, however, that too much household

Jottings 4: Ecology and the environment 161

waste is not recycled; it is dumped in unhygienic, land-hungry landfill and burnt in energy-inefficient incinerators, and so irrecoverably lost • It is estimated that 80 per cent of household waste could be genuinely recycled, that is, reused: Belgium achieves 70 per cent • It is claimed that a third runway at Heathrow would increase CO_2 emissions there by 40 per cent • The EU is committed to reducing CO_2 emissions by 20 per cent by 2020 • The UK target of a 20 per cent reduction by 2020 will not be reached until 2050, by which time the government target will have been raised to a 60 per cent reduction, or even 80 per cent • Conservation bodies have argued that the 2050 target should indeed be a reduction of 80 per cent • An estimate of annual health costs resulting from aviation pollution is £1 billion • Air pollution at rural Stansted affects very few people, whereas at Heathrow the number is 30,000 • However, 14,000 people are affected by noise pollution at Stansted • Airports in the south east are used by 120 million of the 200 million people flying each year • The benefits brought to local economies by airport expansion are questioned: for example, airport employment levels *fall in proportion* to increasing numbers of passengers (although rising in absolute terms) • In EU countries, 70 per cent of air journeys are shorter than 1,000 km, and 45 per cent are shorter than 500 km, suggesting opportunities for alternative modes of transport • The volume of road traffic in the UK has doubled since 1980 • In the UK, road transport contributes 25 per cent of CO_2 emissions • Transport's contribution to climate change could be reduced by 60 per cent by 2030 • In the UK, the length of 61 per cent of car journeys is between one and two miles • Transport and road planning needs to take into account the fact that in the UK 28 per cent of households have no car, and in rural areas 15 per cent of households have no car • Government expenditure on the rail network in the next 10 years will reach £60 billion, but relatively little will be allocated to commuter lines, which would have the greatest impact on the use of cars • Residential area speed limits of 20 mph would contribute to a planned reduction in road deaths, from 3,000 to 1,000 a year (Why 1,000? Why not 100? Or zero?) • A 20 mph urban speed limit would create a safer environment • 9 out of 10 cyclist and pedestrian casualties happen in built-up areas • This safer environment would also contribute to climate change and sustainability • The so-called carbon footprint of the 'average' Briton is 11,000 kg of CO_2 a year, and needs to be reduced to 2,500 kg • It is estimated that a global temperature rise of 4°C would raise sea levels by 59 cm, with 1.8 million people in Britain alone at risk from flooding • Britain's power comes from coal (37 per cent), gas (36 per cent), nuclear (18 per cent), renewables (4 per cent), oil and imports (5 per cent) • British consumers waste £900 million a year by leaving appliances on standby • As oil demands rise, supply is falling; global oil production peaked in 2006, Britain's in 1999 • A government target is for 20 per cent of Britain's energy to come from renewable sources by 2020 • It is reported that revised, lower renewable targets will be set by government • Nuclear power stations and offshore wind farms are the most expensive power sources to build, the latter even more than the former • Wind power is said to be 3 times more efficient than nuclear power • Wind farms cost half as much to build onshore as offshore • Tidal power could provide 10 per cent of the UK's electricity • A barrage built on the River Severn would supply near half of that • It is estimated that such a barrage would cost between £15 and £20 billion to construct • If the barrage were built, up to 75 per cent of the intertidal natural habitat would be lost • During the past 50 years, 95 per cent of wildlife-rich peat has been destroyed • Trials to grow crops of GM (genetically modified) potatoes continue, in spite of widespread consumer opposition • Too little is known about the risks of contamination between GM and non-GM crops, or the potential risks to consumers • GM crops can be used to reduce or eliminate soil and water contamination by major pollutants such as trichloroethylene and chemicals from military explosives (e.g. on moorland firing ranges) • GM crops could also prove to be the only sustainable source of omega-3 nutrients, essential to good health • A counterargument is that more healthy diets would remove a need to look for such additives • Even so, government seems intent on pursuing the argument for GM crops • Each year, air pollution is a cause of 24,000 premature deaths in Britain • Children living within 500 metres of a motorway have more lung damage and lower life expectancy than others • If the government house-building targets for building new homes are to be met, 2 million of them will have to be built on green belt • The UK has less available water per head of population than most EU countries • The south east of England has less available water per head of population than Sudan • Each person in the UK

Jottings 4: Ecology and the environment

uses 150 litres (33 gallons) of water a day • A garden sprinkler uses up to 1,000 litres (220 gallons) an hour—more than 6 people normally use in a day • Washing a car with a hose uses 300 litres of water (66 gallons) rather than 36 litres (8 gallons) with a bucket • The key to water efficiency is reducing waste, not restricting use.

- As a result of researching and studying the theme of Ecology and the environment introduced by these jottings, what action are we planning to take?

Jotting 5: Education

Equality of educational opportunity has long been an ideal, but one by no means realised. Quite apart from differences between state schools and fee-paying 'public' and independent schools, there are variations within the state system itself. If there is no equality of access to what continues to be privileged education, at least there should be opportunity for equality in educational achievement. However, evidence continues to suggest that while children from more affluent families tend to sail through the educational system, achieving good results, the same cannot be said for poorer children.

In addition to examining the social problem of educational underachievement, questions might include: What is meant by 'education' and what is its purpose? Is its prime aim to prepare young people for the world of work? Is the endpoint of education the attainment of academic qualifications? Is there an 'endpoint' anyway? Or does education have a broader and continuing purpose? If so, what is that purpose? And is education related only to children and young people?

Learning is or should be a lifelong process. But to what extent are education and learning the same thing? Lifelong learning clearly has a place in enhancing Britain's work skills, necessary for keeping up with or getting ahead of the country's foreign competitors. But hopefully it is clear by now that lifelong learning should have a much deeper and broader purpose.

It has already been noted that in thinking and speaking about 'problems' it is too easy in the process to overlook success and achievement, too simple to concentrate on the negative at the expense of the positive. So, in examining aspects of education which clearly require attention and solutions, it is important also to keep in mind the improvements and achievements of recent years.

While the emphasis here is on problems within primary and secondary education, since those are the principal areas of concern for the majority of people, other aspects of education must not be ignored. Higher education has its problems. And, at the other end of the scale of concerns, there may be 7 million adults in Britain who cannot read and write.

*

In a national survey of issues considered to be priorities for government action, education came third, after crime and health • Overcrowding at home profoundly affects underachievement at school • Compared with those in more affluent families, poor children are more likely to underachieve at school and/or have behavioural problems • Pupils from better-off families are twice as likely to get good GCSE qualifications as those from low-income families • Poorer children's development is hindered by missing out on school trips, for example, and after-school activities • By the age of 3, the social and educational development of children in poorer families lags a year behind that of children from more affluent families • By the age of 7, the least able children of affluent families outperform the most able children of poor families • About 770,000 (7 per cent) of children in the UK have a disability • Children with disability face multiple barriers which make it more difficult for them to achieve their potential and to succeed in education • The educational attainment of children with a disability is unacceptably lower than that of non-disabled children • All schools are required to have an accessibility plan • 29 per cent of children with disability live in poverty • August-born children, i.e. the youngest in their class year, often struggle to keep up with the September-born, older children • This suggests a need for more flexibility in the dates and ages when children start school • Progress in basic skills in primary schools is static or falling • Only 80 per cent of 7 year-olds have achieved the expected standard in writing, and 84 per cent in reading • In maths and science, around 90 per cent of 7 year-olds have reached the expected standard but the proportion is not rising • A 7 year-old poor child in a top attainment group is 40 per cent more likely to drop from it by age 11 than is a child from a more affluent family • A lack of progress has been made in 10 years to raise the numbers of school leavers achieving basic qualifications • However, something like two thirds gain 5 or more A*–C grade GCSEs • The current rate of achievement will have to accelerate rapidly and substantially if the government target of 80 per cent is to be reached by 2020 • 66 per cent of girls achieved 5 good GCSEs compared with 57 per cent of boys • Young people with fewer than 5 GCSEs are 4 times more likely to use alcohol or drugs to deal with mental health problems • If teachers did not have to spend a disproportionate amount of time with boys, girls might perform even better than they do • More girls than boys stay on in sixth forms; and more girls go on to university • By the age of 7, the least able children of affluent families outperform the most able children from poor families • 1 in 5 14 year-old boys has a reading ability half his age • Each year tens of thousands boys leave school without a GCSE qualification • More than a million young people between 16 and 24 are not in education, employment or training • Girls tend to study 'female' subjects and boys study 'male' subjects • This gender divide in study subjects adversely affects girls' career choices and later promotion opportunities • 90,000 boys leave school each year without a GCSE • 30 per cent of 15–19 year-olds are not in education or training and aspire to low-skill jobs • A disproportionate number of black boys are excluded from school • 4 out of 5 children excluded from school are boys • Nearly a third of secondary schools have poor behaviour • More than 200,000 secondary school pupils play truant at least 1 day a week • It is claimed that the younger a person leaves school, the more likely it is that he or she will use drugs, engage in prostitution, commit crime, and end up in prison, unemployed or homeless, and possibly all 3 • Uneducated boys and girls suffer a 'spiral of despair'; a lack of interest in being at school turns into disillusionment and then hostility to society • More than 50 per cent of parents are prepared to move house in order to get a child into a good school • In London, nearly a quarter of parents are prepared to lie (e.g. about their address or their faith) to gain their child's admission to a better school • While there have been an increasing number of successful entrants to Oxford and Cambridge universities from some top public schools (but fewer from some independent schools) the rate of increase from state schools is slow • A third of Oxbridge places go to pupils from 100 schools, 80 per cent of which are private • Only 18 per cent of young people from the poorest families go to university • Only 10 per cent of young people in the poorest fifth of the population have a degree, compared with 44 per cent in the most affluent fifth • While the proportion of full-time first degree students from lower socio-economic groups is at an all-time high, the proportion still needs to increase • The number of A grades awarded in A-level examinations has risen more rapidly in private schools than in state comprehensives • Girls outperform boys in all A-level subjects except further mathematics and modern languages • Students in fee-paying schools have gained 4 times more GCSE A* grades than the UK average • Increasing numbers of children (in a few local authorities, as many as 10 per cent) are being taken out of state schools into private education • Social and ability segregation lowers the nation's *overall* level of educational achievement • Segregated education means that children grow up without learning how 'the other half' live • This can also lay the foundation to socially constructed views of 'them' (i.e. those who are 'not one of us') • Social segregation and privileged education seem likely to continue while class distinctions continue • It is reported that the 'extended services' programme will have had a revolutionary effect on developing children's 'social capital', facilitating their learning not only in academic contexts but also in their growth and commitment as members of the community • Experiments have begun in the UK with US-style 'small schools' which have achieved outstanding improvements in 'ghetto' schools • Evidence suggests that these disadvantaged children are being enabled to acquire social skills which middle-class children take for granted • It is argued that a raised school-leaving age, coupled with new apprenticeships and diplomas, may reduce truancy and antisocial behaviour, and increase many children's opportunities to make a better start to their lives.

▪ As a result of researching and studying the theme of <u>Education</u> introduced by these jottings, what action are we planning to take?

Jottings 6: Employment

A sociological view is that work is the primary human activity, potentially the source of fulfilment, but much has been written about 'alienation' from work, the factors which separate people from this potential for fulfilment.

None the less, to work is a human right: the United Nations *Universal Declaration of Human Rights* states that 'Everyone has the right to work, to free choice of employment, to just and favourable conditions of work and to protection against unemployment'. However, the extent to which that right is universally enjoyed is barely a question.

The meaning of 'work' is infinitely variable: a desert nomad following his grazing animals has a quite different perception of his daily occupation from (say) a man or woman commuting to a city office or factory. And yet these people would doubtless agree that their occupations are essential to their subsistence, their ability to pay their way. In that sense, if work provides the means for everything above the subsistence level, it is essential both to individuals and to the society in which they live.

Millions of people gain from their occupation not only the income necessary for their day-to-day living, but also their self-respect and esteem in a society where being employed is the norm. Moreover, occupation is used to define the hierarchy of 'class'. Unemployment, on the other hand, may be the route into poverty, with a downward spiral of loss of self-worth, and ultimately despair.

Unemployment is itself associated with a number of other social problems: areas with high unemployment may also have high levels of poor health, family breakdown, violence and crime.

Although work is thought about mainly within the structured labour market, it must also include those who are unpaid but none the less fully occupied: women (in the main) managing homes and families, carers and those in the voluntary sector.

*

Jottings 6: Employment

At least 10 per cent of under-25s are unemployed • More than a million young people between 16 and 24 are 'NEETs' (not in education, employment or training) and aspire to low-skill jobs • Boys of 16 are twice as likely to be NEETs as are girls of 16 • There are half as many NEETs in the south east of England as in the old coalmining and shipbuilding areas • As unemployment figures fall, so figures for disability rise • Sickness-related benefit is concentrated in areas of industrial decline, suggesting a redefinition of 'unemployment' • Compared with young people in more affluent families, those from poor homes are more likely to have low work skills and aspirations, be unemployed or in low-pay occupations, and/or become welfare-dependent • People with mental health problems are more at risk of losing their jobs than people with physical disability • A government aim is to 'Increase the number of disabled people in employment while providing support and security for those unable to work' • 80 million work days are lost every year through stress, anxiety and depression • An increasing majority of both men and women in full-time employment say that job demands interfere with family life • 82 per cent of full-time working men and 84 per cent of full-time working women would like to spend more time with their family • New rights will enable more adults to request to work flexibly — parents of older schoolchildren, for example • Some form of flexible working is now offered by 95 per cent of employers • Although rights to flexible working may prove beneficial, reduced stress in the workplace is said to be a more effective goal • More than half of senior managers and directors have difficulty in getting home as early as they would wish • And only 1 in 10 of them said they could relax in their spare time • The hourly rate of pay for a woman working full-time is 17 per cent lower than that of a man working full-time • And a part-time woman's hourly rate of pay is 36 per cent lower than that of a full-time man • Women managers earn 35 per cent less than their male colleagues • In 2014, 30 per cent of 18–30 year-olds were classed as low-paid (under two thirds of median hourly rate) • More than a quarter of the workforce work at home some of the time • Foreign nationals account for perhaps 8 per cent of the workforce • There is evidence that immigrant workers are employed for lower wages and with less favourable working conditions than British workers • Unions argue for equal rights for agency workers, who tend to be immigrants, and are said to be exploited, with low wages and poor conditions • A survey suggests that 40 per cent of unemployed young people have mental health problems • In 2014 there were 900,000 unemployed 16–24 year-olds • Of these, 400,000 may face long-term unemployment • 1 in 10 people aged 65 and over are in employment • Between 2010 and 2014 the number of people aged over 64 had increased by a third • In 2013 nearly 4 per cent of employed people were 65 or older • Many older people postpone retirement because of a need to earn to maintain their living standards • 1 in 3 long-term unemployed young people have contemplated suicide • Women make up about half the workforce • Although women are increasingly engaged in paid employment, and are at least as committed to a career as men are, they still carry out most of the housework and child care • Everyone, without any discrimination, has the right to equal pay for equal work • 3 years after graduation, 40 per cent of men are earning more than £25,000 compared with 26 per cent of women • Girls tend to study 'female' subjects and boys study 'male' subjects at school; and this gender divide in study subjects adversely affects girls' career choices and later promotion opportunities • Only 23 executive directors of top UK companies are women: only 3 chief executives are women • This gender divide is also evidenced in figures for apprenticeships: only 3 per cent of engineering apprentices and 1 per cent of construction apprentices are women; only 8 per cent of hairdressing apprentices and 3 per cent of those on childcare courses are men • In a survey, 56 per cent of senior managers believed the UK's management skills undermine national productivity • Only 28 per cent of senior managers interviewed demonstrated faith in those skills • Less than one third of employees trust their manager • This lack of trust is more noticeable among long-term employees; 75 per cent of those employed for at least 10 years do not trust their manager completely, and 61 per cent say their managers look after their interests only when it suits them • Only 34 per cent of UK employees see their manager as a role model • Nearly a quarter of employees feel that their line manager takes little or no account of their views or does not consult them when making decisions • Nearly half of all employees say that their employers withhold information which affects them • Nearly half of employees say that lack of trust in their managers would lead them to look for a new job • A majority of

Jottings 6: Employment

employees believe they could make a greater contribution to their firm's success if their ideas were sought or listened to • Employers frequently state that they wish employees would show more initiative.

- As a result of researching and studying the theme of Employment introduced by these jottings, what action are we planning to take?

Jottings 7: Equality of opportunity

It will be seen that there is extensive overlap between these jottings and 'Gender and sexuality', and it may prove beneficial to take the two together.

Inequality of opportunity, or rather the denial of equality of opportunity, is an age-old function of patriarchal cultures and societies, where the levers of power and authority are in the hands of men. There, roles are determined by gender: men, the 'stronger sex', are destined to control, dominate, as masters, breadwinners, decision makers, free to come and go as they please; while women, the 'weaker sex', remain submissively in their place in the kitchen, looking after the home and the children. That may reflect so-called Victorian values, but today, patriarchy and gendered roles are alive and well and living in Britain.

The Equal Opportunities Commission (now a part of the Equality and Human Rights Commission) expressed a concern that it will take generations to close the gender equality gaps and achieve parity in Britain, if the present rate of change does not accelerate significantly.

It is relevant to add a note almost in parenthesis, however, that although gender equality gaps mainly favour men, they do not do so exclusively: for example, men under 45 years of age are half as likely as women to consult their GP, with the result that diagnoses are delayed and may come too late to deal effectively with serious illness; and young men are 80 per cent more likely than young women to be the victim of serious crime, which is not to suggest that the level of female victims should be raised to equal that of the men!

Although gender inequality is the focus here, there are other aspects of inequality of opportunity in the UK. How true is it that Britain is a country where anyone can succeed, where opportunity is open to all? (Admittedly, 'succeed' needs to be defined, but let us take it to mean becoming what one is capable of becoming.) To what extent does disablement, education, ethnicity or poverty affect one's ability to progress or achieve success? Many women are successful,

Jottings 7: Equality of opportunity

people of colour occupy senior positions, some from 'the wrong side of the tracks' make it to the top. Why should these be seen as exceptions?

*

In total, the wealth of the top 3 per cent of Britons is 3 times greater than the total wealth of the bottom 50 per cent • Everyone, without any discrimination, has the right to equal pay for equal work • The hourly rate of pay for a woman working full-time is more than 17 per cent lower than that of a man working full-time • A part-time woman's hourly rate of pay is 36 per cent lower than that of a part-time man • In her lifetime, a woman working full-time earns about £300,000 less than a man doing similar work • In some firms, male managers earn 46 per cent more than their female counterparts • At board level, women directors earn up to 26 per cent less than their male colleagues • On the boards of FTSE 100 companies, women total 21 per cent of the directors • Only 3 chief executives of top UK companies are women • The highest-paid woman director in the UK received more than £4 million, 25 per cent below the average for FTSE 100 senior executives • A quarter of the 16 non-executive directors with places on 3 or more FTSE 100 boards are women • It has been calculated that at the present rate of change it may take 65 years before the pay of men and women is equal • Only 20 per cent of MPs are women • At the present rate of change, it will take 200 years to achieve parity of numbers in parliament • There are 27 MPs from ethnic minorities • 42 members of the Lords are from ethnic minorities • Only 6 per cent of directors of FTSE 100 companies are from ethnic minorities • 8 black women are directors of FTSE 100 companies, but none of them are British • There are only 2 black women MPs • There are only 4 non-white directors of FTSE 100 companies • Only 9 top civil servants are from ethnic minority background • If the current rate of improvement continues, it will take another 20 years to achieve equality in the civil service, and 40 years in the judiciary • In 2006, more women than men were ordained as clergy in the Church of England; but fewer than a quarter of the women were ordained to full-time or paid positions • In 2014, for the first time, more women than men were included in the New Year's honours list • A retired woman has 40 per cent less income than a retired man; this 'pension gap' could take 45 years to eliminate • Women are less able than men to save for a pension • Single mothers can rarely earn enough to lift their families out of poverty • People with disability tend to be out of work for longer periods than other unemployed people • 90 per cent of unemployed people with mental problems would like to work • When they are employed, people with a disability tend to work in low-pay occupations with comparatively poor working conditions • People with mental health problems are at greater risk of losing their jobs than people with physical disability • Employers' discrimination against people with disability means they are more likely to be unemployed than able-bodied people, even though (apart from an identifiable disability) they may otherwise have similar abilities or potential • 40 per cent of people who have had psychiatric treatment say that they have been denied jobs because of their medical history • Only 5 per cent of police officers in England and Wales are from ethnic minorities • There are high levels of unemployment in ethnic minority communities living in inner city areas, where traditional manufacturing industries have long been in decline • 42 per cent of people in minority communities mistakenly believe they are not eligible to adopt children • There is clear evidence that immigrant workers are employed for lower wages and with less favourable working conditions than British workers • At school, girls tend to study 'female' subjects and boys study 'male' subjects • This gender divide in study subjects adversely affects girls' career choices and later promotion opportunities • 3 years after graduation, 40 per cent of men earn more than £25,000 compared with 26 per cent of women • 82 per cent of full-time working men and 84 per cent of full-time working women would like to spend more time with their family • Women are 63 per cent more likely than men to seek flexible working arrangements • Evidence suggests that while half of men say they would like to work flexibly, they will be less likely than women to request a flexible working arrangement, seeing it as potentially career limiting (thus influencing pay prospects) • In consequence, men work long hours in full-time employment, while many women have flexible hours and/or low-paid occupations • Women continue to have prime responsibility for housework and child care: women spend 78 per cent more time on housework than do their domestic

Jottings 7: Equality of opportunity

partners • Poor people in employment do essential work on which society depends, but do not earn enough to support a family • Large numbers of people on low pay and the 'seeming acceptance of gross inequalities of rates of pay' mean future poverty remains inevitable.

- As a result of researching and studying the theme of <u>Equality of opportunity</u> introduced by these jottings, what action are we planning to take?

Jottings 8: Ethnicity, 'race' and immigration

Official statistics separate the UK population into two categories, white (88 per cent) and minority ethnic groups (12 per cent): that is to say, white and not-white. One quarter of this not-white population is specifically defined as black, with either Caribbean or African origins. However, when asked to give their religion in the national census, most of this 'black' population ticked the 'Christian' box. So it is not their religion which constitutes black people's perceived 'otherness', but only the colour of their skin.

One half of the 'minority ethnic' population is Asian, also identifiable by skin colour *but also by religion* — principally Muslim, Hindu and Sikh. Here, religious practice is far more discernable as an integral part of people's culture than is true of the 'Christian' population, and to that extent colour *and* religion ('race' and ethnicity) may be considered to be synonymous.

This perception is most marked, perhaps, in the case of the million and a half Muslims in Britain. White Britons' attitude toward Islam and 'the mosque' is unquestionably more acute than toward (say) Hinduism and 'the temple'. When words such as immigration, integration and citizenship are used — or, more markedly, terrorism, radicalising, extremism, militancy — the link is readily made with Muslims and Islam. There is, however, an imperative to accept that the Muslims within our society are by no means the only ones subject to prejudice and exclusion.

Thought needs to be given to the words immigrant, race and ethnic. The more politically correct phrase 'ethnic minorities' seems largely to have replaced the word 'immigrants', but both continue to racialise groups and communities. Physical attributes, which may be taken to mean colour or facial features, are instantly recognisable and are used as the construct of 'race'. Ethnicity, on the other hand, is more commonly linked to cultural attributes, such as language, religion, dress, diet. Both 'race' and 'ethnicity' are used in the social construction of 'difference'.

Jottings 8: Ethnicity, 'race' and immigration

The topic of immigration extends beyond this duality of colour and religion. While the largest single group of immigrants to Britain continues to be Asian, the people classified as 'other ethnic minorities' include large numbers from the enlarged EU.

The need for new perspectives on cohesion and integration is similar to the earlier discussion of 'disablement'. It is not as much a question of what ethnic minorities should do to 'fit in' with British society, as what can be done to remove the barriers which set them apart.

*

Minority ethnic groups account for approximately 14 per cent of the total population of Britain • About 4 per cent of the UK population is Asian (Indian, Pakistani, Bangladeshi) • And about 2 per cent of the population have black Caribbean or black African origins • However, uncertainty about government statistics indicates that insufficient is known about the scale of immigration and population changes • Only 5 per cent of police officers in England and Wales are from ethnic minorities • There may be 500,000 illegal immigrants in Britain • A majority of Britons believe that immigrants without papers who have been in the country for at least 4 years should be allowed to stay and not be termed illegal • A similar majority believe that asylum seekers should be permitted to work while their cases are being considered • A poll showed that 82 per cent of Britons think that religion is a cause of division between people • Another survey indicated that 58 per cent of white people believe that racial prejudice has worsened • In 2014, 30 per cent of Britons were reported to have racist views • A large majority of white people have few friends from ethnic minorities • It is thought that more than 120 different languages are spoken in the UK's major cities • It is said that, on average, migrant workers are more skilled than British workers • Local authorities in 7 of England's 8 regions say that migration puts pressure on housing; in 5 regions, difficulties with crime and education were reported • Only 10 per cent of Gypsy and Roma children achieve 5 GCSE A*–C, compared with the national average of 59 per cent • The modern western lifestyle of young Indian people born in Britain may clash with their parents' traditions • Not to agree to an arranged marriage, denying their parents' wishes, would be a sign of deep disrespect and cause distress in the family • The first two mosques in Britain were built in the last decade of the nineteenth century, in Liverpool and Woking; there are now 1,350 across the country • A new regulatory body established by Muslim groups in Britain seeks among other things to develop mosques as centres of community cohesion, citizenship and dialogue • Surveys show that in London Muslims have a greater sense of identity with their locality than non-Muslims have • Citizenship denotes integration; how does that sit with the retention of indigenous customs and culture? • Questions of the law may arise from this ideal; for example, what is the potential for abuse, where violence may punish a breach of codes of family honour? • A great majority of national newspaper articles about Muslims have been shown to be negative; only 4 per cent of several hundred studied were positive • In the year following the 2005 London bombings, Asians experienced an 84 per cent increase in police stop-and-search • At the same time, there was a 51 per cent increase in black people being stopped and searched, and 36 per cent for people from other ethnic backgrounds • The increase for white people was 24 per cent • Anti-Muslim crime in the UK increased in 2013, with 500 reported in London alone • Black people are 6 times more likely than white to be stopped and searched; Asian and mixed race, twice as likely • Each year there are 3,000 cases of disputes about the age of asylum seekers; minors qualify for more support and protection • There are high levels of unemployment in ethnic minority communities living in inner city areas, where traditional manufacturing industries have long been in decline • 25 per cent of white children live in poverty, contrasted with 74 per cent of Bangladeshi children, 60 per cent of Pakistani children and 56 per cent of black children • Immigration officers at British airports are 10 times more likely to stop non-white South Africans for questioning than their white fellow countrymen • Although the ratios are smaller, the same treatment is given to non-white Canadians and Americans • Some immigration officers perceive certain nationalities as devious, difficult or arrogant • The social construction of 'race' extends beyond non-white people; consider, for example, how jokes racialise Irish and Jewish people, creating negative stereotypes • Violence and discrimination on the basis of 'race' and religion can be seen in the growth in anti-Semitism • There is

Jottings 8: Ethnicity, 'race' and immigration

increasing evidence of anti-Semitic literature, personal violence, attacks on Jewish schools and synagogues, desecration of Jewish burial grounds • 42 per cent of people in minority communities mistakenly believe they are not eligible to adopt children • 76 per cent of the population disagree that gun crime is only a black youth problem • There is a disproportionate rate of arrest of young black males, and they are over-represented within the criminal justice system • Compared with white youths, a young black person is 6 times more likely to be stopped and searched, and 3 times more likely to be arrested • Of those arrested, twice as many black youths as white were detained in custody • Young black people are nearly 3 times more likely to be a victim of violent crime • It is already foreseen that 75 per cent of the young black population will be registered on the national DNA database • It is claimed that social exclusion is the cause of high levels of crime among young black people—being excluded from school, educational underachievement, poor housing and other deprivation • It is suggested that absentee fathers may be a cause of young people's involvement in gangs, significantly in black communities • There is clear evidence that immigrant workers are employed for lower wages and with less favourable working conditions than British workers • Unions argue for equal rights for agency workers, who tend to be immigrants, and are said to be exploited, with low wages and poor conditions • There are 27 MPs from ethnic minorities • 42 members of the Lords are from ethnic minorities • Only 6 per cent of directors of FTSE 100 companies are from ethnic minorities • 8 black women are directors of FTSE 100 companies, but none of them are British • 9 per cent of civil servants are from ethnic minorities; this falls to 5 per cent in the top ranks • 41 per cent of hospital and community services doctors are from ethnic minorities • It has been reported that more than a dozen central government departments failed to comply with race relations legislation • It has been disclosed that several thousand illegal immigrants have been working for security firms in the UK

▪ As a result of researching and studying the theme of <u>Ethnicity, 'race' and immigration</u> introduced by these jottings, what action are we planning to take?

Jottings 9: Family and marriage

For countless generations, the unquestioned concept of the family was that, after a legal ceremony in a church, a man and a woman would live together in their first and lasting marriage, with children conceived and born in wedlock (although that could often be questioned), the man providing for the family as a full-time worker, and the woman managing the home as a full-time carer. Further, it was not unusual for members of the extended family to be living nearby — the parents' parents, for example, aunts and uncles, or brothers and sisters, and so on.

Jottings in this section indicate the extent to which that long-lived standard no longer holds good: that is to say, it is by no means universally accepted as the norm today.

There are varying responses to these changes from the old model. A conservative belief is that the breakdown of family life is at the root of many social problems, and so there is a need to get 'back to basics', re-establishing what are considered to be the traditional family values. A liberal stance is to accept that changing family structures are an inevitable function of wider social developments, values and norms, and have to be recognised as such. A radical response — one that may be labelled a 'feminist' position, but one held also by many others, significantly by gay and lesbian people, for example — sees many of these changes as a welcome and overdue acknowledgment that people should be free to enjoy lifestyles of their own choosing.

Clearly, our understanding of the word 'marriage' is changing. Perhaps most significant in this context is the fact that the law has been changed to allow same-sex marriage. Thus, the essential definition of a word which once signified the union of a man and a woman, simply because that had always been the social norm, no longer holds good.

*

Everyone has the right to a standard of living adequate for the health and well-being of himself [sic] and of his family, including food,

Jottings 9: Family and marriage

clothing, housing and medical care and necessary social services, and the right to security in the event of unemployment, sickness, disability, widowhood, old age or other lack of livelihood in circumstances beyond his control • In 2012 there were 18.2 million families in the UK: of these, 12.2 million consisted of a married couple with or without children • In 2013, there were 120,000 families classified as 'troubled families' in England and Wales • Government initiatives aim to get children of 'troubled families' back into school, reduce youth crime and antisocial behaviour, put adults on a path back to work, and reduce the high costs these families place on the public sector each year • It is estimated that £9 billion is spent annually on troubled families—an average of £75,000 per family each year • Of this, an estimated £8 billion is spent reacting to the problems these families have and cause • The remaining £1 billion is spent on helping families to solve and prevent problems in the longer term.• In 2012 one local authority identified 94 police calls to a 'troubled family'—34 for domestic violence, 6 overdoses, 9 self-harm (including 6 children) • In 2012 it was estimated that there were nearly 9,000 'troubled families' in Greater Manchester; it was questioned to what extent these families had problems or whether they were people who caused problems, or in some cases both • In 2011 1.2 million women experienced domestic violence • While the population of the UK has grown by 8 per cent since 1971, the number of households has increased by 30 per cent • In the last 35 years, the percentage of children born outside marriage has more than quadrupled • There were 26.4 million households in the UK in 2012; 29 per cent of them consisted of only one person • The proportion of British couples getting married continues to decline • The number of religious marriages continues to decline: by 2011, fewer than 30 per cent were religious marriages—the lowest percentage on record • In 1994 (the earliest date for which figures are available) 75 per cent of couples marrying in a civil ceremony lived together before getting married; that increased steadily to 88 per cent in 2011 • People are marrying later: men at 32, women at 30 • It is suggested that living together first and getting married later may contribute to more stable marriages • Even so, a third of the population is now directly affected by divorce • Children of co-habiting parents achieve less well at school than children of married parents, leave education earlier, and are more at risk of serious illness • In the UK, 40 per cent of the poorest children, and 25 per cent of all children, live in lone-parent households • 2 per cent of single mothers are teenagers • The proportion of births registered to a single parent is declining • In a survey, 9 out of 10 people described 'the single parent' as a young female, probably unemployed • Mothers can rarely earn enough to lift their families out of poverty • A fifth of families with children under 17 cannot afford to heat their homes adequately • New policies may require single parents of primary schoolchildren to be available for part-time work, and full-time work when children are at secondary school • The life expectancy of children born in a poor family is 13 years less than those in an affluent family • 80 per cent of Britons believe that a major contributor to crime is family breakdown and lack of discipline in the home • There is some suggestion that absentee fathers may be a cause of young people's involvement in gangs, significantly in black communities • 50 per cent of children of parents with learning disability are removed from their homes • Only 12 per cent of children in care achieve the minimum school-leaving qualifications • Children in care are 8 per cent more likely than average to be excluded from school • Only 4 per cent of children with disability are supported by social services • Families needing support for children with a disability experience a 'lottery' of provision, confusing eligibility criteria, and are subjected to long waits, having to 'jump through hoops' to get support • Families with disabled children report particularly high levels of unmet needs, isolation and stress • The number of people taking on a carer's role is increasing by 300,000 a year • The total number of carers may have reached 9 million by 2040 • Women make up about half the workforce • Although women are increasingly engaged in paid employment, they still carry out most of the housework and child care • 82 per cent of men working full-time and 84 per cent of women working full-time would like to spend more time with their family • Women are 63 per cent more likely than men to seek flexible working arrangements • Evidence suggests that men may be less likely than women to request flexible working, seeing it as potentially career limiting, therefore influencing pay prospects • Consequently, men work long hours in full-time employment, while many women have flexible hours and/or low-paid occupations • When parents split, 10 per cent are unable to agree with whom their

Jottings 9: Family and marriage 183

children should live • In-court conciliation has ensured that more fathers continue seeing their children • However, within 2 years, more than two thirds of agreed cases return to court • In one recent year, 30 per cent of children placed with families for adoption had experienced neglect, 20 per cent were behind in their development, and 18 per cent had a background of parental alcohol or drug misuse • Within minority communities, 42 per cent believe (incorrectly) that they are ineligible to adopt • Almost 10 per cent of children under 16 will have spent at least one night absent from home as runaways • The majority will have run away from family conflict or abuse • Only 12 per cent of local authorities have established services specifically to aid runaway children.

▪ As a result of researching and studying the theme of <u>Family and marriage</u> introduced by these jottings, what action are we planning to take?

Jottings 10: Gender and sexuality

A number of issues surrounding gender have already been touched upon in the sections on education, employment, equality of opportunity and family and marriage. A few of those jottings are repeated here as reminders and for ease of reference, and others have been added.

By linking the topics of gender and sexuality in this section, the aim is to give thought to inequalities and prejudice: inequalities which are a function of gender stereotyping, and prejudice which disadvantages and damages the lives of lesbian, gay, bisexual and transgender (LGBT) people.

There are a number of theories which attempt to explain gender differences and inequalities. Perhaps the most fundamental argument is based on the observable fact that men and women are physically different, and that their biological and genetic differences—the most obvious one being the reproduction processes—give rise to inequality. We are built differently and function differently and are thus deemed to be unequal.

Then, the socialisation theory argues that males and females have prescribed, socially-constructed gender 'scripts', and social expectations are such that boys and girls, men and women, unavoidably act out their stereotypical gender 'roles'. These roles are not to be found in all cultures, though, but are those which seem to be embedded in the 'norms' of many white, western, industrialised societies.

Another argument, not exclusively a feminist one, is that gender inequality derives from the age-old patriarchal structures within society: power and influence are in the hands of men, both in public and in private life, and mechanisms are in place to exclude women from participating, or participating fully or on an equal basis, in this 'man's world'.

In practice, it can be seen that there are few clear boundaries between these arguments for the bases of gender inequality, which merge and overlap. It is not the prejudice itself that is the topic of this section, however, but the hostility and destructive behaviour which prejudice engenders.

*

Women make up about half the workforce • Everyone, without discrimination, has the right to equal pay for equal work • The hourly rate of pay for a woman working full-time is more than 12 per cent lower than that of a man working full-time • And a part-time woman's hourly rate of pay is more than 40 per cent lower than that of a man working full-time • 3 years after graduation, 40 per cent of men are earning more than £25,000 compared with 26 per cent of women • Although women are increasingly engaged in paid employment, they still carry out most of the housework and child care: women spend 78 per cent more time on housework than their domestic partners do • At school, girls tend to study 'female' subjects and boys study 'male' subjects • This gender divide in study subjects adversely affects girls' career choices and later promotion opportunities • The gender divide is also evidenced in figures for apprenticeships: only 3 per cent of engineering apprentices and 1 per cent of construction apprentices are women; only 8 per cent of hairdressing apprentices and 3 per cent of those on childcare courses are men • On the boards of FTSE 100 companies, women total 21 per cent of the directors • The government wants 25 per cent of FTSE 100 directors to be women by 2015—to meet that target, more than 50 women need to be appointed • There are now only 2 all-male boards left among FTSE 100 companies • Out of a total of 650 members of parliament, 146 are women • A traditional gender role is that of men as priests and clergy • More women than men are now being ordained as clergy in the Church of England • However, fewer than a quarter of these women were ordained to full-time or paid positions • Until 2014, women were barred from becoming bishops of the Church of England • A 'gender equality duty' requires public authorities to demonstrate the elimination of sexual discrimination, and the promotion of equality between men and women • More women hold top jobs in the public sector than in the private sector • Between a third and a half of chief executives in voluntary organisations, the health service and other senior public appointments are women • Even so, fewer than a quarter of the most senior people in Whitehall are women • British attitudes surveys show that in 20 years the number of people who thought that homosexuality was always or mostly wrong fell from 75 per cent to 32 per cent • A Stonewall report found that 64 per cent of Britons had negative feelings towards at least one minority group • Those most frequently cited included gay or lesbian people (17 per cent); others were travellers and gypsies (35 per cent), refugees and asylum seekers (34 per cent), people from ethnic minorities (18 per cent) • Prejudice against one group tended to be linked with prejudice against others: for example, people prejudiced against an ethnic minority are twice as likely as the population as a whole to be prejudiced against gay and lesbian people • Knowing someone who is gay or lesbian halves the likelihood of being prejudiced against gay or lesbian people as a group • More than 60,000 civil partnerships have been formed in the UK since the legislation came into force • In 2013, 7,037 civil partnerships were entered into in the UK • The average age of men forming a civil partnership in 2012 was 40, while for women it was 37.6 • In 2012, the number of civil partnership dissolutions rose by 20 per cent, to 794 from 663 in 2011 • In spite of more liberal legislation in aspects of sexuality, homophobia and the results of homophobic attitudes or prejudice have not been reduced significantly, certainly not eliminated • Schism or threat of schism within the Anglican communion over the appointment of gay bishops is a clear example of this • According to a survey of gay, lesbian and bisexual people, 34 per cent of men and 23 per cent of women had experienced violence because of their sexual orientation, being punched, kicked or attacked with a weapon • Many had experienced other harassment: blackmail, graffiti written about them, vandalism, hate mail • More than three quarters of respondents to the survey had been called names by parents or families • Of those aged under 18, nearly half had experienced violence • Half of these violent attacks involved fellow students, many actually taking place at school • Many under 18s had been harassed or attacked by their parents or family • In the workplace, according to another report, 1 in 6 gay, lesbian, bisexual and transgender people had been discriminated against at least once because of their sexuality • A further 20 per cent suspected they had been discriminated against • Of those interviewed, 8 per cent had actually been dismissed • Nearly half of the respondents said they

Jottings 10: Gender and sexuality

had been harassed at work because of their sexuality • The harassment included unwanted jokes, innuendo, verbal abuse, being sent to Coventry, malicious gossip, name-calling, bullying and victimisation, being 'outed', false accusations of child abuse, graffiti, abusive telephone calls, anonymous mail, damage to property, blackmail, violence and even death threats • Nearly a quarter of respondents had avoided certain jobs, careers or employers for fear of discrimination because of their sexuality • Two thirds of respondents who were working concealed their sexuality from those with whom they worked • Only 11 per cent of all respondents in this survey never concealed their sexuality at work • Other findings report that 43 per cent of lesbian and gay people had experienced insults shouted in a public place; 32 per cent kept their homosexuality secret from their employers and colleagues; 25 per cent had been physically threatened or attacked; 21 per cent had been harassed at work; 11 per cent had suffered other forms of discrimination or ill treatment; and 8 per cent had been refused promotion.

▪ As a result of researching and studying the theme of <u>Gender and sexuality</u> introduced by these jottings, what action are we planning to take?

Jottings 11: Health

In a national survey of issues considered to be priorities for government action, health came second, after crime but ahead of education and the environment. The provision of 'health services' is clearly seen to be a government's responsibility; but the issue of health extends far beyond political interventions. While a number of the jottings in this section do indeed relate directly or indirectly to the National Health Service (NHS), many others focus on what might be termed lifestyle choices, actions that individuals take which adversely affect their health or well-being, as well as options which they have to improve their own or others' health: a healthy diet and exercise are two examples; others are the moderate use of alcohol, the avoidance of tobacco and illegal drugs, and taking advantage of available screening services. Unfortunately, the clear evidence is that too many Britons continue to suffer ill-health by making unhealthy choices.

Healthy choices, on the other hand, clearly benefit the individual's sense of well-being, not only enhancing the quality of his or her personal life, but also positively affecting those around them, their family, their work colleagues and their friends.

Some of the jottings which follow give some indication, not only of the cost of personal suffering, but also of the financial cost of health problems. One example of how health becomes a social issue is to be found in accidents and injury at work. Here, the problems are experienced primarily by the injured people, of course, and that is regrettable and serious enough; but also affected are the employers or their industry and ultimately the national economy. With a 10 per cent reduction in workplace accidents since 1997, the UK has one of the best industrial health and safety records in the world. And yet 40 million working days are still lost every year through occupational ill-health and injury.

Individuals' and the nation's health, then, continues to be an area demanding urgent attention and action.

*

Jottings 11: Health

More than 15 million Britons have at least one long-term health problem • The number with 3 or more long-term health conditions is likely to rise to nearly 3 million by 2018 • These problems derive largely from lifestyle choices such as smoking, alcohol, overeating and unhealthy diet • More than 1 in 10 Britons have private health insurance • People over 45 drink more alcohol than young people do • Between 2007 and 2011 the percentage of young men (16 to 24) drinking more than 8 units on at least one day a week fell from 32 to 22 per cent, and young women from 24 to 18 per cent • Harmful use of alcohol costs the NHS £2.7 billion annually • In Britain, 3.8 million people have diabetes • 37 per cent of 11 year-olds are overweight • 1 in 7 hospital patients in Britain has diabetes • It is estimated that by 2050, 60 per cent of men, 50 per cent of women and 25 per cent of children will be obese • Obesity costs billions of NHS pounds each year • By 2050, the annual cost of lost productivity through obesity-related health problems will be £45 billion • Studies indicate that obesity can weaken the immune system • Obesity is principally a disorder of those less well-off, reducing life expectancy by 9 years • Fewer than half of 1 per cent of teenage girls get enough physical exercise • Compared with those in more affluent families, poor children are more likely to suffer ill-health • It has been suggested that TV advertising of 'junk' food should be restricted to post-9pm watershed • Cocaine users are thought to be unconcerned about the associated risks of heart disease and mental health problems • Each year, nearly 9,000 Britons die from alcohol-related diseases • In the UK, the annual social cost of alcohol is £20 billion, one third attributed to crime and public nuisance • 75 per cent of Asian women are non-drinkers, 38 per cent of black women and 23 per cent of white women • Non-drinkers who are inactive are twice as likely to risk heart disease as moderate drinkers who take exercise • In one recent year, more than 5,000 children under 16 were admitted to hospital as a result of alcohol abuse; more than half were girls • 40 per cent of unemployed young people may have mental health problems • In a poll of MS sufferers, 67 per cent worried about their ability to manage because of benefits changes • Binge drinking is likely to lead to unsafe sex • Problems facing 16 year-old binge drinkers: 60 per cent more likely to be alcoholics by age 30, 40 per cent more likely to be users of illegal drugs, 40 per cent more likely to suffer mental health problems,

60 per cent more likely to be homeless • Government investment in enforcement, education and treatment has resulted in a fall in the overall level of drug usage in the UK • However, 13 per cent of British schoolchildren say they have tried cannabis before they were 13 • Although the overall number of deaths in the UK from drug misuse has fallen, the numbers in Scotland have risen • Cannabis contains similar carcinogens to cigarette tobacco, and cannabis smoke is even more toxic than tobacco smoke • Nearly a quarter of British adults still smoke cigarettes • The NHS spends £1.7 billion annually treating smoking-related disease • Smoking-related diseases kill 106,000 people a year in Britain • People with mental health problems are more at risk of losing their jobs than people with physical disability • Each year, nearly a third of the workforce will have a mental health problem at some time • Depression, anxiety and stress account for 80 million work days lost each year • In the UK, 150,000 people a year suffer a stroke • After heart disease and cancer, strokes are the third biggest killer in the UK (50,000 deaths a year) — that is, 9 per cent of all deaths in men and 13 per cent of deaths in women • In the UK, strokes are the largest single cause of severe disability, with a greater disability impact than any other chronic disease • Over 300,000 people in the UK are living with moderate to severe disabilities as a result of a stroke • In the UK, more than 2 million women a year are screened for breast cancer • Women not screened for breast cancer are twice as likely to die from the disease as women who are screened • Asian women are 18 per cent less likely than white women to get breast cancer and black women 15 per cent less likely • In poorer areas, death rates from cancer are dramatically higher than in wealthier areas: 70 per cent for men, 41 per cent for women • Each year, air pollution is a cause of 24,000 premature deaths in Britain • Children living within 500 metres of a motorway have more lung damage and lower life expectancy than others • Unpaid care in the UK is valued at £87 billion annually • By 2030 the total of 6 million unpaid carers will have grown to 9 million • Osteoarthritis affects 2 million people in Britain and there is no known cure • Studies suggest that 50 per cent of knee osteoarthritis and 60 per cent of hip osteoarthritis is linked to genetic factors • More than 2 million people in the UK buy prescription drugs on the internet; but 50 per cent of drugs seized by the healthcare regulatory authority (MHRA) were fake • About half a

million people in Britain are thought to be suffering from Alzheimer's • The risk of suffering from Alzheimer's and other dementia may be more than halved by eating an omega-3 rich diet • Omega-3 is said to give protection not only against dementia but also cardiovascular disease • The recommended daily intake of omega-3 is about 450 mg • Most adults eat around half that amount; teenagers eat perhaps 100 mg a day • Healthier diet could prevent something like 70,000 premature deaths a year • One third of heart disease and perhaps a quarter of cancers may in some way be diet-related • There is a north–south divide as well as a gender gap in life expectancy: for men, 72.5 years in the north, 82.6 in the south; and for women, 78.1 years in the north, 86.2 in the south • A substantial minority of dissatisfied NHS patients do not complain because they expect no improvements or changes; others fear that their complaints might lead to reprisals of some kind • A majority of NHS staff say they would welcome patients expressing their concerns, but get insufficient feedback.

▪ As a result of researching and studying the theme of Health introduced by these jottings, what action are we planning to take?

Jottings 12:
Housing and homelessness

The *Universal Declaration of Human Rights* states that 'Everyone has the right to a standard of living adequate for the health and well-being of himself [sic] and of his family, including… housing'. Clearly this basic human right is far from universally experienced in Britain.

In thinking about housing in the context of social construction (no pun intended), it is important to remember the difference between people who *have* a problem and people who may be considered to *be* a problem. People who are homeless clearly *have* a problem. As a result of being homeless, they experience a whole range of physical and emotional difficulties and misery. Why they are in the position of being homeless or remain in that situation is a question.

People who are homeless may also be perceived to *be* a problem. 'They' intrude into 'our' lives. For example, 'the homeless' may be thought to be a nuisance in our towns and cities, begging or sleeping rough in doorways, or drinking in public places.

It seems that for those who *have* the problem of homelessness, there is a need for the ways in which housing provision is arranged to be changed very radically. On the other hand, those who *are* a problem may benefit from being helped to understand that there may be some options, and to see that there are advantages to be had by conforming to 'normal' standards. Ultimately, of course, the choice would be theirs to make.

People are homeless if they do not have a legal right to occupy any accommodation, or if the accommodation they do have is unsuitable to live in. In reality, the majority of 'the homeless' are not sleeping rough; they may be families or single people staying with relatives or friends on a temporary basis, or in bed and breakfast accommodation, hostels, night shelters or some other temporary provision. For many, the poor quality of such accommodation is detrimental to their health and well-being.

Jottings 12: Housing and homelessness

Having a home is not simply having a roof over one's head. A home is a place which one calls 'one's own', an affordable place providing security and privacy, with links to a supportive community.

It is the norm to be housed. However, it must be questioned how a society which fails to invest adequately in social housing can be justified in treating as 'other' those who are marginalised and socially excluded by the lack of such housing.

*

England has 710,000 empty homes • The number of homeless households in the UK has doubled in 10 years • There are 1.5 million households on waiting lists in England alone • 94,000 homeless households are in temporary accommodation • In 2011, 1.06 million households in England (nearly 5 per cent of the population) were classified as overcrowded, double 10 ago • Overcrowding at home profoundly affects underachievement at school • In 2012 nearly 6,000 people were sleeping on London streets • In 2012 people sleeping rough in England had increased by 23 per cent over the previous year • In 2013 house prices rose by an average of over 8 per cent—in Manchester by 21 per cent, in London by 15 per cent • In 2014, only 3 per cent of 18–30 year-olds were home buyers • Owner occupation accounts for 72 per cent of all domestic accommodation • Local authority and housing association homes form 18 per cent of the total, and private landlords the remaining 10 per cent • The value of property in Britain now accounts for 60 per cent of the nation's wealth • The combined value of privately owned housing is 3 times the whole economy's annual output • Increasing numbers of people cannot afford to buy their own home • In the past decade, house prices have risen by more than 200 per cent, while average wages have risen by 94 per cent • The average house price is in the order of 7 times annual earnings; some foresee that rising to 8 times • The average house price has been forced up as a result of a huge increase in buying-to-let • The concept of a property-owning democracy implies that home ownership confers full citizenship • There is also an implication that not wishing to own one's home is deviant • The right-to-buy transferred 1.7 million council houses to private ownership • Failure to replace those sold properties has reduced the stock of social housing by a third • Social housing is reducing as a proportion of the total housing stock • There is a political intention to extend the right-to-buy • The incidence of damp reports in social housing has risen in line with energy bills • 9 out of 10 housing associations noted increased condensation damp in social housing, caused by inadequate heating • Housing has significant influence on social justice: those living in poor areas suffer a number of disadvantages: health, education, opportunities • In London, 1 in 3 socially-housed families lives in overcrowded conditions • It is thought that, nationally, half a million families live in overcrowded conditions • Approval of social housing applications outstrips supply of new homes by 4 to 1 • Only 23 per cent of housing association tenants work and do not claim housing benefits • 63 per cent of housing association tenants are on benefits, almost 20 per cent are single parents, 33 per cent are retired • It is questioned whether social tenancy for life encourages welfare dependency • It is calculated that if the wages of a family in social housing increased from £100 to £400 a week, they would be only £23 a week better off (if they then rented from a private landlord) or £55 a week better off (if they remained as social housing tenants), since they would lose housing benefit • There are therefore questions about incentives for socially-housed tenants to seek and gain employment • An argument is that an affordable rent helps socially-housed tenants back into the labour market • When it comes to seeking and gaining employment, tenants of social housing tend to be disadvantaged—as lone parents, for example, or with lack of qualification or skills, or high levels of ill health or disability • Of the 4 million people living in social housing, 2.6 million are of working age, but more than half of these are unemployed • Almost three quarters of social tenants under 25 are unemployed • If the government's house-building targets are to be met, 1.8 million will have to be built on green belt • The current rate of new house building needs to increase six-fold if the government's target is to be met • Some estimate that far more new houses will be needed, to enable a whole generation to get on to the property ladder • New households are increasing at more than 200,000 a year, all needing housing • In rural areas, 45 per cent of new households aged between 16 and 35 cannot afford housing in their home communities • Only 5 per cent of housing in rural communities is social housing, compared with 23 per cent nationally • Government claims that half

Jottings 12: Housing and homelessness

of the extra 40,000 new homes planned each year will be social housing • A new government body, the Homes and Communities Agency, aims to increase the supply of new affordable homes in England • By 2015, this agency will have invested £4.5bn through its Affordable Homes Programme • It remains to be seen how the agency will have improved ways in which land is made available for social housing • Such land has tended to be low-cost land 'on the wrong side of the tracks' • Almost half of all social housing is located in a fifth of the most deprived areas • The criteria set by planning authorities for 'much sought-after' new housing developments may be questioned: how efficient is land usage in such developments? • It is suggested that the land occupied by an owner-occupied house has a rental value and should be taxed • The top 20 per cent of the population more than recoup their annual income tax through their homes' appreciating value • The bottom 20 per cent do not have this benefit because they live in rented property • A survey of recent housing developments reported that only 18 per cent were 'very good' and 25 per cent should never have been built • These developments were criticised for being poorly planned and badly located: to what extent did that criticism reflect privileged and elitist values? • Specially adapted accommodation is needed by 1.4 million people living in social housing • Home modifications would allow people with disability to move out of residential care into their own homes, reducing residential home costs by £10 million a year in England alone • However, this would put yet more pressure on social housing • Anti-discrimination legislation requires landlords to make 'reasonable adjustments' for disabled tenants • Local authorities maintain registers of adapted and accessible properties • Even so, there are far too few properties which are suited to the needs of people with disability.

▪ As a result of researching and studying the theme of Housing and homelessness introduced by these jottings, what action are we planning to take?

Jottings 13: Media

This topic merits a place in a discussion of social issues, since media feed into a number of problems highlighted in other sections. The reason for the prime focus being on computers, the internet and other digital devices is that, while they have such remarkably innovative and positive potential, they can at the same time be the source of major problems. Child pornography and paedophile grooming of young people are perhaps two of the most obvious and serious examples; cyberbullying is another.

Increasingly, questions are being asked about the 'digital insurgency', and the ways in which shadowy organisations are tuning in to our private communication. There is a need to balance the interests of national security with our personal privacy and civil rights. None the less, 'they' are monitoring our habits and interests, in effect watching our every move, 'harvesting' and storing untold quantities of personal data. What may in fact be unauthorised or uncontrolled third party access to Twitter, Facebook and Skype, for example, facilitates an understanding of the influence that social media has on our everyday lives, invaluable information for governments and commercial interests. And the instant exchange of digital information facilitates synchronised collective action—illustrated, further afield, by the Arab spring in north Africa, and nearer home by student protests in London, and riots in London and other English towns in 2011.

But there are other questions, not implying a criminal quality, certainly, but having social significance none the less. For example, what is meant by the freedom of the press? What controls, if any, should be in place, and who decides what those controls should be? What of television—when it comes to drama, for example, does anything go?

There is no intention here of taking Mrs Grundy's position, siding with those who volubly attack books which they have not read, or films or plays or television programmes they have not seen. But there is every intention of encouraging an examination of these and other

Jottings 13: Media

questions, questions about the negative influence and power of the media, as well as their potential for good.

*

In 3 recent years, the number of child abuse images for sale on the internet more than quadrupled, from 7 per cent of images monitored to 29 per cent • In one year, the internet watchdog investigated nearly 32,000 reports of illegal images, mainly of children under 12 • Contrary to a common view, it is over-65s who use the internet most • On average, over-65s use the internet for 42 hours a month, compared with 25 hours by teenagers • Women aged between 25 and 34 spend more time on the internet than men in the same age group, forming a valuable and receptive market for online advertisers • Money spent on online advertising is two and a half times more effective than the same amount spent on other media, a clear indicator of the power of the internet • Online advertising spend is around £2.5 billion a year, and is increasing at around 30 per cent annually • Analysts forecast that online advertising spend will soon surpass television advertising expenditure, which grows at only 2 to 3 per cent a year • Online advertisers are able to use 'behavioural targeting' to deliver their sales message direct to the computers of individual potential customers, after tracking their internet search usage • Individual use of the internet, watching television and listening to the radio, and time spent on the telephone, occupies an average of 50 hours a week • Identity theft, largely via the internet, costs the UK economy £1.7 billion a year, at the very least • Three quarters of 11 year-olds have their own television set, games console and mobile telephone • More children watch television in bed before going to sleep (63 per cent) than read a book each day • 80 per cent of children read a book at some point in their own time, 53 per cent once a week, but only 25 per cent do so daily • Popularity of internet social networks is measured in literally tens of millions of users • Nearly a fifth of 16 to 25 year-olds have published sensitive information in an internet chat room or social network • Almost 60 per cent of these young people were unaware that personal information placed online remains permanently linked to them • More than 50 per cent of young people have had an unwelcome experience following use of social network websites, including sexual abuse and bullying • To what extent is there generational prejudice against video games and similar electronic pursuits? • Advertising standards require that all marketing communications are prepared with a sense of responsibility to consumers and society • Ofcom aims to ensure that television and radio audiences are adequately protected from harmful or offensive material, and that people are protected from unfair treatment in television and radio programmes and from infringements of privacy • A third of complaints to the Advertising Standards Authority are about online advertisements • There are calls for more control on inappropriate marketing to children via internet, television and mobile phone messaging • Teachers believe that advertisers infiltrate children's lives, and undermine education's role of developing children's ability to think critically and draw their own conclusions • Specifically, there are concerns about the 'sexualisation' of adolescent (and younger) girls through marketing messages which 'reinforce the notion that image and fashion are everything' • Magazine websites are encouraging young teenage girls to upload photographs of themselves and compare their bodies • The internet and television commercials commonly portray female body images in ways which are considered to debase women sexually • This raises questions about what girls think they need to do or look like in order to please boys... and what expectations boys may have about relationships when they see such images • Nearly three quarters of 18 year-olds say internet pornography leads to unrealistic views about sex • More than half of young women aged between 16 and 25 say the media make them believe the most important thing is to be pretty and thin • Is this an issue relating only to women's bodies? • Photographs in advertisements for male toiletries, for example, show 'ideal' beautiful, barely-clothed young men • Major brands promote expensive clothing, toys and electronic items to families unable to afford them • Questions have been asked about changes in film/DVD classification and changing (lower?) standards: films of a kind once classified as 18 may now be 15; and 18 DVD/films may now be pornographic • Long-banned video 'nasties' are now readily available on the high street • There is criticism of films which juxtapose (for example) the sound of calls to prayer and images of mosques with explosions and indiscriminate killing, thus demonising Islam • You cannot believe every-

Jottings 13: Media

thing you read in the papers: a study of 2,000 newspaper stories revealed that the information in only 12 per cent had been thoroughly checked by the writer: 80 per cent of the news items were based on second hand and unverified information • Tabloid journalists are trusted by only 10 per cent of the population • A great majority of national newspaper articles about Muslims have been shown to be negative; only 4 per cent of several hundred studied were positive • Is it permissible for television comedy programmes to portray any group (racial, religious, ethnic, disabled, sex-orientation) in a negative or derisory way? • How would the television series from the 1960s and 1970s, *Till Death Us Do Part*, screen today? • Is it permissible for comedians to tell jokes through public media, on the basis of 'anything goes'? • Are there different rules for such jokes to be told in private? • Is there any argument for media censorship? • How would so-called 'top shelf' magazines feature within such an argument, if at all? • What are the links, if any, between under-age drinking and advertising and other media images? • Advertisements for alcohol appear in commercial breaks during popular television programmes screened between 3 and 5pm, when children are watching • Should television advertising of 'junk' food, high on fat, salt and sugar, be restricted to (say) a post-9pm watershed? • For discussion: mass media has reduced or removed much long-established prejudice against regional accents: what are the pros and cons of young people taking (say) East End voices or so-called Estuary English as a speech standard?

▪ As a result of researching and studying the theme of <u>Media</u> introduced by these jottings, what action are we planning to take?

Jottings 14: Old age

By the end of 2014, nearly half of the country's 'senior citizens' possessed a smartphone. That consumerist statistic may be put forward by some as a measure of progress. Others may not consider it to be deserving of a place high on the agenda here, but think other issues to be more pressing.

Ten million people in the UK are over 65 years of age. It is expected that there will be five and a half million more elderly people in twenty years' time, and the number will have nearly doubled to around 19 million by 2050. Within this total, the number of very old people grows even faster. There are currently three million people aged more than 80 years and that may have doubled by 2030 and reach eight million by 2050. While one in six of the UK population is currently aged 65 or over, by 2050 it will be one in four.

The pensioner population is expected to increase despite the rise in women's state pension age to 65 by 2020 and the rise for both men and women from 65 to 68 between 2024 and 2046. In 2008 there were 3.2 people of working age for every person of pensionable age; this ratio is projected to fall to 2.8 by 2033.

Those relegated to Class E in the coldly-named National Statistics Socio-Economic Classification (the model used for compiling UK government statistics) are the people described as being 'at the lowest levels of subsistence', and that, according to the definition, includes pensioners and others depending on the state for their income. So, although quite clearly there are other issues affecting pensioners, and they are touched on below, it is largely with poverty and the difficulties that old people experience as a result of poverty (or at least, low incomes) that these jottings are concerned.

*

In the final decade of the twentieth century and the first decade of this, official figures show a fall in poverty among pensioners, down from 27 per cent of old people to 17 per cent • Even so, an estimated 1.8 million pensioners still live in poverty • Many pensioners are

Jottings 14: Old age

unaware of their entitlement to benefits • If they were to claim the pension credit due to them, 30,000 elderly home owners would be lifted out of poverty • 2 million pensioners are in poverty before housing costs • Almost 70 per cent of pensioners depend on state benefits for at least half of their income • Government proposals should make state pensions more generous, ensuring that pensioners have a greater share in rising national prosperity • The state pensionable age is to be equalised for men and women, and will continue to rise in line with life expectancy • The over-80s are the fastest growing age group in Britain • In 2008 for the first time there were more people of retirement age than children under 16 • Within 20 years, nearly one fifth of the population will be over retirement age • In that time, the older black and minority ethnic population will have doubled to 2 million • 1 in 10 people aged 65 and over are in employment • Between 2010 and 2014 the number of people aged over 64 had increased by a third • In 2013 nearly 4 per cent of employed people were 65 or older • Many older people postpone retirement because of a need to earn to maintain their living standards • 73 per cent of people over 65 are homeowners, and only 3 per cent rent private accommodation • 22 per cent of people aged over 65 rent their home from a local authority or housing association — a third of all tenants of social housing • Of those over 75, more women than men live alone — nearly two thirds of women, more than a quarter of men • Older Asian people are less likely to live alone than are other older people • People over 65 are more likely than those from other age groups to have contact with friends or neighbours less frequently than once a month • Women over 75 are more likely to end their own lives than any other group of women • 1 in 4 people over 65 have symptoms of depression, and 2 in 5 over 85 • Around 10 per cent of older people live in sheltered or retirement accommodation, or in a residential or care home • About 450,000 people live in care homes • Pensioners are more likely to live in energy-inefficient homes than are other age groups • It is thought that 9 per cent of pensioners live in damp homes — proportionally half as many again as the rest of the population • Government figures suggest that there are problems in the homes of 10 per cent of older people — problems of damp, infestation by vermin or insects, or poor lighting • Perhaps 40 per cent of older people spend between 5 and 10 per cent of their income on fuel (fuel poverty is basically defined as 10 per cent or more of the household income spent on necessary energy) • Something like 60 per cent of care homes fall short of the required standard for safe medication management • The prospect of having to go into a care home frightens two thirds of adults • 40 per cent of Britons fear loneliness in old age • 1 in 5 adults with a father over 60 does not have contact with him • On admission to hospital, 40 per cent of older people are malnourished • For many elderly people in hospital, meal times are an unpleasant experience, being given inappropriate food, perhaps, or insufficient time or help to eat their meal • As a result, older people in hospital are becoming malnourished • It is estimated that more than 280,000 frail old people need help with everyday life-sustaining tasks, but get none from care providers • Some 450,000 old people get limited assistance, but insufficient to ensure a decent level of wellbeing • Those with 'moderate needs' must pay for private care, or rely on family or neighbours to help • We are living longer, but our extra years are lived with poor quality of life—increasing disability, for example • 58 per cent of people dying at 95 or older have dementia, and 80 per cent have serious mental problems • It is thought that in the UK there are more than 10,000 people over 100, and by midcentury it is estimated that this could be 250,000 • The number of people with dementia is likely to increase to nearly a million in the next 10 to 15 years • In residential homes, insufficient attention is paid to basic standards of dignity and respect for people with dementia • Over the next 20 years it is estimated that the number of people over 85 will increase six times faster than the population as a whole, with a proportionate increase in the number of elderly people with disability • It is possible that 500,000 older people are being abused or maltreated, mainly in their own home, but also in care homes • This may involve verbal or emotional abuse, financial or other theft, and even physical assault • More than three quarters of such abuse is against people aged 70 and over • Age discrimination is a major problem, for example in the workplace • More adults complain about being discriminated against because of their age than about any other form of discrimination • In one study, a third of respondents had the view that people over 70 are incompetent and incapable • One study of older homeless people in day centres revealed that more than a quarter had been homeless for 25 years or longer • Elderly people have the highest fear of crime, but are the group least likely to become a victim · However, if they are attacked, older people suffer disproportionately.

▪ As a result of researching and studying the theme of <u>Old age</u> introduced by these jottings, what action are we planning to take?

Jottings 15: Poverty

There is no poverty in Britain. That is true if poverty is taken to be an absolute, the total lack of resources necessary for existence. Of the two billion people in the world without the basics for survival, it is unlikely that any of them are in Britain.

What is true, however, is that poverty is widespread in Britain, *relative to society as a whole*. A lack of money limits the choices which are readily available to the more affluent. Those experiencing social exclusion and inequality through poverty will not be intent on acquiring luxuries, but merely access to the minimum standard of living.

Polarised beliefs about poverty derive largely from a wish to find an explanation for the absence or existence of poverty in Britain: that is to say, they are socially constructed. There are things that 'everyone knows' about poverty and 'the poor'. Take the poverty trap, for example, implying that poor people are caught by circumstances beyond their control. Or the concept of opportunities for all, and the idea that there is no need for anyone to be poor in Britain; all one needs to do is see and seize the opportunities which are there.

To state that there is no *absolute* poverty in Britain, then, is to say that poverty is not a social problem. However, to state that *relative* poverty is widespread in Britain is to say that poverty is very much a social problem.

So there is a need to explore ways in which people may *have* a problem, and the extent to which people *are* a problem. Are there external conditions which create poverty and make people poor, and if so, what are they? Can those conditions be changed, to reduce or eliminate social exclusion and inequality? Or do people bring poverty on themselves, have they only themselves to blame? If so how does that come about, and what can be done to change it?

*

Relative poverty is defined here as *a household income below 60 per cent of the national average* • Absolute poverty is the deprivation of basic human needs, including food, safe drinking water, sanitation facilities, health, shelter and education • In the UK, something approaching a third of children live in poor families (perhaps as many as 3.8 million) • 25 per cent of white children live in poverty, contrasted with 74 per cent of Bangladeshi children, 60 per cent of Pakistani children and 56 per cent of black children • 29 per cent of disabled children live in poverty • A government objective is to eliminate child poverty by 2020 • A study suggests that there will be 400,000 more children in poverty in the UK by 2015 • In 2013, 47 per cent of children in Greater Manchester lived in poverty • In 2013, in at least two London boroughs 42 per cent of children lived in poverty — contrasted with 7 per cent in a wealthier borough • Although a government target to lift 1 million children out of poverty by 2006 was missed, 600,000 *were* lifted out of poverty • It is said that the government needs to invest a further £4 billion to hit the 2020 target • Increasing the top rate of income tax by one penny would raise that £4 billion in three years • Something like 40 per cent of adults believe there is little child poverty in the country • Poor people in employment do essential work on which society depends, but do not earn enough to support a family • Large numbers of people on low pay and the 'seeming acceptance of gross inequalities of rates of pay' mean future poverty remains inevitable • There are 1.5 million households whose weekly income is only £10 (or less) above the poverty line • One third of the 1.3 million families living in poverty have only one bread winner — twice as many as those with two earning • Fuel poverty is experienced by 2.4 million households • There is food poverty, too: nearly one million people received food parcels in 2013-14 • The wealth of the top 3 per cent of Britons is 3 times greater than that of the whole bottom half of the population • The top 10 per cent of households own 54 per cent of the nation's wealth, with 26 per cent of all disposable income; while the bottom 10 per cent have only 3 per cent of the disposable income between them • In 2013, the poorest quarter of the population gambled £13.2 billion pounds in betting shops • The top 10 per cent pay less than the average ratio of tax to income, whereas the bottom 10 per cent pay more than the average • The average pay of chief executives values them 100 times higher than the average employee • Even larger differentials are apparent in (for example) supermarkets, where the chief executive's remuneration is likely to be several hundred times higher than that of the average employee, typically women and part-time staff • Nearly 300,000 working adults in Britain earn less than the minimum wage • 60 per cent of people believe the government should set a limit to senior management earnings • Government use of targeted benefits rather than resolving underlying issues such as workplace inequality is to be questioned • Half of the 3.8 million children living in poverty have a parent already in paid work • A low-paid couple can only avoid poverty if both are working • Services such as fuel, energy and banking cost poor families £1,000 a year more than better off households, because they do not have access to preferential deals and offers •. Poor families using pre-paid gas and electricity meters are charged substantially more than more affluent households paying by direct debit • Extra charges can be £100 or more a year • More than 3 million families have their energy supply metered • Adequate heating is seen by 90 per cent of people as the number one necessity for a family in their home (the next in the top five were an indoor toilet, not shared with others; freedom from damp; a bathroom, not shared with others; beds for everyone[1]) • A fifth of families with children under 17 cannot afford to warm their homes adequately • 15 per cent of households have to choose between paying for heating and how much they can spend on food • Mothers (especially single parents) rarely earn enough to lift their families out of poverty • Official figures show a fall in poverty among pensioners, from 27 per cent in the 1990s to 17 per cent, and among single pensioners from 33 per cent to 17 per cent • Even so, an estimated 1.8 million pensioners live in poverty • Many pensioners seem unaware of their entitlement to benefits: of those eligible, perhaps 30 per cent are not claiming pension credit, 10 per cent are not claiming housing benefit, and 40 per cent are not claiming council tax benefit • If they were to claim the pension credit due to them, 30,000 elderly home owners would be lifted out of poverty • 2 million pensioners are in poverty before housing costs • Almost 70 per cent of pensioners depend on state benefits for at least half of their income • Perhaps 40 per cent of older people spend between 5 and 10 per cent of their income on fuel: fuel poverty is basically defined as 10 per cent or more of the household income needing to be spent to maintain satisfactory heating • Poor children living in affluent areas are bullied by their better-off peers • Poor

Jottings 15: Poverty

families feel less able to depend on their neighbours' help than do more affluent households • Only 45 per cent of poor families feel safe at night in their neighbourhood, compared with 86 per cent of the more well-to-do • Surveys suggest that the great majority of people believe that we are judged by class: the poorest people are those who experience this most acutely, with 55 per cent saying that class and not ability influences the way they are treated • Obesity tends to be more common among poorer people, with adverse effects on already low self-image and quality of life • The lowest performing group of school-leavers are white boys from disadvantaged areas: 85 per cent fail to achieve 5 good GCSEs.

▪ As a result of researching and studying the theme of Poverty introduced by these jottings, what action are we planning to take?

1 In the 1980s, a MORI survey identified thirty-five 'necessities of life', of which these are the top five. The complete list is in J. Mack and S. Lansley, 'Absolute and Relative Poverty' in A. Giddens (ed.), *Sociology: Introductory Readings*.

Jottings 16: Other concerns

By definition, this final section is for you and your learning community to complete. The first fifteen sets of jottings were provided to enable you to take a look at and think about a number of issues, some of which you may have agreed are social problems (or you may not), others may link to social problems, or they may have acted as prompts for you to think about issues which are not included in this book. Here is your opportunity to compile your own agenda for study and action.

It may be that the list is endless, all the way from major, global matters which affect the whole of humankind, such as war and peace, and food and water for all, to local issues such as the motorists who ignore the speed limit in my village.

A social attitudes survey indicated that a majority of Britons believe that doctors should be allowed legally to end the life of terminally ill patients, at their request: so, what are the issues surrounding euthanasia? And what of loneliness, civil liberties, abortion, human rights, animal rights, people trafficking, the trading policies of multinational corporations, slavery, prostitution, investing in the arms industry, gambling, and countless other issues of which you are doubtless aware?

Over to you!

Epilogue

Where to now?

2020 Vision

The two ideas which '2020 Vision' is intended to suggest are these: first, looking ahead to the year 2020, visualising ways in which the fulfilment society is beginning to develop, and ways in which a new social order is being built. The year 2020 provides a short-term, interim goal towards which the fulfilment society can progress, putting its agenda into effect. That vision for the year 2020 and beyond will have as its focus what it means *in practice* to love God (that shorthand form just one more time!) and to love our neighbour as ourselves.

The second idea has to do with 20/20 vision as the 'normal acuity' of eyesight. But that does not accurately enough express this second meaning of 2020 Vision. It is not *normal* vision but *extraordinary* vision that is needed, creative imagination and insight, if the world is to be remade. More of the same will not be good enough.

The underlying theme of this book has been the need to learn, and to go on learning, in order to stay ahead in a fast-changing world, in this 'fugitive present'. The challenge has been, and continues to be, for learning communities within the fulfilment society constantly to question orthodoxy, the 'body of knowledge', finding ways to deconstruct and then reconstruct words and concepts—both in what it means to believe, and how to give expression to belief in remaking the world. That learning will itself be an unending process.

In this age of discontinuity, then, the only permanence on which the fulfilment society will be able to rely is change. Change is here to stay. The fulfilment society's goals will need to be updated constantly, and so the year 2020 must not be seen as an endpoint: it is merely an early staging post.

There will be a continuing need to enable others to catch the vision, to recruit others to the community of learners, welcoming their questions and challenges and inputs, however uncomfortable that may be. New worlds require new thinkers.

Transformative leaders are needed now, those rare people who are remarkable for their organising skills but who will on no account be seduced into the dead-end of creating an organisation.

If at any time the fulfilment society believes the job is done, it will have lost sight of the transient nature of an impermanent world. If at any point the fulfilment society believes it has arrived at journey's end, it will in fact have lost its way.

>This journey has no end.
>Each new day,
>the horizon beckons still.

Appendix 1
A Supreme Court opinion on 'religion'

In July 2013, an appeal was heard by five justices in the Supreme Court in London. The leading judgment was given by Lord Toulson in December 2013. The appeal concerned the question whether a church of the Church of Scientology might be recorded as a 'place of meeting for religious worship'.

A summary of the judgment is included here,[1] not as a comment on Scientology, but simply to provide an example of current thinking about words such as religion, belief and spiritual (as seen from a legal standpoint) and how understanding changes over time.

The Church of Scientology had made a similar application in 1970; but the Court of Appeal rejected it on the grounds that 'Scientology did not involve "religious worship" since it did not involve "reverence or veneration of God or of a Supreme Being", but rather instruction in philosophy'. Making that judgment, Lord Denning added, 'there may be a belief in the spirit of man, but there is no belief in a spirit of God'.

In hearing the new appeal, the first question that the court had to answer was whether Scientology is to be regarded as a religion. The interpretation of 'religious worship' in the Court of Appeal judgment in 1970 implied a theistic definition of religion: what that court's definition required was reverence for God. However, there has never been a universal legal definition of religion in English law, given the variety of world religions, changes in society and the different legal contexts in which the issues arise.

It was Lord Toulson's suggestion now that the concept of 'religion' should not be confined to faiths involving a supreme deity, since to do so would exclude Buddhism, Jainism, Taoism and other faiths. The court heard evidence that Scientologists do believe in a supreme deity, but one of an abstract and impersonal nature. In a different context, the Charities Act 2006 states that 'religion' includes faiths not involving belief in a god.

Religion could summarily be described as a belief system held by a group of adherents, which claims to explain mankind's place in the universe and relationship with the infinite, and to teach its adherents how they are to live their lives in conformity with the spiritual understanding associated with the belief system. On this approach, Scientology was clearly a religion.

By spiritual or non-secular, Lord Toulson said he meant a belief system which goes beyond what can be perceived by the senses or ascertained by the application of science. Such a belief system may or may not involve belief in a supreme being, but it does involve a belief that there is more to be understood about humankind's nature and relationship to the universe than can be gained from the senses or from science. He emphasised, however, that this was intended to be a description and not a definitive formula.

[1] Source: www.supremecourt.gov.uk. For the full text of the judgment, see Decided cases, 11 December 2013, Case number UKSC 2013/0030.

Appendix 2
Developing the effective working group

A number of ideas are included here to help the working group to develop its effectiveness. Clearly it is for the group itself to determine how to use these checklists, of course, and there is no one right way. In fact, it is for the group to decide whether or not it agrees with the factors listed. Some groups have found it useful to work though the lists, first prioritising the attributes as (for example) must-have, should-have, could-have. Then, an assessment is made of the extent to which the 'must-haves' are present in the group; and if they are not present, or not well-developed as characteristic of the group's working methods, decisions are made on how to develop those characteristic behaviours.

*

First and foremost, the members of an effective work group establish and share explicit goals or objectives • The effective work group is synergetic: that is to say, its achievements are greater than the sum of its individual parts • The working group gets moving quickly, and maintains a rapid pace • Even so, a high level of personal attention and economy of expression mean that all relevant issues are explored • Its members participate willingly in tackling individuals' problems • The working group is not leader dependent: that is, all members share responsibility for success and failure • Early questions for the learning community include: what will leadership mean, how will it be established, is formal leadership necessary? • Members are clear on roles and relationships within the group (the concept of 'team' roles is introduced in Chapter 4) • There are flexible and explicit ways of working, which are understood and observed by all • The working group allocates time to 'process' issues: structure, relationships, objectives, how time is used, how conflict is resolved and so on • Openness is such that relationship issues can always be discussed in a mature way • There is an air of competence, and boredom is rarely felt at meetings • Over a period of time, levels of individual contribution are more or less equal • Individual members have developed personal skills that are appreciated and valued by the group • Members learn while they work • The working group thinks results first, then method, but acknowledges that both are equally important • An effective working group will hone its working methods so that they become an informal discipline • Each member values and respects the contribution of the others • Each member can and does use the other members, including the leader, as a resource • Disagreements are worked through by discussion, and the use of voting is sparing and normally only as a last resort • Members enjoy the group's meetings.

* * *

Other criteria against which the work group might assess itself are:
 • *Task effectiveness* • *Positive atmosphere* • *Absence of negative behaviour.*

1: Task effectiveness

Does the working group use a methodical approach? • Are resources (time, people's skills and knowledge) used effectively? • How are ideas co-ordinated? By a facilitator? (The facilitator's role is not to teach, but to help the group focus on *learning*, encourage positive contributions, and ensure that all contribute.) • Do members seek and give information and opinions? • Are ideas expanded and tested in the group? • Are summarising and restating of ideas and suggestions used to aid understanding and progress? • Is action initiated and are members committed to it?

2: Positive atmosphere

Are members' contributions valued and accepted? • Are members brought into discussion and given the chance to be heard? • Does the

Appendix 2: Developing the effective working group 215

working group set standards for itself to use in choosing procedures and evaluating decisions? • Are feelings expressed and are personal issues dealt with? • Do members thoughtfully, rather than grudgingly, accept the decisions of the group?

3: Absence of negative behaviour

Do members withdraw by daydreaming, chatting with others, or wandering from the subject? • Is competition with other members expressed by attempts to offer the most ideas, play the most roles, talk the most? • Are members aggressive, criticising or blaming others and showing hostility or deflating others? • Do members use the group for self-confession, excessively delving into personal, non-group oriented feelings or points of view? • Do members disrupt by being flippant? • Do members block progress by going off at tangents, arguing too much on a point, or rejecting ideas without consideration?

Appendix 3

A learning review

What have I learnt today?
What do I know now that I did not know before?
What can I do now that I could not do before?

Learning has been defined as a more or less permanent change in behaviour, as a result of a specific experience. Acquiring new skills means that we are now able to do something that we could not do before, or do better something that we were already able to do, but now can improve upon. Acquiring new knowledge also means that our behaviour is likely to be modified in some way.

While it is true that in one way or another we learn something every day, much of it is random, unplanned, accidental and is 'learnt' rather passively. Something happens, but we are not quite sure what or why, and so the quality or the effectiveness of the 'learning' must be questioned.

This learning review (or better still, learning journal) is intended to encourage you to practise being an active learner: actively seeking learning opportunities, and taking some simple steps to analyse the experience — that is, to learn from it.

These are suggestions for the kind of questions that you may ask, but over time you will develop your own methods for analysing your learning experiences.

It is important that you keep a written journal, in a notebook or literally in a diary. You may prefer to keep an electronic notebook, of course. Just how often you make entries is for you to decide. Some studies suggest that once a week is sufficient; others recommend a daily journal, as far as is possible. You may wish to vary the frequency from time to time. Your ability to put the process to good use will determine which frequency is right for you.

- *First, make a note of the event or experience: for example*
  What happened? To what extent did I initiate it?
  Other questions or observations

- *Review the experience: for example*
  How did it come about? How did I feel? Who else was involved?
  How did we interact? What went well? What did not go so well?
  What did I do?
  Other questions or observations

- *Draw some conclusions: for example*
  How did this compare with earlier similar experiences (if any)?
  What would I want to repeat? What would I want to avoid in future?
  What would I do differently? What did I learn about other people?
  Other questions or observations

- *Think about the next steps: for example*
  What are the applications for what I have learnt?
  How will I use what I have learnt?
  What would I do in similar circumstances in future?
  Is there anything about my learning style that I would like to change?
  Other questions or observations

Appendix 4

A personal check-up: For your eyes only

The purpose of this personal check-up is to help you focus on the topics of social problems and social exclusion, which are at the heart of the third part of this book, and to give thought to your own values and attitudes.

Remember that *this is for your eyes only* and there is no expectation that you will share your findings with anyone else, unless you choose to do so.

Here are the main section headings in Part 3: tick any which you consider to be social problems.

- ☐ Children and young people
- ☐ Crime
- ☐ Disablement
- ☐ Ecology and the environment
- ☐ Education
- ☐ Employment
- ☐ Equality of opportunity
- ☐ Ethnicity, 'race' and immigration
- ☐ Family and marriage
- ☐ Gender and sexuality
- ☐ Health
- ☐ Housing
- ☐ Media
- ☐ Old age
- ☐ Poverty

Perhaps you do not see these at social problems in themselves, but can think of social problems which might be included under one or more of the headings.

What are they?

What words would you use to describe the people who *have* these problems, or the people who *are* these problems?

Appendix 4: A personal check-up

To what extent would you identify those 'problem' people as 'them', while you/your family/your friends are identified as 'us'?

What would you say 'everybody knows' about those 'problem' people?

Which of those people (if any) would you describe as being socially excluded?

If so, would you say they have been excluded by an 'official' agency of some kind (for example), or by other circumstances, or have they excluded themselves?

If you have negative thoughts or feelings about, or consider it possible that you have prejudice towards, any of those 'problem' people, what are they?

To what extent will these questions and your answers to them affect your thinking as you work through the remainder of the book?

Bibliography

Aikman, D., *Billy Graham: His Life and Influence*, Thomas Nelson 2007.

Aland, K., et al. (eds.), *Novum Testamentum Graece*, 26th edition, Stuttgart: Deutsche Bibelstiftung 1979.

Alcock, P. and Erskine, A., 'Divisions, Difference and Exclusion' in *The Student's Companion to Social Policy*, 1998; 2nd edn. 2003, Alcock, P., Erskine, A. and May, M. (eds.), Blackwell 1998.

Aldridge, F. and Tuckett, A., *The Road to Nowhere?* NIACE 2007.

Armstrong, K., *A History of God*, Heinemann 1993.

Barclay, W., *Jesus as They Saw Him*, SCM Press 1962.

Berger, P.L. and Luckmann, T., *The Social Construction of Reality*, Penguin University Books 1971.

Berne, E., *Games People Play*, André Deutsch 1966.

Betjeman, J., *John Betjeman's Collected Poems*, John Murray 1984.

Betjeman, J., *Sweet Songs of Zion: Selected Radio Talks*, Stephen Games (ed.), Hodder and Stoughton 2007.

Bloch, E., *The Principle of Hope (Das Prinzip Hoffnung)*, N. Plaice, S. Plaice and P. Knight (trs.), Blackwell 1986.

Bonhoeffer, D., *Letters and Papers from Prison*, SCM Press 1953.

British Social Attitudes Survey, National Centre for Social Research: http://www.natcen.ac.uk.

Brown, C.G., *Religion and Society in Twentieth-Century Britain*, Pearson Education 2006.

Buber, M., *Tales of the Hasidim: The Early Masters*, Schocken Books 1947.

Cameron, R. (ed.), *The Other Gospels: Non-Canonical Gospel Texts*, Lutterworth Press 1983.

Copley, T., *Indoctrination, Education and God: The Struggle for the Mind*, SPCK 2005.

Cupitt, D., *The Sea of Faith*, BBC Publications 1984; 2nd edn, revised, SCM Press 1994.

Cupitt, D., 'After Religion—What?' in *Sofia* No. 80, Journal of the Sea of Faith Network, November 2006.

Davies, O. and Bowie, F., *Celtic Spirituality: Medieval and Modern*, SPCK 1995.

Dawes, H., *Freeing the Faith: A Credible Christianity for Today*, SPCK 1992.

Bibliography

Dawkins, R., *The God Delusion*, Bantam Press 2006.
de Bono, E., *Lateral Thinking*, Penguin Books 1977.
de Botton, A., *A Religion for Atheists*, Hamish Hamilton 2012.
De Graaf, N.D. and Need, A., 'Losing Faith: Is Britain Alone?' in *British Social Attitudes: the 17th Report*, Jowell, R. *et al.* (eds.), Sage 2000.
Durkheim, E., *The Elementary Forms of the Religious Life*, Collier 1961.
Eagleton, T., *Literary Theory*, Blackwell Publishers 1983.
Eliot, T.S., *Collected Poems*, Faber and Faber 1963.
Field, J., *Lifelong Learning and the New Educational Order*, 2nd edn, Trentham 2006.
Fielding, H. (1749), *Tom Jones*, Penguin Classics 1985.
Fisher, E.A., *The Saxon Churches of Sussex*, David and Charles 1970.
Fox, G. (1694), *Journal*, J M Dent 1924.
Francis, L. and Roberts, C., 'Growth or Decline in the Church of England During the Decade of Evangelism' in *Journal of Contemporary Religion*, Routledge January 2009.
Freeman, A., *God in Us: A Case for Christian Humanism*, SCM Press 1993; 2nd edn, Imprint Academic 2001.
Furlong, A., *Tried for Heresy: A Twentieth Century Journey of Faith*, O Books 2003.
Furlong, M., *C of E: The State It's In*, Hodder and Stoughton 2000.
Geering, L., *Christianity without God*, Bridget Williams Books 2002.
Geering, L., *Wrestling With God*, Bridget Williams Books 2006.
Gibbon, E., *Decline and Fall of the Roman Empire*, D.M. Low (ed.), Chatto and Windus 1960.
Giddens, A. (ed.), *Sociology: Introductory Readings*, revised edn., Polity Press 2001.
Grayling, A.C., *The God Argument: The Case against Religion and for Humanism*, Bloomsbury 2013.
Greene, G., *Complete Essays*, Bodley Head 1969.
Hamilton, M., 'Secularisation? Now You See it, Now You Don't' in *Sociology: Introductory Readings*, A. Giddens (ed.), Polity Press/Blackwell 1997.
Haralambos, M., *Sociology: Themes and Perspectives*, HarperCollins 2009.
Harris, T.H., *I'm OK – You're OK*, Harper & Row 1967.
Harvey, A.E., *The New English Bible: Companion to the New Testament*, Oxford University Press 1970.
Hertz, J.H., *Authorized Daily Prayer Book*, Bloch Publishing 1948.

Hick, J., *Christianity at the Centre*, SCM Press 1968.
Hick, J., *Who or What is God?* SCM Press 2008.
Hitchens, C. (ed.), *The Portable Atheist: Essential Readings for the Nonbeliever*, Da Capo Press (a member of The Perseus Books Group) 2007.
Holloway, R., *Looking in the Distance*, Canongate 2004.
Honderich, E. (ed.), *The Oxford Companion to Philosophy*, Oxford University Press 1995.
Honey, P., *The Learning Styles Questionnaire*, Pearson Education 2006.
Horan, M., *Jesus and the Trojan War: Myth and Meaning for Today*, Imprint Academic 2007.
Hull, J.M., *What Prevents Christian Adults from Learning?* SCM Press 1985.
Huxley, J., 'The Coming New Religion of Humanism' in *The Humanist* (Washington DC) January/February 1962.
Jerusalem Bible, The, Darton, Longman and Todd 1966.
Kahneman, D., *Thinking, Fast and Slow*, Allen Lane 2011.
Lampe, G., 'The Essence of Christianity' in *Explorations in Theology*, SCM Press 1981.
Larkin, P., 'Church Going' in *Philip Larkin: The Complete Poems*, A. Burnett (ed.), Faber and Faber 2012.
Lombardo, S. (trs.), *Hesiod: Works and Days* and *Theogony*, Hackett 1993.
Luft, J. and Ingham, H., 'The Johari Window: A Graphic Model of Interpersonal Awareness' in *Proceedings of the Western Training Laboratory in Group Development*, University of California 1955.
McNeile, A.H., *An Introduction to the Study of the New Testament*, 2nd edn., Oxford University Press 1953.
Moore, J.R. (ed.), *Religion in Victorian Britain* vol. 3: *Sources*, Manchester University Press/The Open University 1988.
New Revised Standard Version of the Holy Bible, Anglicized Edition, Oxford University Press 1995.
Parsons, G. (ed.), *The Growth of Religious Diversity*, Routledge with the Open University 1993.
Pevsner, N. et al., *The Buildings of England*, 46 volumes, Penguin 1951–1974.
Religious Society of Friends (Quakers), *Quaker Faith and Practice*, 5th edn 2013.
Revans, R., *ABC of Action Learning*, Gower 2011.
Revised English Bible, The, Cambridge University Press 1989.
Rogers, C.R., *On Becoming a Person*, Constable 1961.

Simpson, W.W., *Jewish Prayer and Worship*, SCM Press 1965.
Souter, A., *A Pocket Lexicon to the Greek New Testament*, Oxford University Press 1916.
Thomas, D., *Under Milk Wood*, Dent 1954.
Throckmorton, B.H. (ed.), *Gospel Parallels: A Comparison of the Synoptic Gospels*, 5th edn, Thomas Nelson 1992.
Tillich, P., *The Courage to Be*, Nisbet 1952.
United Nations, *Universal Declaration of Human Rights*, General Assembly of the UN 1948.
Vidler, A.R., *20th Century Defenders of the Faith*, SCM Press 1965.
Yeats, W.B., *Yeats's Poems*, A. Norman Jeffares (ed.), Macmillan 1989.

Acknowledgments

The author and publisher thank the following for their kind permission to quote from copyright material:

Canongate Books: *Looking in the Distance* by Richard Holloway.

Da Capo Press (a member of The Perseus Books Group), *The Portable Atheist: Essential Readings for the Nonbeliever* edited by Christopher Hitchens (ed.).

The Friend magazine: editorial in vol. 123 (1962).

HarperCollins Publishers Ltd: *Sociology: Themes and Perspectives* © M. Haralambos 1980.

Hodder and Stoughton: *C of E: The State It's In* by M.Furlong; *Sweet Songs of Zion: Selected Radio Talks* by John Betjeman; and *John Betjeman's Collected Poems*.

Dr Peter Honey and Pearson TalentLens Division of Pearson Education: *Learning Styles Questionnaire* by Peter Honey.

The Humanist magazine: 'The Coming New Religion of Humanism' by Sir Julian Huxley.

Penguin Random House (USA): *Tales of the Hasidim: the Early Masters* by Martin Buber.

Polity Press: *Sociology: Introductory Readings*, A. Giddens (ed.).

SCM Press: *Jesus as They Saw Him* by William Barclay; *Letters and Papers from Prison* by Dietrich Bonhoeffer; *The Sea of Faith* by Don Cupitt; *Twentieth Century Defenders of the Faith* by Alec R. Vidler; *The Essence of Christianity* by G. Lampe; *What Prevents Christian Adults from Learning?* by John Hull; and *Who or What is God?* by John Hick.

SPCK: *Freeing the Faith* by Hugh Dawes.

Taylor & Francis Group: *The Growth of Religious Diversity*, G. Parsons (ed.); and *Religion and Society in Twentieth Century Britain* by Callum G. Brown.

Index

Abraham 2, 74, 91, 101, 125
Abrahams, Israel 79n9
activist 47, 58ff
Adam and Eve 5, 87, 91, 125, 127, 128
'Adult' 131n25
afterlife 132ff
aggression 55
agnostics 4, 7, 9, 10, 11, 14, 67, 73
agnostos/unknown, unknowable 76, 77
aionios/unending 134
akrasia/intemperance 128
Aldridge, F. 56n13
Alpha course 16, 17
Alternative Service Book 18
ambiguity 9, 43, 49
Anglican church ix, 15, 16, 18, 19, 21, 23, 25n17, 32, 35, 36, 68, 121
Apostles' Creed 9, 22, 68, 71, 71n1, 73, 82, 95, 119, 125
Aristotle 10
Armstrong, Karen 12n20
Arnold, Thomas 23
ascension 22, 106ff, 110, 111, 114
assertiveness 55
Athanasian creed 72n1
atheists 4, 5, 7, 9, 10, 11, 67, 73

Barclay, William 109n13, 109n16, 113n11
Belbin, Meredith 50
Belbin team roles 50ff
believers-in-exile 5, 10, 68, 73
believing without belonging 31
Berger, Peter 39n15
Berne, Eric 56n17
Betjeman, John 13, 24n3, 34
Bloch, Ernst 10
Bonhoeffer, Dietrich 4, 12n11, 24
Book of Common Prayer 18, 19, 71n1
Bowie, F. 25n15
British Humanist Association 33
British Social Attitudes Survey 39n19, 40n24
Brown, Callum 25n8
Buildings of England, The 28

Caesar *see* Tiberius
Cain 125
Canter, Bernard 39n9
Canterbury, Archbishop of xn2, 17, 23, 25n9, 25n18
Carey, George xn2, 25n18
Celtic Christianity 21
census, national 31
census of religion (1851) 14

change 44, 49, 209
Chesterton, G.K. 43
'Child' 128, 129, 131n25
Christian humanism ix, 27, 78
Christian ideal 43
Christian Research 15, 16
christos/Christ 80ff, 85n8, 97, 120
church 119ff
church attendance 14, 15, 16, 23, 26, 30, 31, 67
Church Going (Larkin) 13
church in decline ix, x, 1, 7, 9, 14–17, 23, 26, 73
Church of England *see* Anglican church
Cicero 38
Clinard, M.B. 147n3
Common Worship 19
communitas/community 38
Constantine 30
Copley, Terence 48
Cranmer 18, 19
creation 67, 87, 127
creative thinking 44
creator God 22, 73ff, 87
credo/I believe 76
creeds 22, 30, 32, 68, 69, 119 *also see* Apostles' Creed
'Critical Parent' 128, 131n25
crucifixion 94ff
Cupitt, Don 12n19, 25n20, 40n29, 79n19

Daniel 108, 110
David, king 81, 82, 88, 89, 90, 91, 114
Davies, O. 25n15
Dawes, Hugh 25n11, 105n28

Dawkins, Richard 5, 12n10
de Bono, Edward 44, 57
de Botton, Alain 5
Decade of Evangelism 16
Decline and Fall of the Roman Empire 39n10
deconstruction 4, 9, 36, 37, 70, 71, 123, 143, 209
de Graaf, N.D. 40n26
deviance 68, 70, 140, 142, 143
disclosure 54
discontinuity 49, 209
Disraeli 34
dissenters 21
diversity 41, 42, 46, 51, 67, 70, 145
Durham, Bishop of 104, 105n29
Durkheim, Emile 27

Eagleton, Terry 40n28
Ebionites 90
Einstein, Albert 29, 56n5
ekklesia/assembly 38, 119, 120, 123
Elijah 103, 107
Eliot, T.S. 10, 11
Elisha 103, 107
Elizabeth I, queen 21
End of Days 107
Enoch 107
Evangelical Alliance 32, 104, 112, 132, 135n9
evangelical churches xn3, 18
evolution 127
exaleipho/obliterate 129

father God 73ff, 80, 83
Fawkes, Guy 21
feedback 54

Field, J. 56n12
Fisher, E.A. 25n14
Fisher, Geoffrey 25n9
forgiveness 125ff
Fox, George 2
Freeman, Anthony 32
fugitive present 44, 49, 57, 209
fulfilment society: definition 4
fulfilment society 3-9, 10, 37, 41, 46, 52, 123, 130, 209, 210
Furlong, Andrew 32
Furlong, Monica 25n12

Garden of Eden 128
Geering, Lloyd 32
generational shift 34
Giddens, Anthony 207n1
Gideon 114
goal setting 146
Good Samaritan 139
Gospel Parallels (Throckmorton) 85n2, 92n25, 105n18, 109n1
Graham, Billy 17, 25n9
Grayling, A.C. 5
greatest commandment 43, 64, 139
Greene, Graham 24n4
guilt 128-129

hagios/set apart 122
Hamilton, Malcolm 27, 31
Haralambos, M. 155n1
Harris, Thomas 131n25
Harvey, A.E. 92n15
heaven 22, 106ff, 110ff
Hebrew Bible 2, 73, 74, 75, 87, 89, 91, 97, 106, 107, 114, 119, 125, 134
hell 100

heresy trials 32
Herod 94
Hertz, Joseph 79n10
Hesiod 105n1
Hick, John 12n20, 56n10
Holloway, Richard 3
Holy Spirit 87, 88, 90, 91, 92, 114ff, 125
Holy Trinity church, Brompton 16
Honderich, Ted 12n13
Honey, Peter 64n4
Hull, John 39n13, 49
Humanist magazine 3
humanist religion 3, 4, 5
humanists ix, 5, 11
human spirit x, 1, 4
Husén, Torsten 56n12
Huxley, Julian 3, 4, 5, 27, 39n2, 130

Immaculate Conception 91
Immortality 132
I'm OK, you're OK 55, 56n17, 129, 131n25
Ingham, Harry 56n16
Isaac 74, 89, 125
Ishmael 89
Israel 2, 80

Jacob 125
James, king 21
Jenkins, David 104, 105n29
Johari Window 53-54, 56n16
John the Baptist 89, 90, 103, 115
Joseph 114
Joseph of Arimathæa 95, 96, 102
Josephus 81, 96
Jowell, Nick 56n9

Judaism 75
Judgment Day 22, 110ff

Kahneman, Daniel 45
koinonia/fellowship 122, 123
Kolb, David 64n3
kurios/lord 82, 83

Lampe, G. 104
Lansley, S. 207n1
Larkin, Philip 13, 14, 24n1, 29
lateral thinking 44, 45, 57
learning 7, 9, 46, 47, 57ff
learning communities 10, 37, 38, 39, 41ff, 46, 49, 51, 62, 135, 145, 146
learning cycle/process 58, 61
learning styles 47, 58ff
learning theorists 58, 64n3
learning to learn 46ff, 57ff
Les Misérables 11n5
logos/word, expression 107
Luckmann, Thomas 39n15
Luft, Joseph 56n16

Mack, J. 207n1
Magnificat 91
Mann, Horace 39n4
Mary, mother of Jesus 81, 87ff
Mary, queen 21
McNeile, A.H. 92n15
Meditations of Marcus Aurelius 10
Mencap 149
messiah 85n8, 91, 97, 98, 103, 107, 110
metaphysics 4, 12n13, 133
Metropolitan Police 143
monotheism 74
Moore, J.R. 39n4
Moses 2, 74, 114, 119, 122, 125

Murray, Douglas 12n17

Napoleonic wars 14
Need, A. 40n26
New Age cults 2
Newman, Cardinal 134
new religion of humanism 39n2
Nicene creed 72n1, 119
Noah 102, 125
nonconformist churches ix, 28, 32, 68
Northern Ireland 2

Old Testament *see* Hebrew Bible
openness 52ff
Orthodox church 121
Other Gospels: Non-Canonical Gospel Texts (Cameron) 85n1, 92n20, 92n28, 98n5, 99n11, 105n9, 105n17
'Other-than-oneself' ix, 2, 3, 6, 30, 64, 73, 78, 117
outdated beliefs/teaching x, 9, 17, 19, 22, 24, 69, 78

parakletos/helper, comforter 115
'Parent' 131n25
parousia/second coming 110, 111
Parsons, Gerald 25n6
parthenos/virgin 89
Passover 94, 101, 115
Paul (Saul), apostle 75, 76, 80, 82, 89, 104, 108, 111, 112, 115, 116, 121, 122, 128, 132, 133
Pentateuch 119
Pentecost 88, 115
Pentecostal churches 15, 16

Index

Peter, apostle 83, 85, 102, 103, 104, 111, 112
Peterloo massacre 15
petros/rock 120
Pevsner, Nikolaus 39n6
Philip, apostle 84
Philo of Alexandria 96
Picasso, Pablo 45
Plato 10
pneuma/breath, wind 88
Polish Roman Catholics 16
Pontius Pilatus 81, 83, 94ff, 127
post-religious religion 24
post-Roman Britain 20
pragmatist 47, 58ff
Prayer Book Society 18
predestination 133
Protestant religion/churches 35, 91, 121

Quakers 2, 11n6, 29, 40n31, 121

Ratzinger, Joseph 124n12
reconstruction 8, 36, 37, 70, 71, 209
re-evangelisation of England 16
reflector 58ff
religion, definition 27
religionless Christianity 4, 24
Religious Society of Friends *see* Quakers
religious values and beliefs *see* spiritual values and beliefs
resurrection 100ff, 106, 111, 120, 132
Revans, Reg 56n3, 57, 64n2
Rogers, Carl 41
Roman Catholic church ix, 15, 16, 21, 29, 31, 91, 121, 122

Rowntree Foundation, Joseph 140

Sacks, Jonathan 11n4
sacrifice 125
Samson 89, 114
Samuel 89, 114
Sanhedrin 94, 95
Saul, king 114
secular humanists ix, 5, 11
secularisation 26
Sentamu, John 16, 24
Septuagint 89, 119
Sermon on the Mount 10, 126
Sheol 101
Simon, magician 115
Simpson, W.W. 79n9
social class 144
social construction 10, 11, 41, 135, 139ff
social exclusion 145
social problems 141
socio-economic classification 144, 147n6
Songs of Praise 34
Son of God 80ff, 107, 133
Son of Man, 101, 107, 108, 110, 133
soter/saviour 81, 111
spiritual values and beliefs x, 1, 4, 6, 8, 9, 10, 28, 67, 78
Stephen, martyr 107
stereotyping 144
sum of our values, the (God as) 5, 78, 85, 117
Sunday assembly 3, 38, 43
supernatural doctrines/beliefs 6, 17, 19, 22, 23, 26, 30, 36, 69, 77, 87, 94, 100, 106, 110, 123

System 1 and System 2 thinking 45
Tacitus 96
teaching/teachers 7, 8, 9, 21, 31, 36, 44, 47ff, 69–70
team roles *see* Belbin
team-working 50ff
theistic religion 6, 9
Theodotion 89
theorist 58ff
Thomas, Dylan 36
Thwackham, parson 35
Tiberius, emperor 95, 96
Tillich, Paul 131n26, 131n27
transcendence 3, 4
trinity 32, 68, 69, 116
trust 52ff
Tuckett, A. 56n13
2020Vision 146, 209

Ultimate Reality 2, 3
unconditional positive regard 41
underworld 100ff

Vatican ix, 121
vertical thinking 44, 57
Victorian church 13ff, 18, 28, 34
Vidler, Alec 8
virgin birth 22, 87ff, 114
vision 43

Warnock, Mary 11n1
Wesleyan revival 21
Wesley, Charles 112
William the Conqueror 31
Wilson, A.N. 25n10
Wordsworth, William 29
Worth church 20

Yeats, W.B. 130
York, Archbishop of 16

Zeitgeist 117
Zeus 74, 100, 111

www.ingramcontent.com/pod-product-compliance
Lightning Source LLC
Chambersburg PA
CBHW070940230426
43666CB00011B/2508